THE LIFE OF
JOHN QUINCY ADAMS

BY
JOSIAH QUINCY

PREFATORY NOTE.

The ensuing Memoir comprises the most important events in the life of a statesman second to none of his contemporaries in laborious and faithful devotion to the service of his country.

The light attempted to be thrown on his course has been derived from personal acquaintance, from his public works, and from authentic unpublished materials.

The chief endeavor has been to render him the expositor of his own motives, principles, and character, without fear or favor,—in the spirit neither of criticism or eulogy.

CHAPTER I.

BIRTH.—EDUCATION.—RESIDENCE IN EUROPE.—AT COLLEGE.—AT THE BAR. —POLITICAL ESSAYS.—MINISTER AT THE HAGUE.—AT BERLIN.—RETURN TO THE UNITED STATES.

John Quincy Adams, son of John and Abigail Adams, was born on the 11th of July, 1767, in the North Parish of Braintree, Massachusetts—since incorporated as the town of Quincy. The lives and characters of his parents, intimately associated with the history of the American Revolution, have been already ably and faithfully illustrated.[1]

The origin of his name was thus stated by himself: "My great-grandfather, John Quincy,[2] was dying when I was baptized, and his daughter, my grandmother, requested I might receive his name. This fact, recorded by my father at the time, is not without a moral to my heart, and has connected with that portion of my name a charm of mingled sensibility and devotion. It was filial tenderness that gave the name—it was the name of one passing from earth to immortality. These have been, through life, perpetual admonitions to do nothing unworthy of it."

At Braintree his mother watched over his childhood. At the village school he learned the rudiments of the English language. In after life he often playfully boasted that the dame who taught him to spell flattered him into learning his letters by telling him he would prove a scholar. The notes and habits of the birds and wild animals of the vicinity early excited his attention, and led him to look on nature with a lover's eye, creating an attachment to the home of his childhood, which time strengthened. Many years afterwards, when residing in Europe, he wrote: "Penn's Hill and Braintree North Common Rocks never looked and never felt to me like any other hill or any other rocks; because every rock and every pebble upon them associates itself with the first consciousness of my existence. If there is a Bostonian who ever sailed from his own harbor for distant lands, or returned to it from them, without feelings, at the sight of the Blue Hills, which he is unable to express, his heart is differently constituted from mine."

These local attachments were indissolubly associated with the events of the American Revolution, and with the patriotic principles instilled by his mother. Standing with her on the summit of Penn's Hill, he heard the cannon booming from the battle of Bunker's Hill, and saw the smoke and flames of burning Charlestown. During the siege of Boston he often climbed the same eminence alone, to watch the shells and rockets thrown by the American army.

With a mind prematurely developed and cultivated by the influence of the characters of his parents and the stirring events of that period, he embarked, at the age of eleven years, in February, 1778, from the shore of his native town, with his father, in a small boat, which conveyed them to a ship in Nantasket Roads, bound for Europe. John Adams had been associated in a commission with Benjamin Franklin and Arthur Lee, as plenipotentiary to the Court of France. After residing in Paris until June, 1779, he returned to America, accompanied by his son. Being immediately appointed, by Congress, minister plenipotentiary to negotiate a treaty of peace and commerce with Great Britain, they both returned together to France in November, taking passage in a French frigate. On this his second voyage to Europe, young Adams began a diary, which, with few intermissions, he continued through life. While in Paris he resumed the study of the ancient and modern languages, which had been interrupted by his return to America.

In July, 1780, John Adams having been appointed ambassador to the Netherlands, his son was removed from the schools of Paris to those of Amsterdam, and subsequently to the University of Leyden. There he pursued his studies until July, 1781, when, in his fourteenth year, he was selected by Francis Dana, minister plenipotentiary from the United States to the Russian court, as his private secretary, and accompanied him through Germany to St. Petersburg. Having satisfactorily discharged his official duties, and pursued his Latin, German, and French studies, with a general course of English history, until September, 1782, he left St. Petersburg for Stockholm, where he passed the winter. In the ensuing spring, after travelling through the interior of Sweden, and visiting Copenhagen and Hamburg, he joined his father at the Hague, and accompanied him to Paris. They travelled leisurely, forming an acquaintance with eminent men on their route, and examining architectural remains, the paintings of the great Flemish masters, and all the treasures of the fine arts, in the countries through which they passed. In Paris, young Adams was present at the signing of the treaty of peace in 1783, and was admitted into the society of Franklin, Jefferson, Jay, Barclay, Hartley, the Abbé Mably, and many other eminent statesmen and literary men. After passing a few months in England, with his father, he returned to Paris, and resumed his studies, which he continued until May, 1785, when he embarked for the United States. This return to his own country caused a mental struggle, in which his judgment controlled his inclination. His father had just been appointed minister at the Court of Great Britain, and, as one of his family, it would have been to him a high gratification to reside in England. His feelings and views on the occasion he thus expressed:

"I have been seven years travelling in Europe, seeing the world, and in its society. If I return to the United States, I must be subject, one or two years, to the rules of a college, pass three more in the tedious study of the law, before I can hope to bring myself into professional notice. The prospect is discouraging. If I accompany my father to London, my satisfaction would possibly be greater than by returning to the United States; but I shall loiter away my precious time, and not go home until I am forced to it. My father has been all his lifetime occupied by the interests of the public. His own fortune has suffered. His children must provide for themselves. I am determined to get my own living, and to be dependent upon no one. With a tolerable share of common sense, I hope, in America, to be independent and free. Rather than live otherwise, I would wish to die before my time."

In this spirit the tempting prospects in Europe were abandoned, and he returned to the United States, to submit to the rules, and to join, with a submissive temper, the comparatively uninteresting associations, of college life. After reviewing his studies under an instructor, he entered, in March, 1786, the junior class of Harvard University. Diligence and punctual fulfilment of every prescribed duty, the advantages he had previously enjoyed, and his exemplary compliance with the rules of the seminary, secured to him a high standing in his class, which none were disposed to controvert. Here his active and thoughtful mind was prepared for those scenes in future life in which he could not but feel he was destined to take part. Entering into all the literary and social circles of the college, he became popular among his classmates. By the government his conduct and attainments were duly appreciated, which they manifested by bestowing upon him the second honor of his class at commencement; a high distinction, considering the short period he had been a member of the university. The oration he delivered when he graduated, in 1787, on the Importance of Public Faith to the Well-Being of a Community, was printed and published; a rare proof of general interest in a college exercise, which the adaptation of the subject to the times, and the talent it evinced, justified.

After leaving the university, Mr. Adams passed three years in Newburyport as a student at law under the guidance of Theophilus Parsons, afterwards chief justice of Massachusetts. He was admitted to the bar in 1790, and immediately opened an office in Boston. The ranks of his profession were crowded, the emoluments were small, and his competitors able. His letters feelingly express his anxiety to relieve his parents from contributing to his support. In November, 1843, in an address to the bar of Cincinnati, Mr. Adams thus described the progress and termination of his practice as a lawyer—

"I have been a member of your profession upwards of half a century. In the early period of my life, having a father abroad, it was my fortune to travel in foreign countries; still, under the impression which I first received from my mother, that in this country every man should have some trade, that trade which, by the advice of my parents and my own inclination, I chose, was the profession of the Law. After having completed an education in which, perhaps, more than any other citizen of that time I had advantages, and which of course brought with it the incumbent duty of manifesting by my life that those extraordinary advantages of education, secured to me by my father, had not been worthlessly bestowed,—on coming into life after such great advantages, and having the duty of selecting a profession, I chose that of the Bar. I closed my education as a lawyer with one of the most eminent jurists of the age,—Theophilus Parsons, of Newburyport, at that time a practising lawyer, but subsequently chief justice of the commonwealth of Massachusetts. Under his instruction and advice I closed my education, and commenced what I can hardly call the practice of the law in the city of Boston.

"At that time, though I cannot say I was friendless, yet my circumstances were not independent. My father was then in a situation of great responsibility and notoriety in the government of the United States. But he had been long absent from his own country, and still continued absent from that part of it to which he belonged, and of which I was a native. I went, therefore, as a volunteer, an adventurer, to Boston, as possibly many of you whom I now see before me may consider yourselves as having come to Cincinnati. I was without support of any kind. I may say I was a stranger in that city, although almost a native of that spot. I say I can hardly call it practice, because for the space of one year from that time it would be difficult for me to name any practice which I had to do. For two years, indeed, I can recall nothing in which I was engaged that may be termed practice, though during the second year there were some symptoms that by persevering patience practice might come in time. The third year I continued this patience and perseverance, and, having little to do, occupied my time as well as I could in the study of those laws and institutions which I have since been called to administer. At the end of the third year I had obtained something which might be called practice.

"The fourth year I found it swelling to such an extent that I felt no longer any concern as to my future destiny as a member of that profession. But in the midst of the fourth year, by the will of the first President of the United States, with which the Senate was pleased to concur, I was selected for a station, not, perhaps, of more usefulness, but of greater consequence in the estimation of mankind, and sent from home on a mission to foreign parts.

"From that time, the fourth year after my admission to the bar of my native state, and the first year of my admission to the bar of the Supreme Court of the United States, I was deprived of the exercise of any further industry or labor at the bar by this distinction; a distinction for which a previous education at the bar, if not an indispensable qualification, was at least a most useful appendage."[3]

While waiting for professional employment, he was instinctively drawn into political discussions. Thomas Paine had just then published his "Rights of Man," for which Thomas Jefferson, then Secretary of State, took upon himself to be sponsor, by publishing a letter expressing his extreme pleasure "that it is to be reprinted here, and that something is at length to be publicly said against the *political heresies* which have sprung up among us. I have no doubt our citizens will rally a second time round the standard of *Common Sense.*"

Notwithstanding the weight of Jefferson's character, and the strength of his recommendation, in June, 1791, young Adams entered the lists against Paine and his pamphlet, which was in truth an encomium on the National Assembly of France, and a commentary on the rights of man, inferring questionable deductions from unquestionable principles. In a series of essays, signed Publicola, published in the *Columbian Centinel*, he states and controverts successively the fundamental doctrines of Paine's work; denies that "whatever a whole nation chooses to do it has a right to do," and maintains, in opposition, that "nations, no less than individuals, are subject to the eternal and immutable laws of justice and morality;" declaring that Paine's doctrine annihilated the security of every man for his inalienable rights, and would lead in practice to a hideous despotism, concealed under the parti-colored garments of democracy. The truth of the views in these essays was soon made manifest by the destruction of the French constitution, so lauded by Paine and Jefferson, the succeeding anarchy, the murder of the French monarch, and the establishment of a military despotism.

In April, 1793, Great Britain declared war against France, then in the most violent frenzy of her revolution. In this war, the feelings of the people of the United States were far from being neutral. The seeds of friendship for the one, and of enmity towards the other belligerent, which the Revolutionary War had plentifully scattered through the whole country, began everywhere to vegetate. Private cupidity openly advocated privateering upon the commerce of Great Britain, in aid of which commissions were issued under the authority of France. To counteract the apparent tendency of these popular passions, Mr. Adams published, also in the *Centinel*, a series of essays, signed Marcellus, exposing the lawlessness, injustice, and criminality, of such interference in favor of one of the belligerents. "For if," he wrote, "as the poet, with more than poetical truth, has said, 'war is murder,' the plunder of private property, the pillage of all the regular rewards of honest industry and laudable enterprise, upon the mere pretence of a national contest, in the eye of justice can appear in no other light than highway robbery. If, however, some apology for the practice is to be derived from the incontrollable law of necessity, or from the imperious law of war, certainly there can be no possible excuse for those who incur the guilt without being able to plead the palliation; for those who violate the rights of nations in order to obtain a license for rapine manifestly show that patriotism is but the cloak for such enterprises; that the true objects are plunder and pillage; and that to those engaged in them it was only the lash of the executioner which kept them in the observance of their civil and political duties."

After developing the folly and madness of such conduct in a nation whose commerce was expanded over the globe, and which was "destitute of even the defensive apparatus of war," and showing that it would lead to general bankruptcy, and endanger even the existence of the nation, he maintained that "impartial and unequivocal neutrality was the imperious duty of the United States." Their pretended obligation to take part in the war resulting from "the guarantee of the possessions of France in America," he denied, on the ground that either circumstances had wholly dissolved those obligations, or they were suspended and made impracticable by the acts of the French government.

The ability displayed in these essays attracted the attention of Washington and his cabinet, and the coïncidence of these views with their own was immediately manifested by the proclamation of neutrality. Their thoughts were again, soon after, attracted to the author, by a third series of essays, published in November, 1793, in the *Columbian Centinel*, under the signature of Columbus, in which he entered the lists in defence of the constituted authorities of the United States, exposing and reprobating the language and conduct of Genet, the minister from the French republic, whose repeated insults upon the first magistrate of the American Union, and upon the national government, had been as public and as shameless as they had been unprecedented. For, after Washington, supported by the highest judicial authority of the country, had, as President of the United States, denied publicly Genet's authority to establish consular courts within them, and to issue letters of marque and reprisal to their citizens, against the enemies of France, he had the insolence to appeal from the President, and to deny his power to revoke the exequatur of a French consul, who, by a process issued from his own court, rescued, with an armed force, a vessel out of the custody of justice.

In these essays Genet is denounced as a dangerous enemy; his appeal "as an insolent outrage to *the man* who was deservedly the object of the grateful affection of the whole people of America;" "as a rude attempt of a beardless foreign stripling, whose commission from a friendly power was his only title to respect, not supported by a shadow of right on his part, and not less hostile to the constitution than to the government."

The violence of the times, and the existence of a powerful party in the United States ready to support the French minister in his hostility to the national government, are also illustrated by the following facts: "That an American jury had been compelled by the clamor of a collected multitude to acquit a prisoner without the unanimity required by law;" "by the circulation of caricatures representing President Washington and a judge of the Supreme Court with a guillotine suspended over their heads;" "by posting upon the mast of a French vessel of war, in the harbor of Boston, the names of twenty citizens, all of them inoffensive, and some of them personally respectable, as objects of detestation to the crew;" "by the threatening, by an anonymous assassin, to visit with inevitable death a member of the

Legislature of New York, for expressing, with the freedom of an American citizen, his opinion of the proceedings of the French minister;" and "by the formation of a lengthened chain of democratic societies, assuming to themselves, under the semblance of a warmer zeal for the cause of liberty, to control the operations of the government, and to dictate laws to the country."

The talent and knowledge of diplomatic relations, thus displayed, powerfully impressed the administration, and the nomination of Mr. Adams as minister from the United States resident at the Netherlands, by Washington and his cabinet, was confirmed unanimously by the Senate, in June, 1794. At the request of the Secretary of State, he immediately repaired to Philadelphia. His commission was delivered to him on the 11th of July, the day he entered his twenty-eighth year. He embarked in September from Boston, and in October arrived in London, where Messrs. Jay and Pinckney were then negotiating a treaty between Great Britain and the United States, who immediately admitted him to their deliberations. Concerning this treaty, which occasioned, soon after, such unexampled fury of opposition in the United States, Mr. Adams, at the time, thus expressed his opinion: "The treaty is far from being satisfactory to either Mr. Jay or Mr. Pinckney. It is far below the standard which would be advantageous to the country. It is probable, however, the negotiators will consent to it, as it is, in their opinion, preferable to a war. The satisfaction proposed to be made to the United States for the recent depredations on their commerce, the principal object of Jay's mission, is provided for in as ample a manner as we could expect. The delivery of the posts is protracted to a more distant day than is desirable. But, I think, the compensation made for the present and future detention of them will be a sufficient equivalent. The commerce with their West India islands, partially opened to us, will be of great importance, and indemnifies for the deprivation of the fur-trade since the treaty of peace, as well as for the negroes carried away contrary to the engagements of the treaty, at least as far as it respects the nation. As to the satisfaction we are to make, I think it is no more than is in justice due from us. The article which provides against the future confiscation of debts, and of property in the funds, is useful, because it is honest. If its operation should turn out more advantageous to them, it will be more honorable for us; and I never can object to entering formally into an obligation to do that which, upon every virtuous principle, ought to be done without it. As a treaty of commerce it will be indeed of little use to us, and we shall never obtain anything more favorable so long as the principles of the navigation act are obstinately adhered to by Great Britain. This system is so much a favorite with the nation that no minister would dare to depart from it. Indeed, I have no idea we shall ever obtain, by compact, a better footing for our commerce with this country than that on which it now stands; and therefore the shortness of time, limited for the operation of this part of the compact, is, I think, beneficial to us."

After remaining fifteen days in London, Mr. Adams sailed, on the 30th of October, for Holland, landed at Hellevoetsluis, and proceeded without delay to the Hague.

His reception as the representative of the United States had scarcely been acknowledged by the President of the States General, before Holland was taken possession of by the French, under Pichegru. The Stadtholder fled, the tree of liberty was planted, and the French national flag displayed before the Stadthouse. The people were kept quiet by seventy thousand French soldiers. The Stadtholder, the nobility, and the regencies of the cities, were all abolished, a provincial municipality appointed, and the country received as an ally of France, under the name of the Batavian Republic; the streets being filled with tri-colored cockades, and resounding with the Carmagnole, or the Marseilles Hymn. Mr. Adams was visited by the representatives of the French people, and recognized as the minister of a nation free like themselves, with whom the most fraternal relations should be maintained. In response, he assured them of the attachment of his fellow-citizens for the French people, who felt grateful for the obligations they were under to the French nation, and closed with demanding safety and protection for all American persons and property in the country.

Popular societies in Holland were among the most efficient means of the success of the revolution, as they had been in France. Mr. Adams, being solicited to join one of them, declined, considering it improper in a stranger to take part personally in the politics of the country. "It was," he wrote, "unnecessary for me to look out for motives to justify my

5

refusal. I have an aversion to political popular societies in general. To destroy an established power, they are undoubtedly an efficacious instrument, but in their nature they are fit for nothing else. The reign of Robespierre has shown what use they make of power when they obtain it."

The station of Mr. Adams at the Hague gave him opportunities to acquaint himself with parties and persons, their motives and principles, of which he availed himself with characteristic industry.

In October, 1795, he was directed by the Secretary of State to repair to England, and arriving there in November ensuing, he found he was appointed to exchange ratifications of Mr. Jay's treaty with the British government. This mission was far from pleasant to him. In effect it was merely ministerial, and so far as it might result in negotiation, he did not anticipate any good. "I am convinced," he wrote, "that Mr. Jay did everything that was to be done; that he did so much affords me a proof of the wisdom with which he conducted the business, that grows stronger the more I see. But circumstances will do more than any negotiation. The pride of Britain itself must bend to the course of events. The rigor of her system already begins to relax, and one year of war to her and peace to us will be more favorable to our interests, and to the final establishment of our principles, than could possibly be effected by twenty years of negotiation or war."

While in England, the duties of his appointment brought him into frequent intercourse with Lord Grenville and other leading British statesmen of the period. After the objects of his mission had been acceptably fulfilled, he received authority from his government to return to his station, at the Hague, in May, 1796. His time was there devoted to official duties, to the claims of general society, to an extensive correspondence, the study of works on diplomacy, the English and Latin classics, and the Dutch and Italian languages.

In August, 1796, he received from the Secretary of State an appointment as minister plenipotentiary to the Court of Portugal, with directions not to quit the Hague until he received further instructions. These did not reach him until the arrival of Mr. Murray, his successor, in July, 1797, when he took his departure for England. Truthfulness to himself, not less than to the public, characterized Mr. Adams. Every day had its assigned object, which every hour successively, as far as possible, fulfilled. Daily he called himself to account for what he had done or omitted. At the close of every month and year he submitted himself to retrospection concerning fulfilled or neglected duties, judging himself by a severe standard.

On arriving in London, he found his appointment to the Court of Portugal superseded by another to the Court of Berlin, with directions not to proceed on the mission until he had received the necessary instructions. While waiting for these, an engagement he had formed during a former visit to England was fulfilled, by his marriage, on the 26th of July, 1797, with Louisa Catharine Johnson, the daughter of Joshua Johnson, American consul at London; a lady highly qualified to support and to ornament the various elevated stations he was destined to fill. Mr. Adams was reluctant to accept the appointment to Berlin, as it had been made by his father, who had succeeded Washington as President of the United States. "I have submitted to take it," he immediately wrote to his mother, "notwithstanding my former declaration to you and my father, made a short time ago. I have broken a resolution I had deliberately formed, and that I still think right; but I never acted more reluctantly. The tenure by which I am for the future to hold an office of such a nature will take from me the satisfaction I have enjoyed, hitherto, in considering myself a public servant." To his father he wrote: "I cannot, and ought not, to discuss with you *the propriety* of the measure. I have undertaken the duty, and will discharge it to the best of my ability, and will complain no further. But I most earnestly entreat that whenever there shall be deemed no further occasion for a minister at Berlin I may be recalled, and that no nomination of me to any other public office whatever may ever again proceed from the present chief magistrate." His continuance in a diplomatic career had been repeatedly urged by President Washington. In August, 1795, he wrote to John Adams, then Vice-President: "Your son must not think of retiring from the walk he is now in (minister from the United States to Holland). His prospects, if he pursues it, are fair; and I shall be much mistaken if, in as short a time as can well be expected, he is not found at the head of the diplomatic corps, let the government be administered by whomsoever the people may choose." In a letter dated 20th February, 1797, addressed to Mr. Adams, just before his entrance on the Presidency, Washington again wrote: "I have a strong hope that you will not withhold merited promotion to Mr. John Quincy Adams because he is your son. For, without intending to compliment the father or the mother, or to censure any others, I give it as my decided opinion that Mr. Adams is the most valuable public character we have abroad, and that he will prove himself to be the ablest of all our diplomatic corps. If he was now to be brought into that line, or into any other public walk, I would not, on the principles which have regulated my own conduct, disapprove the caution hinted at in the letter. But he is already entered; the public, more and more, as he is known, are appreciating his talents and worth; and his country would sustain a loss if these are checked by over delicacy on your part."[4]

This letter, communicated to Mr. Adams by his mother, induced him reluctantly to acquiesce in this appointment. In reply, he wrote: "I know with what delight your truly maternal heart has received every testimonial of Washington's favorable voice. It is among the most precious gratifications of my life to reflect upon the pleasure which my conduct has given to my parents. The terms, indeed, in which such a character as Washington has repeatedly expressed himself concerning me, have left me nothing to wish, if they did not alarm me by their very strength. How much, my dear mother, is required of me, to support and justify such a judgment as that which you have copied into your letter!"

Mr. and Mrs. Adams embarked from Gravesend, and landed at Hamburg on the 26th of October, and reached Berlin early in November. He was received, with gratifying expressions of regard for the United States, by Count Finkenstein, the prime minister; but, owing to the king's illness, an audience could not be granted. After his death Mr. Adams was admitted to presentation and audience by his successor. New credentials, which were required, did not arrive until July, 1798, when Mr. Adams was fully accredited.

The absence of the king from Berlin prevented the renewal of the treaty, which was not commenced until the ensuing autumn, nor completed, in consequence of incidental delays, until the 11th of July, 1799, when it was signed by all the king's ministers and Mr. Adams, and was afterwards unanimously approved by the Senate of the United States. The object of his mission being fulfilled, Mr. Adams immediately wrote to his father that he should, at any time, acquiesce in his recall. While waiting for the decision of his government, he travelled, with his family, in Saxony and Bohemia, and, in the ensuing summer, into Silesia. His observations during this tour were embodied in letters to his brother, Thomas B. Adams, and were published, without his authority, in Philadelphia, and subsequently in England. The work contains interesting sketches of Silesian life and manners, and important accounts of manufactures, mines, and localities; concluding with elaborate historical, geographical, and statistical statements of the province.

The following passages are characteristic, and indicate the general spirit of the work. "Count Finkenstein resides in this vicinity. He was formerly president of the judicial tribunal at Custrin, but was dismissed by Frederic II., on the occasion of the miller Arnold's famous lawsuit; an instance in which the great king, from mere love of justice, committed the greatest injustice that ever cast a shade upon his character. His anxiety, upon that occasion, to prove to the world that in his courts of justice the beggar should be upon the same footing as the prince, made him forget that in substantial justice the maxim ought to bear alike on both sides, and that the prince should obtain his right as much as the beggar. Count Finkenstein and several other judges of the court at Custrin, together with the High Chancellor Fürst, were all dismissed from their places, for doing their duty, and persisting in it, contrary to the will of the king, who, substituting his ideas of natural equity in place of the prescriptions of positive law, treated them with the utmost severity, for conduct which ought to have received his fullest approbation."

"Dr. Johnson, in his Life of Watts, has bestowed a just and exalted encomium upon him for not disdaining to descend from the pride of genius and the dignity of science to write for the wants and the capacities of children. 'Every man acquainted,' says he, 'with the common principles of human action, will look with veneration on the writer who is at one time combating Locke, and at another making *a catechism* for children in their fourth year.' But how much greater still is the tribute of admiration, irresistibly drawn from us, when we behold an absolute monarch, the greatest general of his age, eminent as a writer in the highest departments of literature, descending, in a manner, to teach the alphabet to the children of his kingdom; bestowing his care, his persevering assiduity, his influence and his power, in diffusing plain and useful knowledge among his subjects, in opening to their minds the first and most important page of the book of science, in filling the whole atmosphere they breathed with that intellectual fragrance which had before been imprisoned in the vials of learning, or enclosed within the gardens of wealth! Immortal Frederic! when seated on the throne of Prussia, with kneeling millions at thy feet, thou wert only a king; on the fields of Lutzen, of Torndoff, of Rosbach, of so many other scenes of human blood and anguish, thou wert only a hero; even in thy rare and glorious converse with the muses and with science thou wert only a philosopher, a historian, a poet; but in this generous ardor, this active, enlightened zeal for the education of thy people, thou wert *truly great*—the father of thy country—the benefactor of mankind!"

In 1801, Mr. Adams received from his government permission to return home. After taking leave with the customary formalities, he left Berlin, sailed from Hamburg, and on the 4th of September, 1801, arrived in the United States. During his residence in Berlin his time was devoted to official labor and intellectual improvement; yet his letters show that he was seldom, if ever, self-satisfied, being filled with aspirations after something higher and better than he could accomplish. His translations, at this period, embraced many satires of Juvenal, and Wieland's Oberon from the original, into English verse; the last he intended for the press, had it not been superseded by the version of Sotheby. He also translated from the German a treatise, by Gentz, on the origin and principles of the American Revolution, which he finished and transmitted to the United States for publication, eulogizing it "as one of the clearest accounts that exist of the rise and progress of the American Revolution, in so small a compass; rescuing it from the disgraceful imputation of its having proceeded from the same principles, and of its being conducted in the same spirit, as that of France. This error has nowhere been more frequently repeated, nowhere been of more pernicious tendency, than in America itself."

The last years of Mr. Adams' residence at the Court of Berlin were painfully affected by the bitter party animadversions which assailed his father's administration, and which did not fail to bring within the sphere of their asperities the missions he had himself held in Europe. These feelings became intense on the publication of Alexander Hamilton's letter "On the Public Conduct and Character of John Adams, President of the United States." This letter, with the divisions in the cabinet at Washington, occasioned by the political friends of Hamilton, excited in the breast of Mr. Adams a spirit, which, from affection for his father, and a sense of the injustice done to him, could not be otherwise than indignant. Though concealed, it was not the less understood. He regarded Mr. Hamilton's letter as the efficient cause of his father's loss of power, and attributed its influence to its being circulated at the eve of the presidential election, and to its adaptation to awaken prejudices and excite party jealousies; although it contained nothing that could justly shake confidence in a statesman of long-tried experience and fidelity. He pronounced that letter as not only a full vindication, but the best eulogium on his father's administration.

CHAPTER II.

RESIDENCE IN BOSTON.—RETURNS TO THE BAR.—ELECTED TO THE SENATE OF MASSACHUSETTS.—TO THE SENATE OF THE UNITED STATES.— HIS COURSE RELATIVE TO THE ATTACK OF THE LEOPARD ON THE CHESAPEAKE.—RESIGNS HIS SEAT AS SENATOR OF THE UNITED STATES.— APPOINTED MINISTER TO RUSSIA.—FINAL SEPARATION FROM THE FEDERAL PARTY.

Under the circumstances stated in the preceding chapter, Mr. Adams returned to the United States in no disposition to coälesce with either division of the Federal party. He regarded it as fortunate for himself that events, in producing which he had no agency, had placed him in a position free from any constructive pledges to a party which in its original form no longer existed, and at liberty to shape his future course according to his own independent views of private interest and public duty. Resuming his residence in Boston, and his place at the bar of Massachusetts, under circumstances far from being pleasant or encouraging, after eight years' employment in foreign official stations, he had old studies to revise, and new statutes and recent decisions to explore. To the broad field of diplomacy had succeeded the intricate and narrow windings of special pleading and local laws. His juniors were in the field; by the failure of European bankers his property had been diminished; he had a family to support; yet, neither dispirited nor complaining, he reëntered his profession, and, devoting his leisure hours to literature and science, apparently abandoned the political arena, without manifesting a design or desire to return to it. But he was not destined to remain long in private life. At this period the Federalists had lost the control of national affairs, but they retained their superiority in Massachusetts. Their union as a party was not sustained by the same identity of feeling and view by which, in earlier periods, it had been characterized. It was cemented rather by antipathy to the prevailing power than by any hope of regaining it. A division, more real than apparent, separated the friends of the elder Adams from those who, uniting with Hamilton, had condemned his policy in the presidency. The former were probably larger in number; the latter had the advantage in talent, activity, and influence. Both soon united in placing Mr. Adams in the Senate of the state, without any solicitation or intimation of political coïncidence from him. In this election the opponents of his father's policy were acquiescent rather than content. They knew the independence and self-relying spirit of Mr. Adams, his restiveness in the trammels of party, his disposition to lead rather than follow; and yielded silently to a result which they could not prevent. The spirit which they anticipated was soon made evident.

At the annual organization of the state government it had been usual to choose the members of the Governor's Council from his political friends. Mr. Adams at once proposed to place in it one or more of his political opponents. This measure, which he maintained was wise and prudent, was regarded, according to the usual charity of party spirit, as designed to gain favor with the Democracy, and was immediately rejected. In other instances his disposition to think and act independently of the Federal party was manifested, and was of course not acceptable to its leaders.

In November he was urged to accept a nomination as a member of the House of Representatives in Congress. This he refused, saying that "he would not stand in the way of Mr. Quincy,"[5] who had been the candidate at the preceding election. This objection was immediately removed, by an assurance of the previous determination of the latter to decline, and of the satisfaction with which he regarded the nomination of Mr. Adams. The result was unsuccessful. Out of *thirty-seven hundred votes*, William Eustis was elected by a majority of *fifty-nine*. The newspapers assigned as the cause that the day of the election was rainy. Mr. Adams surmised that it was owing to the indifference to his success of the leaders of the old Federal party, and remarked on the occasion, "This is among the thousand proofs how large a portion of Federalism is a mere fair-weather principle, too weak to overcome a shower of rain. It shows the degree of dependence that can be placed on such friends. As a party their adversaries are more sure and more earnest."

In an oration, delivered in May of this year, before the Massachusetts Charitable Fire Society, Mr. Adams paid a just and feeling tribute to the memory of George Richards Minot, then recently deceased, in which the character of that historian, the purity of his life, moral worth, and intellectual endowments, are celebrated with great fulness and truth. In December he delivered, at Plymouth, an address commemorative of the Pilgrim Fathers.

During the remainder of the civil year Mr. Adams had more than once indicated his independence of party, and his settled purpose of thinking and acting on all subjects for himself. When, therefore, in February, 1803, a vacancy in the Senate of the United States occurred, the nomination of Mr. Adams was opposed by that of Timothy Pickering, who was deemed by his friends better entitled to the office, from age and long familiarity with public affairs. To their extreme disappointment, however, after three ballotings, without success, in the House of Representatives, Mr. Adams was chosen, and his election was unanimously confirmed by the Senate. In March following, another vacancy in the Senate of the United States having occurred, Mr. Pickering was elected. Thus, by a singular course of events, two statesmen were placed as colleagues in the Senate of the United States, from Massachusetts, between whom, from antecedent circumstances and known want of sympathy in political opinion, cordial coöperation could scarcely be anticipated. Apparent harmony of principles and views was, however, manifested. Mr. Adams well understood the delicacy of his position, arising from the ill-concealed jealousy of the Federalists, on the one hand, and the open dislike of the Democracy, on the other. He considered himself placed between two batteries, neither of which regarded him as one of their soldiers. He early adopted two principles, as rules of his political conduct, from which he never deviated,—to seek or solicit no public office, and, to whatever station he might be called by his country, to use no instrument for success or advancement but efficient public service.

In October, 1803, Mr. Adams removed his family to Washington, and took his seat in the Senate of the United States. On the 26th of that month he took ground in opposition to the administration upon the bill enabling the President to take possession of Louisiana, and on which he voted in coïncidence with his Federal colleagues. His objection was to the second section, which provided "*that all the military, civil and judicial powers,* exercised by the officers of the existing government of Louisiana, shall be vested in *such person and persons,* and shall be *exercised in such manner, as the President of the United States shall direct.*" The transfer of such a power to the President of the United States, Mr. Adams deemed and maintained, was unconstitutional; and he called upon the supporters of the bill to point out the article, section, or paragraph, of the constitution, which authorized Congress to confer it on the President. He regarded the constitution of the United States to be one of limited powers; and he declared that he could not reconcile it to his judgment that the authority exercised in this section was within the legitimate powers conferred by the constitution. Many years afterwards, when his vote on this occasion was made a subject of party censure and obloquy, in addition to the preceding reasons Mr. Adams gave to the public the following solemn convictions which influenced his course:

"The people of the United States had not—much less had the people of Louisiana— given to the Congress of the United States the power to form this union; and, until the consent of both people could be obtained, every act of legislation by the Congress of the United States over the people of Louisiana, distinct from that of taking possession of the territory, was, in my view, unconstitutional, and an act of usurped authority. My opinion, therefore, was that the sense of the people, both of the United States and Louisiana, should be immediately taken: of the first, by an amendment of the constitution, to be proposed and acted upon in the regular form; and of the last, by taking the votes of the people of Louisiana immediately after possession of the territory should be taken by the United States under the treaty. I had no doubt that the consent of both people would be obtained as much ease and little more loss of time than it actually took Congress to prepare an act for the government of the territory; and I thought this course of proceeding, while it would terminate in the same result as the immediate exercise of ungranted transcendental powers by Congress, would serve as a landmark of correct principles for future times,—as a memorial of homage to the fundamental principles of civil society, to the primitive sovereignty of the people, and the unalienable rights of man."

On the 3d of the ensuing November he manifested his independent spirit by voting in favor of the appropriation of eleven millions of dollars for carrying into effect the treaty for the purchase of Louisiana, in opposition to the other senators of the Federal party;—a vote which, many years afterwards, in consequence of comments of party, he took the opportunity publicly to explain. The critical nature of the course to which he foresaw he was destined was thus expressed by himself: "I have had already occasion to experience, what I had before reason to expect, the danger of adhering to my own principles. The country is so totally given up to the spirit of party, that not to follow the one or the other is an unexpiable offence. The worst of these has the popular current in its favor, and uses its triumph with all the unprincipled fury of faction; while the other is waiting, with all the impatience of revenge, for the time when its turn may come to oppress and punish by the popular favor. But my choice is made. If I cannot hope to give satisfaction to my country, I am at least determined to have the approbation of my own reflections."

On the 10th of January, 1804, Mr. Adams introduced two resolutions for the consideration of the Senate: the one declaring that "the people of the United States have never, in any manner, delegated to this Senate the power of giving its legislative concurrence to any act imposing taxes upon the inhabitants of Louisiana without their consent;" the other, "that, by concurring in any act of legislation for imposing taxes upon the inhabitants of Louisiana, without their consent, this Senate would assume a power unwarranted by the constitution, and dangerous to the liberties of the people of the United States." After a debate of three hours, both resolutions were rejected, as he anticipated; only three senators—Tracy, of Connecticut, Olcott, of New Hampshire, and White, of Delaware—voting with him in favor of the first, and twenty-two voting in the negative; Mr. Pickering, his colleague, asking to be excused from voting, and Mr. Hillhouse, the remaining Federalist in the Senate, absenting himself, obviously to avoid voting: after which the last was unanimously rejected. Concerning his course on this occasion Mr. Adams wrote: "I have no doubt of incurring much censure and obloquy for this measure. I hope I shall be prepared for and able to bear it, from the consciousness of my sincerity and of my duty."

Mr. Adams alone spoke against the bill for the temporary government of Louisiana, which passed on the ensuing 18th of February; and only four senators—Messrs. Hillhouse, Olcott, Plummer, and Stone—voted with him in the negative; Mr. Pickering absenting himself from the question.

In August, 1805, the corporation of Harvard College elected Mr. Adams Professor of Rhetoric and Oratory on the Boylston foundation. After modifications of the statutes, which he suggested, were adopted, he accepted, and immediately entered upon a course of preparatory studies, reviving his knowledge of the Greek, and making researches among English, Latin, and French writers, relative to the objects of his professorship. In the ensuing December, as a member of the Ninth Congress, he took an active part in the debates and measures of the Senate.

In January, 1806, he was appointed on a committee, of which Mr. Smith, of Maryland, was chairman, on that part of the President's message "relative to the spoliations of our commerce on the high seas, and the new principles assumed by the British courts of admiralty, as a pretext for the condemnation of our vessels in their prize courts." The debates in that committee resulted in two resolutions, both offered by Mr. Adams, adopted, reported, and finally passed by the Senate, with some modifications; Mr. Pickering, Mr. Hillhouse, and Mr. Tracy, the three Federalists in the Senate, voting for them.

British aggressions and British policy towards neutrals were, in the judgment of Mr. Adams, to be resisted at every hazard. His opinions on these subjects had been formed from opportunities which no other American statesman had equally enjoyed. In 1783 he had been present at the signature of the treaty of peace, and had imbibed the opinions and feelings then entertained by the American ministers. In 1795 he had been engaged in negotiations with British statesmen, particularly with Lord Grenville. Their views in respect of American commercial rights he considered selfish and insolent; resistance to them as an emanation from the spirit of patriotism, to which others gave the name of "prejudice," or "antipathy." Of these opinions and feelings he made no concealment; and to them may be traced the course of policy which, shortly after, separated him from the Federal party, and subjected him temporarily to their reproaches and censures.

In June, 1806, Mr. Adams was inaugurated Professor of Oratory in Harvard University, and during the ensuing two years delivered a course of lectures on Rhetoric and Oratory, which have been published in two octavo volumes, and constitute an enduring monument of fidelity, laborious research, and eloquent illustration of the objects and duties of his academic station. While engaged in these labors, an event occurred which intensely excited his feelings as a man and a statesman.

On the 22d of June, 1807, during the recess of Congress, an attack by the British ship Leopard upon the American frigate Chesapeake, by which several of her crew were killed, and four of them taken away, created surprise and indignation throughout the Union. From the previous state of his opinions, no one partook more strongly of these feelings than Mr. Adams. He immediately urged his political friends to call a town-meeting in Faneuil Hall on the subject; but the measure was utterly discouraged by the leaders of the Federal party. Soon, however, a meeting of the inhabitants of Boston and the neighboring towns was called at the Statehouse to consider that outrage. The meeting was not numerous, and consisted almost entirely of the friends of the administration. Mr. Gerry was chosen chairman, and Mr. Adams, who had attended it, was appointed on the committee to prepare appropriate resolutions. These, when reported and modified according to suggestions made by Mr. Adams, were unanimously adopted. When it was intimated to him that his course was regarded as symptomatic of party apostasy, he replied that his sense of duty should never yield to the pleasure of party.

Soon after, in consequence of letters from a committee of correspondence at Norfolk, a town-meeting was called at Faneuil Hall, at which resolutions were passed, reported by a committee of which Mr. Adams was chairman. Mr. Otis offered a resolution calling on government for the protection of a naval force; but, Mr. Adams objecting, it was withdrawn.

On the 27th of October, 1807, Mr. Jefferson called a special meeting of Congress, chiefly on account of the affair of the Chesapeake. On this subject the discrepancy of the opinions and views of Mr. Adams with those of the leaders of the Federal party were so openly manifested, that his separation from it was generally anticipated. He had now been a member of the Senate during four sessions, but had not been permitted to exercise any decided influence on the subjects of debate. Many of his propositions had failed under circumstances which indicated a disposition to discourage him from such attempts. Some, which on his motion had been negatived, had been subsequently easily carried, when moved by members of the administration party. In respect of the general policy of the country, he had been uniformly in a small and decreasing minority. His opinion and votes, however, had been oftener in unison with the administration than with their opponents; and he had met with quite as much opposition from his party friends as from their adversaries. At this crisis, however, he took the lead, and, immediately on the delivery of the President's message, offered to the Senate two resolutions. 1st. "That so much of the President's message as related to the recent outrages committed by British armed vessels within the jurisdiction and in the waters of the United States, and to the legislative provisions which may be expedient as resulting from them, be referred to a select committee, with leave to report by bill or otherwise." 2d. "That so much of the said message as relates to the formation of the seamen of the United States into a special militia, for the purpose of occasional defence of the harbors against sudden attacks, be referred to a special committee, with leave to report by bill or otherwise."

Both these resolutions were adopted, and on the first Mr. Adams was appointed chairman. Soon after, in the course of the same session, Mr. Adams took the incipient step on several important subjects, and was appointed chairman of the committee to whom they were intrusted in each of them; thus manifesting that he intended no longer to take a subordinate part in the proceedings of the Senate, and that a disposition to disappoint him was no longer a feeling entertained by a majority of that body.

On the 24th of November, Mr. Adams reported a bill on the British outrages, and, on a motion to strike out of it a section providing that "no British armed vessel shall be admitted to enter the harbors and waters under the jurisdiction of the United States, except when forced in by distress, by the dangers of the sea, or when charged with public dispatches, or coming as a public packet." Mr. Adams, with twenty-five others, voted in the negative. Messrs. Goodrich, Pickering, and Hillhouse, the only three Federal senators, alone voted in the affirmative. On the final passage of the bill, Mr. Adams voted with the majority, in the affirmative, and the three Federal senators in the negative.

On the 18th of December, 1807, Mr. Jefferson sent a message to Congress recommending an embargo. A bill in conformity having been immediately reported, a motion was made, in the Senate, that the rule which required three different readings on three different days should be suspended for three days. Violent debates ensued. On the vote to suspend, Mr. Adams voted in the affirmative. His colleague and every other Federalist voted in the negative.

On the final passage of the bill laying the embargo, and on the subject of British aggressions, Mr. Adams again repeatedly separated from his colleagues and the other members of the Federal party, and voted in coïncidence with the administration.

Newspaper asperities and severities in debate ensued, which he supported, as he averred, in the consciousness that the course of the administration was the only safe one for his country, and in the belief that it would be justified by events, and receive the sanction of future times. His course had been, however, opposite to that of the other Federal members in both houses of Congress. On a subject so momentous to the commercial states, his colleague, Mr. Pickering, thought proper to justify to the people of Massachusetts the course and motives of the Federal party, and on the 16th of February, 1808, addressed a letter to James Sullivan, Governor of that commonwealth, stating what papers "had been submitted to Congress by the President in justification of the embargo," and endeavored to show, by facts and reasonings, that the measure had been passed "without sufficient motive or legitimate object; that the avowed dangers were imaginary and assumed; and that the real motives for it were contained in those French dispatches which had been confidentially submitted to Congress, and withdrawn by Mr. Jefferson, in which the French emperor had declared that he will have no neutrals;" that the embargo was "a substitute—a mild compliance with this harsh demand;" that he (Mr. Pickering) had reason to believe that the President contemplated its continuance until the French emperor repealed his decrees. He concluded by asserting that an embargo was not necessary to the safety of our seamen, our vessels, or our merchandise, and was calculated to mislead the public mind to the public ruin.

This letter, though intended for the Legislature of Massachusetts, was not communicated to it, the political path of Governor Sullivan not being coïncident with that of Colonel Pickering. But it was soon published by a friend of the writer. In a letter to Harrison G. Otis, on the 31st of March, 1808, Mr. Adams published a reply, stating that Mr. Pickering, in enumerating the *pretences* (for he thinks there were no causes) for the embargo, totally omitted the British orders in council, which, although not made the subject of special communication by the President, had been published in the *National Intelligencer* antecedent to the embargo, the sweeping tendency of whose effects formed, to his understanding, a powerful motive, and together with the papers a decisive one, for assenting to the embargo; a measure which he regarded as "the only shelter from the tempest, the last refuge of our violated peace." He adds: "The most serious effect of Mr. Pickering's letter is its tendency to reconcile the commercial states to the servitude of British protection, and war with all the rest of Europe." Regarding it as a proposition to strike the standard of the nation, he proceeded to investigate the claims of Great Britain in respect of impressment, and to her denying neutrals the right of any commerce with her enemies and their colonies, which was not allowed in time of peace. This result of the rule of 1756, he asserted, was "in itself and its consequences one of the deadliest poisons in which it was possible for Great Britain to tinge the weapons of her hostility." The decrees of France and Spain, by which every neutral vessel which submitted to English search was declared "*denationalized*," and became English property, though cruel in execution, and too foolish and absurd to be refuted, were but the reasoning of British jurists, and the simple application to the circumstances and powers of France of the rule of the war of 1756. Mr. Adams then proceeded to state and reason upon other aggressions of Great Britain on our commerce, and asserted that "between unqualified submission and offensive resistance against the war declared against American commerce by the concurring decrees of all the belligerent powers, the embargo had been adopted; and having the double tendency of promoting peace and preparing for war, in its operation is the great advantage which more than outweighs all its evils."

A course thus independent, and in harmony with the policy of the administration, caused Mr. Adams to become obnoxious to suspicions inevitably incident to every man who, in critical periods, amid party struggles, changes his political relations. Of the dissatisfaction of the Legislature of Massachusetts Mr. Adams received an immediate proof. His senatorial term would expire on the 3d of March, 1809. To indicate their disapprobation of his course, they anticipated the time of electing a senator of the United States, which, according to usage, would have been in the legislative session of that year. James Lloyd was chosen senator from Massachusetts by a vote of two hundred and forty-eight over two hundred and thirteen for Mr. Adams, in the House of Representatives, and of twenty-one over seventeen, in the Senate. On the same day anti-embargo resolutions were passed in both branches by like majorities.

The next day Mr. Adams addressed a letter to that Legislature, in which he stated that it had been his endeavor, deeming it his duty, to support the administration of the general government in all necessary measures to preserve the persons and property of our citizens from depredation, and to vindicate the rights essential to the independence of our country; that certain resolutions having passed the Legislature, expressing disapprobation of measures to which, under these motives, he had given assent, and which he considered as enjoining upon the representatives of the state in Congress a *sort* of opposition to the national administration in which, consistently with his principles, he could not concur, he, therefore, to give the Legislature an opportunity to place in the Senate of the United States a member whose views might be more coincident with those they entertained, resigned his seat in that body. James Lloyd was immediately chosen by the Legislature to take the seat thus vacated.

In the midst of these political agitations Mr. Adams was constantly employed in writing and delivering lectures, as Professor of Rhetoric, and in pursuing his studies of the Greek language and the science of astronomy. During the ensuing summer, the neglect or withdrawal of some former friends, and the open asperities of others, were often trying to his feelings. Rumors were circulated of promises made or of expectations held out to him by the administration; and, although he unequivocally denied their truth, belief in them was in accordance with the party passions of the moment, and was diligently inculcated on the popular mind by pamphlets and newspapers. Also in the summer and winter of 1808 he had to support an oppressive weight of obloquy, from which he had no relief, as he asserted, but an unshaken confidence that his course had been coïncident with the true interests of his country, and would finally be approved by it.

In the winter of 1809 he attended the Supreme Court of the United States at Washington, and while there first received from Mr. Madison, two days after his inauguration as President of the United States, an intimation of his intention to offer him the appointment of minister plenipotentiary to St. Petersburg. When this nomination and the concurrence of the Senate became public, it was seized and commented upon as unquestionable evidence of the motives which had occasioned the change in his political course, and was made the subject of severe animadversions in all the forms in which indignant partisans are accustomed to express censure and reproach. This appointment his political adversaries announced as at once a proof and the reward of his apostasy. Such insinuations were felt by Mr. Adams as an insupportable wrong. For seven years he had previously represented his country at foreign courts, in stations to which he had been first appointed by Washington himself; who had declared that he must not think of retiring from the diplomatic line, and pronounced him the ablest, and destined ultimately to become the head, of the diplomatic corps.[6] Under these circumstances he felt that even party spirit itself might have spared towards him this reproach, and have recognized higher motives than seeking and receiving reward for party services. Actuated by this sense of wrong, while preparing for his departure on the mission to Russia, he issued from the press a series of strictures, at once severe and vindictive, on the policy of the Federal leaders, in the form of a review of the writings of Fisher Ames; which were regarded by the public, and probably intended by himself, as an evidence of irreconcilable abandonment of the party to which he had formerly belonged, and a permanent adhesion to that of the national administration.

CHAPTER III.

VOYAGE.—ARRIVAL AT ST. PETERSBURG.—PRESENTATION TO THE EMPEROR.— RESIDENCE AT THE IMPERIAL COURT.—DIPLOMATIC INTERVIEWS.—PRIVATE STUDIES.—APPOINTED ONE OF THE COMMISSIONERS TO TREAT FOR PEACE WITH GREAT BRITAIN.—LEAVES RUSSIA.

After resigning his professorship at Harvard University, Mr. Adams embarked from Boston, with Mrs. Adams and his youngest son, on the 5th of August, 1809, in a merchant ship, bound to St. Petersburg. During a boisterous and tedious voyage his classical and diplomatic studies were pursued with characteristic assiduity. The English were then at war with Denmark; and, as they entered the Baltic, a British cruiser sent an officer to examine their papers. The same day they were boarded by a Danish officer, who ordered the ship to Christiansand. The captain thought it prudent to refuse, and to seek shelter from an equinoctial gale in the harbor of Flecknoe. The papers of the ship and Mr. Adams' commission were examined, and he afterwards went up to Christiansand, where he found thirty-eight American vessels, which had been brought in by privateers between the months of May and August, and were detained for adjudication. Sixteen had been condemned, and had appealed to the higher tribunals of the country. The Americans thus detained presented a memorial to Mr. Adams, to be forwarded to the President of the United States. The sight of so many of his countrymen in distress was extremely painful, and he determined to make an effort for their relief, without waiting for express authority from his government.

On resuming their voyage, their course was again impeded by a British squadron. An officer was sent on board by Captain Dundas, of the Stately, a sixty-four gun ship, to examine their papers. He compared the personal appearance of each of the seamen with his protection, threatening to take a native of Charlestown because his person did not correspond with the description, and finally ordered the ship to return through the Cattegat.

Mr. Adams immediately went on board the Stately, showed his commission, and remonstrated with Captain Dundas, who referred him to Admiral Bertie, the commander of the squadron, who was in his stateroom on the quarter-deck. After a protracted opposition, the admiral acknowledged the usage of nations, and, as an ambassador, permitted him to pursue his voyage by the usual course through the sound. From these and similar difficulties, Mr. Adams did not land at St. Petersburg until the 23d of October.

The Chancellor of the empire, Count Romanzoff, received Mr. Adams in courtly state, and requested a copy of his credential letter, with an assurance of the pleasure his appointment had given him personally. His presentation was postponed, from the temporary indisposition of the emperor; but he was immediately invited, by Count Romanzoff, to a diplomatic dinner, in a style of the highest splendor. Among the company was the French ambassador, M. de Caulaincourt, Duke de Vicence, the foreign ministers then at the Russian Court, and many of the nobility. In the mansion of the Chancellor Mr. Adams had dined in 1781, as secretary of Mr. Dana, in the same splendid style, with the Marquis de Verac, at that time French minister at the Russian Court. His mind was more impressed with the recollection of the magnificence he had then witnessed on the same spot, and with reflections on the mutability of human fortune, than with the gorgeous scene around him.

The Emperor Alexander received Mr. Adams alone, in his cabinet, and expressed his pleasure at seeing him at St. Petersburg. Mr. Adams, on presenting his credentials, said that the President of the United States had desired him to express the hope that his mission would be considered as a proof of respect for the person and character of his majesty, as an acknowledgment of the many testimonies of good-will he had already given to the United States, and of a desire to strengthen commercial relations between them and his provinces. The emperor replied, that, in everything depending on him, he should be happy to contribute to the increase of their friendly relations; that it was his wish to establish a just system of maritime rights, and that he should adhere invariably to those he had declared. He then entered into a confidential exposition of the obstacles then existing to a general pacification, and of the policy of the different European powers, and said that he considered the system of the United States towards them as wise and just. Mr. Adams replied, that the United States, being a great commercial and pacific nation, were deeply interested in a system which would give security to commerce in time of war. It was hoped this great blessing to humanity would be accomplished by his imperial majesty himself; and that the United States, by all means consistent with their peace, and their separation from the political system of Europe, would contribute to the support of the liberal principles to which his majesty had expressed so strong and just an attachment. The emperor replied, that between Russia and the United States there could be no interference of interests, no cause for dissension; but that, by means of commerce, the two states might be greatly useful to each other; and his desire was to give the greatest extension and facility to these means of mutual interest. Passing to other topics, he made many inquiries relative to the cities of the United States.

The empress and the empress mother each gave Mr. Adams a private audience; and, after Mrs. Adams had also been presented to the imperial family, they were invited to a succession of splendid entertainments. "The formalities of these court presentations," Mr. Adams remarked, "are so trifling and insignificant in themselves, and so important in the eyes of princes and courtiers, that they are much more embarrassing to an American than business of greater importance. It is not safe or prudent to despise them, nor practicable for a person of rational understanding to value them."

As the balls and parties given by the emperor, the foreign ministers, and the nobility, did not usually terminate until four o'clock in the morning, they so essentially interfered with the studies and official engagements of Mr. Adams, that he determined, as far as his station permitted, to relinquish attending them.

In December he requested the Chancellor to solicit the emperor to interpose his good offices with the Danish government for the restoration of American property sequestrated in the ports of Holstein. Count Romanzoff, in reply, stated that the emperor took great pleasure in complying with that request, and was gratified by this opportunity to show his friendly disposition towards the United States, and immediately ordered the Chancellor to represent to the Danish government the wish of the emperor that the American property might be examined and restored as soon as possible. The Danish government acceded at once to the emperor's desire; and the effect of his interposition was gratefully acknowledged by the Americans whose property was liberated.

The residence of Mr. Adams in Russia was during an eventful period. The Emperor Alexander was at first endeavoring to avoid a collision with Bonaparte, by yielding to his policy; and afterwards, on his invasion, was engaged in driving him out of Russia, bereft of his army and continental influence. During these years the release or relief of American vessels and seamen from the effects of the French emperor's Berlin and Milan decrees, and from other seizures and sequestrations, were the chief objects to which Mr. Adams directed his attention.

His subsequent attempts to establish permanent commercial relations between the United States and Russia were favorably received by that government. The chancellor of the empire, Count Romanzoff, acknowledged the importance of a treaty between Russia and the United States, and intimated that the only obstacle was the convulsed state of opinion at that period throughout the commercial world, which was such that "it hardly seemed possible to agree to anything which had common sense in it." Count Romanzoff conducted towards Mr. Adams not only with official respect, but with cordiality. On one occasion he transmitted to him by his private secretary a work relative to an armed neutrality, which was preparing under his auspices for publication, requesting the American minister to make such observations upon it as he thought proper.

The courteous manners of the Emperor Alexander, his apparent desire to conciliate the United States, and the personal intercourse to which he admitted its representative, were frequently acknowledged by Mr. Adams. In the midst of the splendor of the Russian Court, and the magnificent entertainments of its ministers and of resident plenipotentiaries, some of whom expended fifty thousand roubles a year, and the ambassador from the French emperor over four hundred thousand, he maintained the simplicity of style suited at once to his salary and to the character of the country he represented. Loans to an indefinite amount were proffered to him by mercantile houses. These he uniformly declined, though under circumstances of great temptation to accept them. "The opportunities," he wrote, "of thus anticipating my regular income, it is difficult to resist. But I am determined to do it. The whole of my life has been one continued experience of the difficulty of a man's adhering to the principle of living within his income; the first and most important principle of private economy. In this country beyond all others, and in my situation more than any other, the temptations to expense amount almost to compulsion. I have withstood them hitherto, and hope for firmness of character to withstand them in future."

In connection with this topic, the following anecdote was related by Mr. Adams: "As I was walking, this morning (in May, 1811), I was met by the emperor, who was also walking. As he approached he said, 'Monsieur Adams, il y a cent ans que je ne vous ai vu,' and took me cordially by the hand. After some common observations, he asked me whether I intended to take a house in the country this summer. I said 'No; that I had for some time that intention, but I had given it up,'—'And why?' said he. I was hesitating upon an answer, when he relieved me from my embarrassment by saying, 'Peut-être sont-ce des considerations de finance.' As he said it in perfect good humor, and with a smile, I replied, in the same manner, 'Mais, Sire, elles y sont pour une bonne partie.'—'Fort bien,' said he, 'vous avez raison. Il faut toujours proportionner la depense à la recette;' a maxim," remarks Mr. Adams, "worthy of an emperor, though few emperors practise upon it."

The customs, manners, and habits, of the nobility and the people; their public institutions, edifices, monuments, and collections in the fine arts; the overweening influence of the clergy, their power and political subserviency; the character of the foreign ministers, and the policy of the courts they represented, were carefully observed and noted down for future thought and illustration.

Nor were his researches restricted to subjects of diplomatic duty, or to objects immediately connected with his foreign relations. He studied the language and history of Russia, the course and usages of its trade, especially in relation to China, and made laborious inquiries into the proportions of Russian, English, and French weights, measures, and coins. In obtaining a minute accuracy in these proportions, he employed many hours; on which he observed, "I fear I shall never attain them, and the usefulness of which is at least problematical;[7] but *Trahit sua quemque ipsa voluntas*,' my studies generally command me—I seldom control them."

The progress of the seasons in Russia, the rising and the setting of the sun, were daily noted, as also the variation of the climate, by the thermometer. His thirst for knowledge, and his desire of investigating causes and effects, were never satiated.

Astronomy was with him a subject of early and intense interest. He studied the works of Schubert, Lalande, Biot, and Lacroix, and constantly observed the heavens, and noticed their phenomena, according to the calendar. By Langlet's and Dufresnoy's tables he attempted to ascertain with precision the Arabian and Turkish computations of time, comparing them with those of Christian nations. From astronomy and chronology he was drawn into the study of mathematics, and the logarithms in the tables of Collet.

Neither were the works of the ancient philosophers and orators omitted in the sphere of his studies. The works of Plato, the orations of Demosthenes, Isocrates, Æschines, and Cicero, were not only read, but made the subject of critical analysis, comparison, and reflection.

Religion was also in his mind a predominating element. A practice, which he prescribed to himself, and never omitted, of reading daily five chapters in the Bible, familiarized his mind with its pages. In connection with these studies he read habitually the works of Butler, Bossuet, Tillotson, Massillon, Atterbury, and Watts. With such an ardor for knowledge, and universality in its pursuit, it is not surprising that he should say, as on one occasion he did, "I feel nothing like the tediousness of time. I suffer nothing like *ennui*. Time is too short for me, rather than too long. If the day was forty-eight hours, instead of twenty-four, I could employ them all, if I had but eyes and hands to read and write."

In 1810, citizens of the United States, who had formed a settlement on the north-west coast of North America, were embarrassed in their intercourse with China, by the Chinese mistaking American for Russian vessels. In a conversation with Mr. Adams on the means of avoiding this difficulty, Count Romanzoff described the obstacles the Russians had experienced in their commerce with China. He stated that in the reign of Catharine II. the Emperor of China complained of a governor of a province bordering on Russia, as "a bad man;" in consequence of which, the empress caused him to be removed. This concession did not satisfy the Chinese emperor, who declared the punishment insufficient, and demanded that "*the offender should be impaled alive by way of atonement*." This demand so shocked Catharine that she issued an edict prohibiting her subjects from all commercial relations with China. This edict continued in force until the Chinese themselves sought for a renewal of their former intercourse, when the empress yielded her resentment to policy.

The loss of time from the civilities and visits of his numerous diplomatic associates was annoying to Mr. Adams. "I have been engaged," he wrote, "the whole forenoon; and though I rise at six o'clock, I am sometimes unable to find time to write only part of a private letter in the course of the day. These visits take up so much of my time, that I sometimes think of taking a resolution not to receive them; but, on the other hand, so much information important to be possessed, and particularly relative to current political events, is to be collected from them, that they are rather to be encouraged than discountenanced."

"The French ambassador," writes Mr. Adams, "assured me that he hoped the difference between his country and mine would soon be settled, and requested me to inform my government that it was the desire of the Emperor of France, and of his ministers, to come to the best terms with the United States; that they knew our interests were the same, but he was perfectly persuaded that, if any other person but Gen. Armstrong was there, our business might be settled entirely to our satisfaction. I told him that, as I was as desirous that we should come to a good understanding, I regretted very much that anything personal to General Armstrong should be considered by his government as offensive; that I was sure the government of the United States would regret it also, and would wish, on learning it, to be informed what were the occasions of displeasure which he had given. 'C'est d'abord un très galant homme,' said the ambassador; 'but he never shows himself, and upon every little occasion, when by a verbal explanation with the minister General Armstrong might obtain anything, he writes peevish notes.' This appears to me," observes Mr. Adams, "an intriguing manœuvre, of which the minister thinks I might be made the dupe."

On one occasion, Count Romanzoff requested an interview with Mr. Adams, and, among other inquiries, asked what could be done to restore freedom and security to commerce. He replied, that, "setting aside all official character and responsibility, and speaking as an individual upon public affairs," as Count Romanzoff had requested, he thought the best course towards peace was for his excellency to convince the French government that the continental system, as they called it, and as they managed it, was promoting to the utmost extent the views of England, and, instead of impairing her commerce, was securing to her that of the whole world, and was pouring into her lap the means of continuing the war just as long as her ministers should consider it expedient. He could hardly conceive that the Emperor Napoleon was so blind as not to have made that discovery already. Three years' experience, with the effects of it becoming every day more flagrant, had made the inference too clear and unquestionable. The Emperor Napoleon, with all his power, could neither control the elements nor the passions of mankind. He had found his own brother could not or would not carry his system into execution, and had finally cast at his feet the crown he had given him, rather than continue to be his instrument any longer. Count Romanzoff gravely questioned the statement of Mr. Adams respecting the commercial prosperity of England, but admitted his views in general to be correct, saying that, as long as a system was agreed upon, he thought exceptions from it ought not to be allowed. Mr. Adams then asked him how that was possible, when the Emperor Napoleon himself was the first to make such exceptions, and to give licenses for a direct trade with England? Count Romanzoff replied, that he thought all such licenses wrong, and he believed that there were not so many of them as was pretended. There was indeed one case of a vessel coming to St. Petersburg both with an English license and a license from the Emperor Napoleon. He was of opinion that she ought to be confiscated for having the English license. But the French commercial and diplomatic agents were very desirous that she might go free, on account of her French license; and perhaps the Emperor, in consideration of his ally, might so determine. Romanzoff complained bitterly that all the ancient established principles, both of commercial and political rectitude, had, in a manner, vanished from the world; and observed that, with all her faults, England had the advantage over her neighbors, of having hitherto most successfully resisted all the innovations upon ancient principles and establishments. For his own part, since he had been at the head of affairs, he could sincerely protest one wish had been at the bottom of all his policy, and the aim of all his labors,—and that was universal peace.

In 1811 Mr. Adams received from the Secretary of State a commission of an Associate Justice of the Supreme Court of the United States; an appointment which he immediately declined.

In 1812 the emperor directed Count Romanzoff to inquire whether, if he should offer his mediation to effect a pacification between the United States and Great Britain, Mr. Adams was aware of any objection on the part of his government. He replied, that, speaking only from a general knowledge of its sentiments, the proposal of the emperor would be considered a new evidence of his regard and friendship for the United States, whatever determination might be formed. Under this assurance, the offer was made, transmitted, and immediately accepted. In July, 1813, Mr. Gallatin and Mr. Bayard, being associated with Mr. Adams on this mission, arrived at St. Petersburg, bringing credentials, for the purpose of commencing a negotiation, under the mediation of the emperor.

On communicating these credentials to Count Romanzoff, Mr. Adams informed him that he had received instructions from the American government to remain at St. Petersburg under the commission he had heretofore held; and that he had been mistaken in supposing that his colleagues had other destination, independent of this mission. His conjecture had been founded on the doubt whether the President would have appointed this mission solely upon the supposition that the mediation would be accepted by the British government; but he was now instructed that the President, considering the acceptance of the British government as probable, though aware that if they should reject it this measure might wear the appearance of precipitation, thought it more advisable to incur that risk than the danger of prolonging unnecessarily the war for six or nine months, as might happen if the British should immediately have accepted the mediation, and he should have delayed this step until he was informed of it. It was with the President a great object to manifest, not only a cheerful acceptance on the part of the United States, but in a signal manner his sentiments of consideration and respect for the emperor, and to do honor to the motives on which he offered his mediation. After hearing these statements of Mr. Adams, the emperor directed Count Romanzoff to express his particular gratification with the honorable notice the American government had taken of his offer to effect a pacification between Great Britain and the United States.

In September Lord Cathcart delivered to the emperor a memoir from the British government, stating at length their reasons for declining any mediation in their contest with the United States. But, although the British government did not choose that a third power should interfere in this controversy, it had offered to treat directly with the American envoys at Gottenburg, or in London.

This proposition having been accepted by the United States, Mr. Adams was associated with Bayard, Clay, and Russell, in the negotiation. After taking leave of the empress and Count Romanzoff,—the emperor being then before Paris with the allied armies,—he quitted St. Petersburg on the 28th of April, 1814. His family remained in that city, and he travelled alone to Revel. There he received the news of the taking of Paris, and the abdication of Napoleon. From thence he embarked for Stockholm.

CHAPTER IV.

RESIDENCE AT GHENT.—AT PARIS.—IN LONDON.—PRESENTATION TO THE PRINCE REGENT.—NEGOTIATION WITH LORD CASTLEREAGH.—APPOINTED SECRETARY OF STATE.—LEAVES ENGLAND.

Mr. Adams arrived in Stockholm on the 24th of May, and after visiting Count Engerström, the Minister of Foreign Affairs, and meeting the Swedish and foreign ministers at a diplomatic dinner, given by Baron Strogonoff, he left that city on the 2d of June. A messenger from Mr. Clay informed him that, at the request of Lord Bathurst, the negotiation of the treaty of peace had been transferred to Ghent. Passing through Sweden, he embarked from Gottenburg in the United States corvette John Adams for the Texel, landed at the Helder, and proceeded through Holland to Ghent, where his associates met for the first time in his apartments on the 30th of June. The British commissioners did not arrive until the 7th of August, and their negotiations were not concluded until the 24th of December, 1814. On presenting three copies of the treaty, signed and sealed by all the commissioners, to Mr. Adams, and on receiving three from him, Lord Gambier said, he trusted the result of their labors would be permanent. Mr. Adams replied, he hoped it would be the *last* treaty of peace between Great Britain and the United States.

The American commissioners were presented to the Prince of Orange, the sovereign of the Netherlands, and, on the 5th of January, 1815, the citizens of Ghent celebrated the ratification of the treaty, by inviting the representatives of both nations to a public entertainment at the Hotel de Ville. Mr. Adams left that city with characteristic expressions of gratitude for the result of a negotiation which he hoped would prove propitious to the union and best interests of his country.

On the 3d of February he arrived in Paris, and met the American commissioners, and with them was presented by Mr. Crawford, resident minister of the United States, to Louis the Eighteenth, and to the Duke and Duchess of Angoulême. He was also presented to the Duke of Orleans, at the Palais Royal, who spoke with grateful remembrance of hospitalities he had received in America. Mr. Adams was often in the society of Lafayette, Madame de Staël, Humboldt, Constant, and other eminent persons, and was deeply interested in observing the effect of all changes in the laws and government of France.

The intelligence that Napoleon had left Elba soon caused great excitement and anxiety in Paris, which continued to increase until the morning of the 20th of March, when Louis the Eighteenth left the Tuileries. In the evening Napoleon alighted there so silently, that Mr. Adams, who was at the Théatre Français, not a quarter of a mile distant, was unaware of the fact until the next day, when the gazettes of Paris, which had showered execrations upon him, announced "the arrival of his majesty, the Emperor, at *his* palace of the Tuileries." In the Place du Carousel Mr. Adams, in his morning walk, saw regiments of cavalry, belonging to the garrison of Paris, which had been sent out to oppose Napoleon, pass in review before him, their helmets and the clasps of their belts yet glowing with the arms of the Bourbons. The theatres assumed the title of Imperial, and at the opera, in the evening, the arms of the emperor were placed on the curtain and on the royal box.

A few days afterwards, Mr. Adams requested an interview with the emperor's Minister of Foreign Affairs, the Duke de Vicence, with whom he had been previously acquainted at St. Petersburg. He assured Mr. Adams that the late revolution had been effected without effort; that Fouché, the new Minister of Police, who received reports from every part of the country, informed him that there had not been one act of violence or resistance. He said, that if Napoleon had not returned, the misconduct of the Bourbons would have caused an insurrection of the people in less than six months; that the emperor had renounced all ideas of extended conquest, and only desired peace with all the world. Mr. Adams expressed a hope that the relations between France and the United States would become friendly and mutually advantageous, and said he was awaiting orders from his government, and should soon need a passport to England. The duke assured him of his readiness to comply with any request from him or from Mr. Crawford. All the other foreign ministers had already quitted Paris.

After Mrs. Adams had arrived from St. Petersburg, Mr. Adams, having been appointed American minister at the British Court, left Paris, with his family, on the 16th of May, 1815. About the time of his departure he observed: "War appears to be certain. The first thought of the inhabitants of Paris will be to save themselves. They have no attachment either to the Bourbons or Napoleon. They will submit quietly to the victorious party, and do nothing to support either."

On the 25th of May Mr. Adams arrived in London, and on the 29th had an interview with Lord Castlereagh relative to the treaty of peace, and the commercial relations of Great Britain with the United States. The Prince Regent, at a private audience, said the United States might rely with full assurance on his determination to fulfil all engagements with them on the part of Great Britain.

After the convention concerning commerce had been concluded, and Mr. Gallatin and Mr. Clay had departed, Mr. Adams removed his residence to Boston House, Ealing, nine miles from London, where he commanded time for his favorite studies, and reciprocated the civilities paid to him and Mrs. Adams. He continued to receive in public and private the distinguished attentions due to his official station and his personal character and attainments. The queen gave him a private audience, and in May, 1816, with Mrs. Adams, he was present at the marriage of the Princess Charlotte of Wales. His society was sought and highly appreciated by the most eminent men of all classes; and he availed himself, with characteristic assiduity, of all opportunities to acquire information, especially that relative to the science of government, and the political relations of Europe.

Some conversations and opinions his papers preserve tend to throw light upon his course and character. In reply to an inquiry made by Lord Holland concerning the forms and results of representation in the United States, Mr. Adams said that one consequence was that a very great proportion of their public men were lawyers. Lord Holland said it was precisely the same in England; that the theory of their representation in the House of Commons was bad, but perhaps no theory could produce a more perfect practice of representation of all classes and interests of the community. Even the close boroughs often served to bring in able and useful men, who by a more correct theory would find themselves excluded. Men of property could always make their way into Parliament by their wealth. Men of family might go into the House of Commons for a few years in youth, to get experience of public business, and to employ time for useful purposes; and there was no man of real talent who, in one way or another, could fail of obtaining, sooner or later, admission into Parliament. But a great proportion of the House of Commons were lawyers, and most of the business of the house was done by them. In the House of Lords all that was of any use was done by lawyers. The great practical use of the House of Lords was to be a check upon mischief that might be done by the Commons. Many bills passed through that house without sufficient consideration. The Chancellor is under a sort of personal responsibility to examine and stop them. His character depends upon it. He is at the head of the nobility of the country, and his consideration depends upon his keeping this vigilant eye on the proceedings of the Commons. All the ordinary business of the house, therefore, rests upon a lawyer.

Lord Holland observed that from what he heard the most defective part of our institutions was the judiciary; which Mr. Adams admitted.

In August, 1816, at a diplomatic dinner, given on St. Louis' day, by the French ambassador, the Marquis D'Osmond, Mr. Adams first met Mr. Canning, then recently appointed President of the Board of Control. At his request, he was introduced by Lord Liverpool to Mr. Adams. They both spoke of the great and rapid increase of the United States, and Canning inquired when the next presidential election would take place, and who would probably be chosen. Mr. Adams replied, Mr. Monroe. Lord Liverpool observed that he had heard his election might be opposed on account of his being a Virginian. Mr. Adams said that had been a ground of objection, but it would not avail. He afterwards remarks: "Mr. Canning, whose celebrity is great, and whose talents are probably greater than those of any other member of the cabinet, and who has been invariably noted for his bitterness against the United States, seemed desirous to make up by an excess of civility for the feelings he has so constantly manifested against us."

After reading the Gazette Extraordinary sent him by Lord Castlereagh, containing an account of the victory of Lord Exmouth, on the 27th of August, over the Algerines, and that the terms of capitulation had forced them to deliver up all their Christian slaves, to repay ransom-money, and to stipulate for the formal abolition of Christian slavery in Algiers forever, Mr. Adams observed, "This is a deed of real glory."

The Lord Mayor of London introduced Mr. Adams to Sir Philip Francis, then the supposed author of the letters of Junius. On this celebrated work, on a subsequent occasion, Mr. Adams remarked: "Sir Philip Francis is almost demonstrated to be the culprit. The speeches of Lord Chatham bear the stamp of a mind not unequal to the composition of Junius. Those of Burke are of a higher order. Were it ascertained that either of them were the political assassin who stabbed with the dagger of Junius, I should not add a particle of admiration for his talents, and should lose all my respect for his morals. Junius was essentially a sophist. His religion was infidelity, his abstract ethics depraved, his temper bitterly malignant, and his nervous system timid and cowardly. The concealment of his name at the time when he wrote was the effect of dishonest fear. The perpetuation of it could only proceed from the consciousness that the disclosure of his person would be discreditable to his fame. The object of Junius, when he began to write, was merely to overthrow the administration then in power. He attacked them in a mass and individually; their measures, their capacities, their characters public and private; charged them with every crime and every vice. Afterwards, he followed up his general assault by singling out, successively, the Dukes of Grafton and Bedford, Lord Mansfield, Sir William Blackstone, and the King himself. He magnified mole-hills into mountains, inflamed pin-scratches into deadly wounds, and at last abandoned his course in despair at the very time when he might have pursued it with the most effect. But while he was battering the ministry upon paltry topics, which had neither root or stem, he had declared himself emphatically and repeatedly upon their side on the only subject on which their fate and the destiny of the nation altogether depended—the controversy with America. The course he took in the early stage of that conflict, and his disappearance from the theatre of politics at the time when it was ripening into the magnitude of its nature, have marked Junius in my mind as a man of small things—a splendid trifler, a pompous and shallow politician."

In July, 1816, Mr. Adams showed Lord Castlereagh his authority and instructions to negotiate a new commercial convention with the British government, stating "that one object was to open the trade between the United States and the British colonies in North America and the West Indies, as great changes had occurred since the existing convention between the countries was signed. That convention equalized the duties upon British and American vessels, in the intercourse between Europe and the United States, and thereby admitted British vessels into the ports of the United States upon terms of equal competition with American vessels. But, since that time, the exclusive system of colonial regulations had been resumed in the West Indies with extraordinary rigor. American vessels had been excluded from all the ports, and some seizures had been made with such severity that there were cases upon which it would soon become his duty to address the British government in behalf of individuals who had suffered, and deemed themselves entitled to the restitution of their property. The consequence of these new regulations, as combined with the operation of the commercial convention, was, that British vessels being admitted into our ports upon equal terms with our own, and then being exclusively received in the British West India ports, not only thus monopolized the trade between the United States and the West Indies, but acquired an advantage in the direct trade from Europe to the United States, which defeated the main object of the convention itself, of placing the shipping of the two countries upon equal terms of fair competition. In North America the same system was pursued by the colonial government of Upper Canada. An act of the Colonial Legislature was passed at their last session, vesting in the Lieutenant-Governor and Council of the province the power of regulating its trade with the United States; and immediately afterwards a new tariff of duties was issued, by an order of the previous Council, dated the 18th of April, laying excessively heavy duties upon all articles imported into the province from the United States, with the exception of certain articles of provision of the first necessity; and a tonnage duty of twelve and sixpence per ton upon American vessels, which was equivalent to a total prohibition."

Lord Castlereagh said "that he had not been in the way of following the measures adopted in that quarter, and was not aware that there had been any new regulations either in the West Indies or in North America. In time of war he knew it had been usual to open the ports of the West India Islands to foreigners, merely as a measure of necessity; and it was not until the Americans attempted to starve them by their embargo acts that they were driven to the resort of finding resources elsewhere. But in time of peace it had been usual to exclude foreigners from these islands."

He then asked if the trade was considerable. Mr. Adams replied that it was. "Even in time of peace it was highly necessary to the colonies, in respect to some of the imports indispensable to their subsistence; and, by the exports, extremely advantageous to the interests of Great Britain, by furnishing a market for articles which she does not take herself, and which could not be disposed of elsewhere. At the very time of the embargo, the governors of the Islands, so far from adhering to the principle of excluding American vessels, issued proclamations inviting them, with promises even that the regular papers should not be required for their admission, and encouraging them to violate the laws of their own country by carrying them supplies. In time of peace it was undoubtedly not so necessary. Even then, however, it was so in a high degree. The mother country may supply them in part, but does not produce some of the most important articles of their importation,—rice, for example, and Indian corn, the best and cheapest articles for the subsistence of negroes. Even wheat and flour, and provisions generally, were much more advantageously imported from the United States than from Europe, being so much less liable to be damaged in those hot climates, from the comparative shortness of the voyage. Another of their importations was lumber, which is necessary for buildings upon the plantations, and which, after the hurricanes to which the islands are frequently exposed, must be had in large quantities."

Mr. Adams added, "that the American government did not on this ground now propose that these ports should be opened to their vessels. They did not seek for a participation in the British trade with them. Great Britain might still prohibit the importation from the United States of such articles as she chose to supply herself. But they asked that American vessels be admitted equally with British vessels to carry the articles which could be supplied only from the United States, or which were supplied only to them. The effect of the new regulations had been so injurious to the shipping interest in America, and was so immediately felt, that the first impression on the minds of many was that they should be at once met by counteracting legislative measures of prohibition. A proposal to that effect was made in Congress; but it was thought best to endeavor, in the first instance, to come to an amicable arrangement of the subject with the British government. Immediate prohibitions would affect injuriously the British colonies; they would excite irritation in the commercial part of the British communities. The consideration, therefore, of enacting legislative regulations, was postponed."

Lord Castlereagh, after expressing the earnest disposition of his government to promote harmony between the two countries, said "he was not then prepared to enter upon a discussion on the points of the question, but would take it into consideration as soon as possible."

Mr. Adams then said "that the American government was anxious to settle by treaty all the subjects of collision between neutral and belligerent rights which, in the event of a new maritime war in Europe, might again arise:—blockade, contraband, searches at sea, and colonial trade, but most of all the case of the seamen,—concerning whom the American government proposed that each party should stipulate not to employ, in its merchant ships or naval service, the seamen of the other."

Lord Castlereagh inquired "whether the proposal in the stipulation related only to native citizens and subjects; and, if not, how the question was to be escaped,—whether any act of naturalization shall avail to discharge a seaman from the duties of his original allegiance."

Mr. Adams replied, "that it was proposed to include in the arrangement only natives and those who are on either side naturalized already; so that it would not extend to any hereafter naturalized. The number of persons included would, of course, be very few." Lord Castlereagh inquired "what regulations were proposed to carry the stipulation into effect." Mr. Adams replied, "that if it was agreed to, he thought there would be no difficulty in concerting regulations to carry it into execution; and that the American government would be ready to agree to any Great Britain might think necessary, consistent with individual rights, to secure the bona fide fulfilment of the engagement." "But," said Lord Castlereagh, "by agreeing to this stipulation, is it expected we should abandon the right of search we have heretofore used; or is this stipulation to stand by itself, leaving the rights of the parties as they were before?" Mr. Adams replied, "that undoubtedly the object of the American government was that the result of the stipulation should ultimately be the abandonment of the practice of taking men from American vessels." "How, then," said Lord Castlereagh, "shall we escape the old difficulty? The people of this country consider the remedy we have always used hitherto as the best and only effective one. Such is the general opinion of the nation, and there is a good deal of feeling connected with the sentiment. If we now give up that, how will it be possible to devise any regulation, depending upon the performance of another state, which will be thought as efficacious as that we have in our own hands? He knew that the policy of the American government had changed; that it was formerly to invite and encourage British seamen to enter their service, but that at present it was to give encouragement to their own seamen; and he was in hopes that the effect of these internal legislative measures would be to diminish the necessity of resorting to the right of search." Mr. Adams, in reply, said, "that his lordship had once before made a similar observation, and that he felt it his duty to take notice of it. Being under a perfect conviction that it was erroneous, he was compelled to state that the American government never did in any manner invite or encourage foreign seamen generally, or British seamen in particular, to enter their service." Lord Castlereagh said "that he meant only that their policy arose naturally from circumstances,—from the extraordinary, sudden, and almost unbounded increase of their commerce and navigation during the late European wars; they had not native seamen enough to man their ships, and the encouragements to foreign seamen followed from that state of things." Mr. Adams replied, "that he understood his lordship perfectly; but what he asserted was his profound conviction that he was mistaken in point of fact. He knew not how the policy of any government can be manifested otherwise than by its acts. Now, there never was any one act, either of the legislature or executive, which could have even a tendency to invite British seamen into the American service." "But," said Lord Castlereagh, "at least, then, there was nothing done to prevent them." Mr. Adams replied, "That may be; but there is a very material distinction between giving encouragement and doing nothing to prevent them. Our naturalization laws certainly hold out to them nothing like encouragement. You naturalize every foreign seaman by the mere fact of two years' service on board of your public ships, *ipso facto*, without cost, or form, or process. We require five years' residence in the United States, two years of notice in a court of record, and a certificate of character, before the act of naturalization is granted. Thus far only may be admitted,—that the great and extraordinary increase of our commerce, to which you have alluded, had the effect of raising the wages of seamen excessively high. Our government certainly gave no encouragement to this; neither did our merchants, who would surely have engaged their seamen at lower wages, if possible. These wages, no doubt, operated as a strong temptation to your seamen to go into the American service. Your merchant service could not afford to pay them so high. The wages in the king's ships are much lower, and numbers of British seamen, accordingly, find employment on board American vessels; but encouragement from the American government they never had in any manner. They were merely not excluded; and even now, in making the proposal to exclude them, it is not from any change of policy, but solely for the purpose of giving satisfaction to Great Britain, and of stopping the most abundant source of dissension with her. It proves only the earnestness of our desire to be upon good terms with you."

Mr. Adams said, with regard to his proposal of excluding each other's seamen, "that he was not prepared to say that an article could not be framed by which the parties might stipulate the principle of mutual exclusion, without at all affecting or referring to the rights or claims of either party. Perhaps it might be accomplished if the British government should assume it as one of the objects to be arranged by the convention." On which Lord Castlereagh said: "In that case there will not be so much difficulty. If it is a mere agreement of mutual exclusion, tending to diminish the occasion for exercising the right of search, and undoubtedly if it should prove effectual, it would in the end operate as an inducement to forbear the exercise of the right entirely."

Discussions with the same nobleman on other topics bearing upon the commercial relations between the two nations are preserved among the papers of Mr. Adams.

On the 16th of April, 1817, Mr. Adams received letters from President Monroe, with the information that, with the sanction of the Senate, the Department of State had been committed to him; a trust which he accepted with a deep sense of its weight and responsibility. In compliance with Mr. Monroe's request, he made immediate arrangements to return to the United States. On presenting his letters of recall to Lord Castlereagh, congratulations on his appointment were attended with regrets at his removal from his mission. Mr. Adams stated that the uncertainty of his acceptance of the office of Secretary of State had prevented an immediate appointment of his successor, but that he was instructed in the strongest manner to declare the earnest desire of President Monroe to cultivate the most friendly intercourse with Great Britain. He gave the same explanation to the Prince Regent, at a private audience, who replied by an assurance of his disposition to continue to promote the harmony between the two nations which was required by the interests of both. There was no formality in the discourse on either side, and the generalities of mutual assurance were much alike, and estimated at their real value. In reply to the inquiries of the Prince, the names of the members of Mr. Monroe's cabinet were mentioned. He was not acquainted with any of them, but spoke in handsome terms of Mr. Thomas Pinckney and Mr. Rufus King, and asked many questions concerning the organization of the American government. Lord Castlereagh, in his final interview with Mr. Adams, made numerous inquiries relative to the foreign relations of the United States, especially in regard to Spain,

defender against Spain and England, I shall come in for my share of the obloquy so liberally bestowed upon him."

Mr. Adams had the satisfaction of receiving from Hyde de Neuville, the French minister, an assurance of his coincidence of opinion with him, and that he had written to his own government that the proceedings of General Jackson had been right, particularly in respect of the two Englishmen. Although there was a difference of opinion on the subject among the members of the diplomatic body, he declared that his own was that such incendiaries and instigators of savage barbarities should be put to death.

On one occasion, the President expressed to Mr. Adams his astonishment at the malignancy of the reports which some newspapers were circulating concerning him, and asked in what motives they could have originated. Mr. Adams replied, that the motives did not lie very deep; that there had been a spirit at work, ever since he came to Washington, very anxious to find or make occasions of censure upon him. That spirit he could not lay. His only resource was to pursue his course according to his own sense of right, and abide by the consequences. To which the President fully assented.

While these events were agitating the political world, Mr. Adams was called to lament the death of his mother, dear to his heart by every tie of affection and gratitude. His feelings burst forth, on the occasion, in eloquent and touching tributes to her memory. "This is one of the severest afflictions," he exclaimed, "to which human existence is liable. The silver cord is broken,—the tenderest of natural ties is dissolved,—life is no longer to me what it was,— my home is no longer the abode of my mother. While she lived, whenever I returned to the paternal roof, I felt as if the joys and charms of childhood returned to make me happy; all was kindness and affection. At once silent and active as the movement of the orbs of heaven, one of the links which connected me with former ages is no more. May a merciful Providence spare for many future years my only remaining parent!"

The policy of the friends and enemies of Mr. Monroe's administration was developed by the debates in the House of Representatives on the Seminole war, and the spirit of intrigue began to operate with great publicity. Some of the Western friends of Mr. Adams proposed to him measures of counteraction, on which he remarked: "These overtures afford opportunities and temptations to intrigue, of which there is much in this government, and without which the prospects of a public man are desperate. Caballing with members of Congress for future contingency has become so interwoven with the practical course of our government, and so inevitably flows from the practice of canvassing by the members to fix on candidates for President and Vice-President, that to decline it is to pass a sentence of total exclusion. Be it so! Whatever talents I possess, that of intrigue is not among them. And instead of toiling for a future election, as I am recommended to do, my only wisdom is to prepare myself for voluntary, or unwilling, retirement." On the same topic, in February, 1819, he thus expressed himself: "The practice which has grown up under the constitution, but contrary to its spirit, by which members of Congress meet in caucus and determine by a majority the candidates for the Presidency and Vice-Presidency to be supported by the whole meeting, places the President in a state of undue subserviency to the members of the legislature; which, connected with the other practice of reëlecting only once the same President, leads to a thousand corrupt cabals between the members of Congress and heads of departments, who are thus made, almost necessarily, rival pretenders to the succession. The only possible chance for a head of a department to attain the Presidency is by ingratiating himself with the members of Congress; and as many of them have objects of their own to obtain, the temptation is immense to corrupt coalitions, and tends to make all the public offices objects of bargain and sale."

The treaty with Spain, by which the United States acquired the Floridas, was signed by Onis and Adams on the 22d of December, 1819. To effect this treaty, so full of difficulty and responsibility, Mr. Adams had labored ever since he had become Secretary of State. His success was to him a subject of intense gratification; especially the acknowledgment of the right of the United States to a definite line of boundary to the South Sea. This right was not among our claims by the treaty of peace with Great Britain, nor among our pretensions under the purchase of Louisiana, for that gave the United States only the range of the Mississippi and its waters. Mr. Adams regarded the attainment of it as his own; as he had first proposed it on his own responsibility, and introduced it in his discussions with Onis and De Neuville. Its final attainment, under such circumstances, was a just subject of exultation, which was increased by the change of relations which the treaty produced with Spain, from the highest state of exasperation and imminent war, to a fair prospect of tranquillity and secure peace. The treaty was ratified by the President, with the unanimous advice of the Senate.

In 1819 a committee of the Colonization Society applied to the President for the purchase of a territory on the coast of Africa, to which the slaves rescued under the act of Congress, then recently passed, against piracy and the slave-trade, might be sent. The subject being referred to Mr. Adams, he stated in reply that it was impossible that Congress could have intended to authorize the purchase of territory by that act, for they had only appropriated for its object *one hundred thousand dollars*, which was a sum utterly inadequate for the purchase of a territory on the coast of Africa. He declared also that he had no opinion of the practicability or usefulness of the objects proposed by the Colonization Society, of establishing in Africa a colony composed of the free blacks sent from the United States. "The project," said he, "is professedly formed, 1st, without making use of any compulsion on the free people of color to go to Africa. 2d. To encourage the emancipation of slaves by their masters. 3d. To promote the entire abolition of slavery; and yet, 4th, without in the slightest degree affecting what they call 'a certain species of property in slaves.' There are men of all sorts and descriptions concerned in this Colonization Society: some exceedingly humane, weak-minded men, who really have no other than the professed objects in view, and who honestly believe them both useful and attainable; some speculators in official profits and honors, which a colonial establishment would of course produce; some speculators in political popularity, who think to please the abolitionists by their zeal for emancipation, and the slaveholders by the flattering hope of ridding them of the free colored people at the public expense; lastly, some cunning slaveholders, who see that the plan may be carried far enough to produce the effect of raising the market price of their slaves. But, of all its other difficulties, the most objectionable is that it obviously includes the engrafting a colonial establishment upon the constitution of the United States, and thereby an accession of power to the national government transcending all its other powers."

The friends of the measure urged in its favor that it had been recommended by the Legislature of Virginia. They enlarged on the happy condition of slaves in that state, on the kindness with which they were treated, and on the attachment subsisting between them and their masters. They stated that the feeling against slavery was so strong that shortly after the close of the Revolution many persons had voluntarily emancipated their slaves. This had introduced a class of very dangerous people,—the free blacks,—who lived by pilfering, corrupted the slaves, and produced such pernicious consequences that the Legislature was obliged to prohibit their further emancipation by law. The important object now was to remove the free blacks, and provide a place to which the emancipated slaves might go; in which case, the legal obstacles to emancipation being withdrawn, Virginia, at least, might in time be relieved from her black population.

A committee from the Colonial Society also waited on Mr. Adams, repeating the same topics, and maintaining that the slave-trade act contained a clear authority to settle a colony in Africa; and that the purchase of Louisiana, and the settlement at the mouth of Columbia River, placed beyond all question the right of acquiring territory as existing in the government of the United States. Mr. Adams, in reply, successfully maintained that the slave-trade act had no reference to the settlement of a colony on the coast of Africa; and that the acquisition of Louisiana, and the settlement at the mouth of Columbia River, being in territories contiguous to and in continuance of our own, could by no reason warrant the purchase of countries beyond seas, or the establishment of a colonial system of government subordinate to and dependent upon that of the United States.

In July, 1819, Mr. Adams, writing concerning the failure at the preceding session of Missouri to obtain admission as a state into the Union, from the restriction, introduced by the House of Representatives, excluding slavery from its constitution, thus expressed himself: "The attempt to introduce that restriction produced a violent agitation among the members from the slaveholding states, and it has been communicated to the states themselves, and to the territory of Missouri. The slave-drivers, as usual, whenever this topic is brought up, bluster and bully, talk of the white slaves of the Eastern States, and the dissolution of the Union, and of oceans of blood; and the Northern men, as usual, pocket all this hectoring, sit down in quiet, and submit to the slave-scourging republicanism of the planters."

Being urged to use his influence that the language and policy of the government should be as moderate and guarded as possible, from the consideration that both England and France were profoundly impressed with the idea that we were an ambitious, encroaching people, Mr. Adams replied: "I doubt if we should give ourselves any concern about it. Great Britain, who had been vilifying us for twenty years as a low-minded nation, with no generous ambition, no God but gold, had now changed her tune, and was endeavoring to alarm the world at the gigantic grasp of our ambition. Spain and all Europe were endeavoring to do the same; being startled at first by our acquisition of Louisiana, and now by our pretensions to extend to the South Sea. Nothing we can say will remove this impression until the world shall be familiarized with the idea of considering the continent of North America to be our proper dominion. From the time we became an independent people, it was as much a law of nature that this should become our pretension, as that the Mississippi should flow to the sea. Spain had pretensions on our southern, Great Britain on our northern borders. It was impossible that centuries should elapse without finding them annexed to the United States; not from any spirit of encroachment or of ambition on our part, but because it was a physical, and moral, and political absurdity, that such fragments of territory, with sovereigns fifteen hundred miles beyond sea, worthless and burdensome to their owners, should exist, permanently, contiguous to a great, powerful, enterprising, and rapidly-growing nation. Most of the territories of Spain in our neighborhood had become ours by fair purchase. This rendered it more unavoidable that the remainder of the continent should ultimately be ours. It was but very lately we had seen this ourselves, or that we had avowed the pretension of extending to the South Sea; and, until Europe finds it to be a settled geographical element that the United States and North America are identical, any effort on our part to reason the world out of the belief that we are an ambitious people will have no other effect than to convince them that we add to our ambition hypocrisy."

Concerning the discords which arose in the cabinet, on policy to be pursued, Mr. Adams remarked: "I see them with pain, but they are sown in the practice which the Virginia Presidents have taken so much pains to engraft on the constitution of the Union, making it a principle that no President can be more than twice elected, and whoever is not thrown out after one term of service must decline being a candidate after the second. This is not a principle of the constitution, and I am satisfied it ought not to be. Its inevitable consequence is to make every administration a scene of continuous and furious electioneering for the succession to the Presidency. It was so through the whole of Mr. Madison's administration, and it is so now."

The signature of the treaty for the acquisition of Florida, sanctioned by the unanimous vote of the Senate, had greatly contributed to the apparent popularity of Mr. Monroe's administration. But the postponement of its ratification by Spain soon clouded the prospect; and the question whether Missouri should be admitted into the Union as a slave or free state, in which Mr. Adams took a deep interest, immediately rendered the political atmosphere dark and stormy. "There is now," Mr. Adams observed, "every appearance that the slave question will be carried by the superior ability of the slavery party. For this much is certain, that if institutions are to be judged by their results in the composition of the councils of the Union, the slaveholders are much more ably represented than the simple freemen. With the exception of Rufus King, there is not, in either house of Congress, a member from the free states able to cope in powers of the mind with William Pinkney and James Barbour. In the House of Representatives the freemen have none to contend on equal terms either with John Randolph or Clay. Another misfortune to the free party is that some of their ablest men are either on this question with their adversaries, or lukewarm in the cause. The slave men have indeed a deeper immediate stake in the issue than the partisans of freedom. Their passions and interests are more profoundly agitated, and they have stronger impulses to active energy than their antagonists, whose only individual interest in this case arises from its bearing on the balance of political power between the North and South."

The debate on this subject commenced in the Senate. In the course of January and February, 1820, Rufus King, senator from New York, delivered two of the most well-considered and powerful speeches that this Missouri question elicited. The remarks they drew forth from Mr. Adams render it proper that some idea of their general course should be stated, although it is impossible that any abstract can do justice to them. Disclaiming all intention to encourage or assent to any measure that would affect the security of property in slaves, or tend to disturb the political adjustment which the constitution had established concerning them, he enters at large into the power of Congress to make and determine whatever regulations are needful concerning the territories. He maintained that the power of admitting new states is by the constitution referred wholly to the discretion of Congress; that the citizens of the several states have rights and duties, differing from each other in the respective states; that those concerning slavery are the most remarkable—it being permitted in some states, and prohibited in others; that the question concerning slavery in the old states is already settled. Congress had no power to interfere with or change whatever has been thus settled. The slave states are free to continue or abolish slavery. The constitution contains no provision concerning slavery in a new state; Congress, therefore, may make it a condition of the admission of a new state that slavery shall forever be prohibited within it.

Mr. King then enters upon the history of the United States relative to this subject, and to the rights of the citizens of Missouri resulting from the terms of the cession of Louisiana, and of the act admitting it into the Union. From this recapitulation and illustration he demonstrates, beyond refutation, that Congress possesses the power to exclude slavery from Missouri. The only question now remaining was to show that it ought to exclude it. In discussing this point, Mr. King passes over in silence arguments which to some might appear decisive, but the use of which in the Senate of the United States would call up feelings that he apprehended might disturb or defeat the impartial consideration of the subject.

Under this self-restraint he observed that slavery, unhappily, exists in the United States; that enlightened men in the states where it is permitted, and everywhere out of them, regret its existence among us, and seek for the means of limiting and of eradicating it. He then proceeds to state and reason concerning the difficulties in the apportionment of taxes among the respective states under the old confederation, and in the convention for the formation of the constitution, which resulted in the provision that direct taxes should be apportioned among the states according to the whole number of free persons and three fifths of the slaves which they might respectively contain. The effect of this provision he then analyzes, and shows that, in consequence of it, *five* free persons in Virginia have as much power in the choice of representatives, and in the appointment of presidential electors, as *seven* free persons in any of the states in which slavery does not exist. At the time of the adoption of the constitution no one anticipated the fact that the whole of the revenue of the United States would be derived from indirect taxes; but it was believed that a part of the contribution to the common treasury would be apportioned among the states, by the rule for the apportionment of representatives. The states in which slavery is prohibited ultimately, though with reluctance, acquiesced in the disproportionate number of representatives and electors that was secured to the slaveholding states. The concession was at the time believed to be a great one, and has proved the greatest which was made to secure the adoption of the constitution. Great as is this concession, it was definite, and its full extent was comprehended. It was a settlement between the thirteen states, and not applicable to new states which Congress might be willing to admit into the Union.

The equality of rights, which includes an equality of burdens, is a vital principle in our theory of government. The effect of the constitution has been obvious in the preponderance it has given to the slave-holding states over the other states. But the extension of this disproportionate power to the new states would be unjust and odious. The states whose power would be abridged and whose burdens would be increased by the measure would not be expected to consent to it. The existence of slavery impairs the industry and power of a nation. In a country where manual labor is performed by slaves, that of freemen is dishonored. In case of foreign war, or domestic insurrection, slaves not only do not add to, but diminish the faculty of self-defence.

If Missouri, and the states formed to the west of the River Mississippi, are permitted to introduce and establish slavery, the repose, if not the security, of the Union, may be endangered. All the states south of the River Ohio, and west of Pennsylvania and Delaware, will be peopled with slaves; and the establishment of new states west of the River Mississippi will serve to extend slavery, instead of freedom, over that boundless region. But, if slavery be excluded from Missouri and the other new states which may be formed in that quarter, not only will the slave-markets be broken up, and the principles of freedom be extended and strengthened, but an exposed and important frontier will present a barrier which will check and keep back foreign assailants, who may be as brave, and, as we hope, as free as ourselves. Surrounded in this manner by connected bodies of freemen, the states where slavery is allowed will be made more secure against domestic insurrection, and less liable to be affected by what may take place in the neighboring colonies.

At the delivery of these speeches Mr. Adams was present, and thus expressed his opinion in writing: "I heard Mr. King on what is called the Missouri question. His manner was dignified, grave, earnest, but not rapid or vehement. There was nothing new in his argument, but he unravelled with ingenious and subtle analysis many of the sophistical tissues of slaveholders. He laid down the position of the natural liberty of man, and its incompatibility with slavery in any shape; he also questioned the constitutional right of the President and Senate to make the Louisiana treaty; but he did not dwell upon those points, nor draw the consequences from them which I should think important. He spoke on that subject, however, with great power, and the great slaveholders in the house gnawed their lips and clenched their fists as they heard him."

"At our evening parties," he adds, "we hear of nothing but the Missouri question and Mr. King's speeches. The slaveholders cannot hear of them without being seized with the cramps. They call them seditious and inflammatory, which was far from being their character. Never, since human sentiment and human conduct were influenced by human speech, was there a theme for eloquence like the free side of this question, now before the Congress of the Union. By what fatality does it happen that all the most eloquent orators are on its slavish side? There is a great mass of cool judgment and of plain sense on the side of freedom and humanity, but the ardent spirits and passions are on the side of oppression. O! if but one man could arise with a genius capable of comprehending, a heart capable of supporting, and an utterance capable of communicating, those eternal truths which belong to the question,—to lay bare in all its nakedness that outrage upon the goodness of God, human slavery,—now is the time, and this is the occasion, upon which such a man would perform the duties of an angel upon earth."

About this time Mr. Calhoun remarked to Mr. Adams, that he did not think the slave question, then pending in Congress, would produce a dissolution of the Union, but, if it should, the South would, from necessity, be compelled to form an alliance, offensive and defensive, with Great Britain. Mr. Adams asked if that would not be returning to the old colonial state. Calhoun said, Yes, pretty much, but it would be forced upon them. Mr. Adams inquired whether he thought, if by the effect of this alliance, offensive and defensive, the population of the North should be cut off from its natural outlet upon the ocean, it would fall back upon its rocks, bound hand and foot, to starve; or whether it would retain its power of locomotion to move southward by land. Mr. Calhoun replied, that in the latter event it would be necessary for the South to make their communities all military. Mr. Adams pressed the conversation no further, but remarked: "If the dissolution of the Union should result from the slave question, it is as obvious as anything that can be foreseen of futurity, that it must shortly afterwards be followed by an universal emancipation of the slaves. A more remote, but perhaps not less certain consequence, would be the extirpation of the African race in this continent, by the gradually bleaching process of intermixture, where the white is already so predominant, and by the destructive process of emancipation; which, like all great religious and political reformations, is terrible in its means, though happy and glorious in its end. Slavery is the great and foul stain on the American Union, and it is a contemplation worthy of the most exalted soul, whether its total abolition is not practicable.

This object is vast in its compass, awful in its prospects, sublime and beautiful in its issue. A life devoted to it would be nobly spent or sacrificed."

On the 26th of February, Mr. John Randolph spoke on the Missouri question in the House of Representatives between three and four hours, on which speech Mr. Adams observed: "As usual, it had neither beginning, middle, nor end. Egotism, Virginian aristocracy, slave-purging liberty, religion, literature, science, wit, fancy, generous feelings, and malignant passions, constitute a chaos in his mind, from which nothing orderly can ever flow. Clay, the Speaker, twice called him to order; which proved useless, for he can no more keep order than he can keep silence." On the 1st of March the Missouri question came to a crisis in Congress. The majorities in both branches were on opposite sides, and in each a committee was raised to effect a compromise. This endeavor resulted in the abandonment by the House of Representatives of the principle it had inserted, that slavery should be prohibited in the Missouri constitution, and in annexing a section that slavery should be prohibited in the remaining parts of the Louisiana cession, north of latitude thirty-six degrees thirty minutes. This compromise, as it was called, was finally carried in the House of Representatives, by a vote of ninety to thirty-seven, after several successive days, and almost nights, of stormy debate.

On the 3d of March, a member of the house from Massachusetts told Mr. Adams that John Randolph had made a motion that morning to reconsider one of the votes of yesterday upon the Missouri bill, and of the trickery by which his motion was defeated. The Speaker (Mr. Clay) declared it when first made not in order, the journal of yesterday's proceedings riot having been then read; and while they were reading the journal, the clerk of the house carried the bill as passed by the house to the Senate; so that, when Randolph, after the reading of the journal, renewed his motion, it was too late, the papers being no longer in the possession of the house. "And so it is," said Mr. Adams, "that a law perpetuating slavery in Missouri, and perhaps in North America, has been smuggled through both houses of Congress. I have been convinced, from the first starting of this question, that it could not end otherwise. The fault is in the constitution of the United States, which has sanctioned a dishonorable compromise with slavery. There is henceforth no remedy for it but a reörganization of the Union, to effect which a concert of all the white states is indispensable. Whether that can ever be accomplished is doubtful. It is a contemplation not very creditable to human nature that the cement of common interest, produced by slavery, is stronger and more solid than that of unmingled freedom. In this instance the slave states have clung together in one unbroken phalanx, and have been victorious by the means of accomplices and deserters from the ranks of freedom. Time only can show whether the contest may ever, with equal advantage, be renewed; but, so polluted are all the streams of legislation in regions of slavery, that this bill has been obtained by two as unprincipled artifices as dishonesty ever devised. One, by coupling it as an appendage to the bill for admitting Maine into the Union; the other, by perpetrating this outrage by the Speaker on the rules of the house."

Mr. Calhoun, after a debate in the cabinet on the Missouri question, said to Mr. Adams that the principles avowed by him were just and noble, but in the Southern country, whenever they were mentioned, they were always understood as applying to white men. Domestic labor was confined to the blacks; and such was the prejudice that, if he were to keep a white servant in his house, although he was the most popular man in his district, his character and reputation would be irretrievably ruined. Mr. Adams replied that this confounding the ideas of servitude and labor was one of the bad effects of slavery. Mr. Calhoun thought it was attended with many excellent consequences. It did not apply to all sorts of labor; not, for example, to farming. He, himself, had often held the plough. So had his father. Manufacturing and mechanical labor was not degrading. It was only menial labor, the proper work of slaves. No white person could descend to that. And it was the best guarantee of equality among the whites. It produced an unvarying level among them. It not only did not excite, but did not admit of inequalities, by which one white man could domineer over another.

Mr. Adams replied, that he could not see things in the same light. "It is in truth all perverted sentiment; mistaking labor for slavery, and dominion for freedom. The discussion of this Missouri question has betrayed the secret of their souls. In the abstract they admit slavery to be an evil. They disclaim all participation in the introduction of it, and cast it all on the shoulders of 'old grandame Great Britain.' But, when probed to the quick upon it, they show at the bottom of their souls pride and vain-glory in their very condition of masterdom. They fancy themselves more generous and noble-hearted than the plain freemen, who labor for subsistence. They look down on the simplicity of Yankee manners, because they have no habits of overbearing like theirs, and cannot treat negroes like dogs. It is among the evils of slavery that it taints the very source of moral principle. It establishes false estimates of virtue and vice; for what can be more false and heartless than this doctrine, which makes the first and holiest rights of humanity to depend on the color of the skin? It perverts human reason, and reduces man endowed with logical powers to maintain that slavery is sanctioned by the Christian religion; that slaves are happy and contented in their condition; that between the master and slave there are ties of mutual attachment and affection; that the virtues of the master are refined and exalted by the degradation of the slave; while, at the same time, they vent execrations on the slave-trade, curse Great Britain for having given them slaves, burn at the stake negroes convicted of crimes for the terror of the example, and writhe in agonies of fear at the very mention of human rights as applicable to men of color."

"'The impression produced on my mind," continued Mr. Adams, "by the progress of this discussion, is, that the bargain between freedom and slavery contained in the constitution of the United States is morally and politically vicious; inconsistent with the principles on which alone our Revolution can be justified; cruel and oppressive, by riveting the chains of slavery, by pledging the faith of freedom to maintain and perpetuate the tyranny of the master; and grossly unequal and impolitic, by admitting that slaves are at once enemies to be kept in subjection, property to be secured and returned to their owners, and persons not to be represented themselves, but for whom their masters are privileged with nearly a double share of representation. The consequence has been that this slave representation has governed the Union. Benjamin's portion above his brethren has ravined as a wolf. In the morning he has devoured the prey, and in the evening has divided the spoil. It would be no difficult matter to prove, by reviewing the history of the Union under this constitution, that almost everything which has contributed to the honor and welfare of this nation has been accomplished in despite of them, or forced upon them; and that everything unpropitious and dishonorable, including the blunders of their adversaries, may be traced to them. I have favored this Missouri compromise, believing it to be all that could be effected under the present constitution, and from extreme unwillingness to put the Union at hazard. But perhaps it would have been a wiser and bolder course to have persisted in the restriction on Missouri, until it should have terminated in a convention of the states to revise and amend the constitution. This would have produced a new Union of thirteen or fourteen states unpolluted with slavery, with a great and glorious object, that of rallying to their standard the other states, by the universal emancipation of their slaves. If the Union must be dissolved, slavery is precisely the question upon which it ought to break. For the present, however, this contest is laid asleep."

Again he says: "Mr. King is deeply mortified at the issue of the Missouri question, and very naturally feels resentful at the imputations of the slaveholders, that his motives on this occasion have been merely personal aggrandizement,—'close ambition varnished o'er with zeal.' The imputation of bad motives is one of the most convenient weapons of political, and indeed of every sort of controversy. It came originally from the devil.—'Doth Job serve God for naught?' The selfish and the social passions are intermingled in the conduct of every man acting in a public capacity. It is right that they should be so. And it is no just cause of reproach to any man, that, in promoting to the utmost of his power the public good, he is desirous; at the same time, of promoting his own. There are, no doubt, hypocrites of humanity as well as of religion; men with cold hearts and warm professions, trading upon benevolence, and using justice and virtue only as stakes upon the turn of a card or the cast of a die. But this sort of profligacy belongs to a state of society more deeply corrupted than ours. Such characters are rare among us. Many of our public men have principles too pliable to popular impulse, but few are deliberately dishonest; and there is not a man in the Union of purer integrity than Rufus King.

"The most remarkable circumstance in the history of the final decision of the Missouri question is that it was ultimately carried against the opinions, wishes, and interests, of the free states, by the votes of their own members. They had a decided majority in both houses of Congress, but lost the vote by disunion among themselves. The slaveholders clung together, without losing one vote. Many of them, and almost all the Virginians, held out to the last, even against compromise. The cause of the closer union on the slave side is that the question affected the individual interest of every slaveholding member, and of almost every one of his constituents. On the other side, individual interests were not implicated in the decision at all. The impulses were purely republican principle and the rights of human nature. The struggle for political power, and geographical jealousy, may fairly be supposed to have operated equally on both sides. The result affords an illustration of the remark, how much more keen and powerful the impulse is of personal interest than is that of any general consideration of benevolence and humanity."

The compromise, by which Missouri was admitted into the Union, did not finally settle the question in. Congress. At the next session it reappeared, in consequence of the insertion into the constitution of Missouri of an article declaring it to be the duty of the Legislature to pass laws prohibiting free negroes and persons of color from coming into Missouri; which declaration was directly repugnant to that article in the constitution of the United States which provides that the citizens of each state shall be entitled to all privileges and immunities of citizens of the other states. The only mode of getting out of this difficulty, said Mr. Adams, was "for Congress to pass a resolution declaring the State of Missouri to be admitted from and after the time when the article repugnant to the constitution of the United States should be expunged from its constitution. This question was much more clear against Missouri than was that of their first admission into the Union; but the people of the North, like many of their representatives in Congress, began to give indications of a disposition to flinch from the consequences of this question, and to be unwilling to bear their leaders out."

Mr. Adams, in conversation with one of the senators of the South, observed, that "the article in the Missouri constitution is directly repugnant to the rights reserved to every citizen in the Union in the constitution of the United States. Its purport is to disfranchise all the people of color who were citizens of the free states. The Legislatures of those states are bound in duty to protect the rights of their own citizens; and if Congress, by the admission of Missouri with that clause in her constitution, should sanction this outrage upon those rights, the states a portion of whose citizens should be thus cast out of the pale of the Union would be bound to vindicate them by retaliation. If I were a member of the Legislature of one of these states, I would move for a declaratory act, that so long as the article in the constitution of Missouri, depriving the colored citizens of the state (say) of Massachusetts of their rights as citizens of the United States within the State of Missouri, should subsist, so long the white citizens of Missouri should be held as aliens within the Commonwealth of Massachusetts, and not entitled to claim or enjoy, within the same, any right or privilege of a citizen of the United States." And Mr. Adams said he would go further, and declare that Congress, by their sanction of the Missouri constitution, by admitting that state into the Union without excepting against that article which disfranchised a portion of the citizens of Massachusetts, had violated the constitution of the United States. Therefore, until that portion of the citizens of Massachusetts whose rights were violated by the article in the Missouri compromise should be reintegrated in the full enjoyment and possession of those rights, no clause or article of the constitution of the United States should, within the Commonwealth of Massachusetts, be so understood as to authorize any person whatsoever to claim the property or possession of a human being as a slave; and he would prohibit by law the delivery of any fugitive upon the claim of his master. All which, he said, should be done, not to violate, but to redeem from violation, the constitution of the United States. It was indeed to be expected that such laws would again be met by retaliatory laws of Missouri and the other slaveholding states, and the consequences would be a dissolution *de facto* of the Union; but that dissolution would be commenced by the article in the Missouri constitution. "That article," declared Mr. Adams, "is itself a dissolution of the Union. If acquiesced in, it will change the terms of the federal compact—change its terms by robbing thousands of citizens of their rights. And what citizens? The poor, the unfortunate, the helpless, already cursed by the mere color of their skin; already doomed by their complexion to drudge in the lowest offices of society; excluded by their color from all the refined enjoyments of life accessible to others; excluded from the benefits of a liberal education,—from the bed, the table, and all the social comforts, of domestic life. This barbarous article deprives them of the little remnant of right yet left them—their rights as citizens and as men. Weak and defenceless as they are, so much the more sacred the obligation of the Legislatures of the states to which they belong to defend their lawful rights. I would defend them, should the dissolution of the Union be the consequence; for it would be, not to the defence, but to the violation of their rights, to which all the consequences would be imputable; and, if the dissolution of the Union must come, let it come from no other cause but this. If slavery be the destined sword, in the hand of the destroying angel, which is to sever the ties of this Union, the same sword will cut asunder the bonds of slavery itself."

"In the House of Representatives, on the 4th of December," writes Mr. Adams, "Mr. Eustis, of Massachusetts, made a speech against the resolution for admitting Missouri into the Union without condition, and it was rejected, *ninety-three* to *seventy-nine*. On the 19th of December he offered a resolution admitting Missouri into the Union conditionally; namely, 'from and after the time when they shall have expunged from their constitution the article repugnant to the constitution of the United States.' On the 24th of January, 1821, this resolution was rejected by a vote of one hundred and forty-six to six. It satisfies neither party. It is too strong for the slave party, and not strong enough for the free party." In December and January the subject was ardently debated in the House of Representatives, and, after commitment and various attempts at amendment, on the 13th of February the report of a committee of the House of Representatives in favor of admitting Missouri into the Union, in conformity with the resolution which had passed the Senate, was rejected, eighty-five to eighty.

The proceedings of the House of Representatives, in counting the votes for President and Vice-President, are thus stated by Mr. Adams: "On the 14th of February, while the electoral votes for President and Vice-President were counting, those of Missouri were objected to because Missouri was not a state of the Union—on which a tumultuous scene arose. A Southern member moved, in face of the rejection by a majority of the House, that Missouri *is* one of the states of this Union, and that her votes ought to be counted. Mr. Clay avoided the question by moving that it should lie on the table, and then that a message should be sent to the Senate informing them that the House were *now* ready to proceed in continuing the enumeration of the electoral votes, according to the joint resolution; which was ordered. The Senate accordingly proceeded to open the votes of Missouri, and they were counted. The result was declared by the President of the Senate, in the alternative that if the votes of Missouri were counted there were two hundred and thirty-one votes for James Monroe as President, and two hundred and eighteen votes for Daniel D. Tompkins as Vice-President; and if not counted, there would be two hundred and twenty-eight votes for James Monroe as President, and two hundred and fifteen for Daniel D. Tompkins as Vice-President; but, in either event, both were elected to their respective offices. He therefore declared them to be so elected.

"After the two houses had separated, Mr. Randolph moved two resolutions: one, that the electoral votes of the State of Missouri had been counted, and formed part of the majorities by which the President and Vice-President had been elected; and the other, that the result of the election had not been declared by the presiding officer conformably to the constitution and the law, and therefore the whole proceedings had been irregular and illegal. This motion, after a very disorderly debate, was disposed of by adjournment. Mr. Randolph was for bringing Missouri into the Union by storm, and by bullying a majority of the House into a minority. The only result was disorder and tumult.

"On the 23d of February, the Missouri question being still undecided, on a motion of Mr. Clay, the House of Representatives chose by ballot a committee of twenty-three members, who were joined by a committee of seven from the Senate. Their object was a last attempt to devise a plan for admitting Missouri into the Union. On the 26th, the committee proposed a *conditional* admission, upon terms more humiliating to the people of Missouri than it would have been to require that they should expunge the exceptionable article from their constitution; for they declared it a fundamental condition of their admission that the article should never be construed to authorize the passage of any law by which any citizen of the states of this Union should be excluded from his privileges under the constitution of the United States; and they required that the Legislature of the state, by a solemn public act, should declare the assent of the state to this condition, and transmit a copy of the act, by the first Monday of November ensuing, to the President of the United States. But, in substance, this condition bound them to nothing. The resolution was, however, taken up this day in the House of Representatives, read three times, and passed by a vote of eighty-seven to eighty-one. On the 28th of February, the Senate, by a vote of twenty-eight to fourteen, adopted the resolution.

"This second Missouri question was compromised like the first. The majority against the unconditional admission into the Union was small, but very decided. The problem for the slave representation to solve was the precise extent of concession necessary for them to detach from the opposite party a number of antiservile votes just sufficient to turn the majority. Mr. Clay found, at last, this expedient, which the slave voters would not have accepted from any one not of their own party, and to which his greatest difficulty was to obtain the assent of his own friends. The timid and the weak-minded dropped off, one by one, from the free side of the question, until a majority was formed for the compromise, of which the servile have the substance, and the liberals the shadow.

"In the progress of this affair the distinctive character of the inhabitants of the several great divisions of this Union has been shown more in relief than perhaps in any national transaction since the establishment of the constitution. It is, perhaps, accidental that the combination of talent and influence has been the greatest on the slave side. The importance of the question has been much greater to them than to the other side. Their union of exertion has been consequently closer and more unshakable. They have threatened and entreated, bullied and wheedled, until their more simple adversaries have been half coaxed, half frightened into a surrender of their principles for a bauble of insignificant promises. The champions of the North did not judiciously select their position for this contest. There must be, some time, a conflict on this very question between slave and free representation. This, however, was not the proper occasion for contesting it."

At this period Mr. Adams considered that the greatest danger of the Union was in the overgrown extent of its territory, combining with the slavery question. The want of slaves was not in the lands, but in their inhabitants. Slavery had become in the South and South-western states a condition of existence. On the falling off of the revenue, which occurred about this time, he observed that "it stirs up the spirit of economy and retrenchment; and, as the expenditures of the war department are those on which the most considerable saving can be made, at them the economists level their first and principal batteries. Individual, personal jealousies, envyings, and resentments, partisan ambition, and private interests and hopes, mingle in the motives which prompt this policy. About one half of the members of Congress are seekers of office at the nomination of the President. Of the remainder, at least one half have some appointment or favor to ask for their relatives. But there are two modes of obtaining their ends: the one, by subserviency; the other, by opposition. These may be called the cringing canvass and the flouting canvass. As the public opinion is most watchful of the cringing canvass, the flouters are the most numerous party."

CHAPTER VI.

SECOND TERM OF MONROE'S PRESIDENCY.—STATE OF PARTIES.—REPORT ON WEIGHTS AND MEASURES.—PROCEEDINGS AT GHENT VINDICATED.—VOTES WHEN HE WAS A MEMBER OF THE SENATE OF THE UNITED STATES DEFENDED.—INDEPENDENCE OF GREECE.—CONTESTS OF PARTIES.—ELECTED PRESIDENT OF THE UNITED STATES.

During the second term of Mr. Monroe's Presidency, Mr. Adams continued to take his full proportion of responsibility in the measures of the administration. Questions concerning the Bank of the United States, the currency, the extinction or extension of slavery, the bankrupt law, the tariff, and internal improvements, brought into discussion the interests of the great States of Virginia, Pennsylvania, and New York, combined with the never-ceasing struggles for power of parties and individuals. Candidates for the office of President and Vice-President were brought into the field by their respective adherents. Every topic which could exalt or depress either was put in requisition, and office-holders and office-seekers became anxious and alert.

In July, 1821, at the request of the citizens of Washington, Mr. Adams delivered an address on the anniversary of American Independence. It did not receive the indulgence usually extended to such efforts, but was made the occasion of severe animadversions on his character and talents. In December his friends called his attention to calumnies and aspersions copied into the *City Gazette*, from papers issued in Georgia and Tennessee, and expressed their opinions that they ought to be answered by him, as they knew they could be most triumphantly. Mr. Adams replied: "Should I comply with your request, it will be immediately said, I was canvassing for the Presidency. I never, that I can recollect, but once, undertook to answer anything that was published against me, and that was when I was in private life. To answer newspaper accusations would be an endless task. The tongue of falsehood can never be silenced. I have not time to spare from public business to the vindication of myself."

To place Philip P. Barbour, of Virginia, in the Speaker's chair, and to prevent the reelection of John W. Taylor, of New York, the tried friend of the administration, became the next object of all those who hoped to rise by opposing it. The partisans of Barbour were successful, and the consequences of his elevation were immediately apparent. As the Committee of Foreign Relations was, by a practical rule, the medium of communication between Congress and the executive government, it was customary for the Speaker to constitute it chiefly of members who coïncided in their views. But many of those now appointed by Barbour, especially the chairman, were hostile to their politics. To this committee all the delicate and critical papers relative to the foreign relations of the United States were to be confidentially communicated. No arrangement could have been more annoying to Mr. Monroe and his cabinet, or more symptomatic of a settled opposition.

By a vote passed in March, 1817, the Senate had required of Mr. Adams a report on weights and measures; and in December, 1819, the House of Representatives had by a resolution made the same requisition. To this subject he had directed his attention when in Russia; and had devoted the leisure his duties as Secretary of State permitted, without approximating to its completion, owing to the number and perplexity of details its pursuit involved.

In the summer of 1820 he relinquished a visit to his father and friends in Massachusetts, and concentrated his attention, during six months, exclusively on this report, which he finished and made to Congress, in February, 1821. At the conclusion of his work he thus expresses himself: "This subject has occupied, for the last sixty years, many of the ablest men in Europe, and to it all the powers, and all the philosophical and mathematical learning and ingenuity, of France and Great Britain, have been incessantly directed. It was a fearful and oppressive task. It has been executed, and it will be for the public judgment to pass upon it."

From the abstruse character of this work, the labor, research, and talent, it evidences have never been generally and justly appreciated. It commences with the wants of individuals antecedent to the existence of communities, and deduces from man's physical organization, and from the exigences of domestic society, the origin of *measures of surface, distance, and capacity*; and that of *weight*, from the difference between the specific gravity of substances and its importance in the exchange of traffic consequent on the multiplication of human wants, with the increase of the social relations. He then proceeds to state and analyze the powers and duties of legislators on the subject, with their respective limitations. The results of his researches relative to the weights and measures of the Egyptians, Hebrews, Greeks, and Romans, are successively stated. From the institutions of the nations of antiquity he derives those of modern Europe and of the United States. He praises the "stupendous and untiring perseverance of England and France" in this field, and explains the causes which have not rendered their success adequate to their endeavors. The system of modern France on this subject he investigates and applauds, as "one of those attempts to improve the condition of human kind, which, although it may ultimately fail, deserves admiration, as approaching more nearly than any other to the ideal perfection of uniformity in weights and measures." After stating the difficulties which prevented other nations from seconding the endeavors of France, Mr. Adams concludes this elaborate treatise with the opinion that universal uniformity on the subject can only be effected by a general convention, to which all the nations of the world should be parties. Until such a general course of measures be adopted, he regards it as inexpedient for the United States to make any change in their present system. After an elaborate enumeration of the regulations of the several states of the Union, accompanied by voluminous documents, he concludes with proposing, "first, to fix the standard with the partial uniformity of which it is susceptible for the present, excluding all innovation. Second, to consult with foreign nations for the future and ultimate establishment of *permanent* and *universal* uniformity."

The Senate ordered six hundred copies of this report to be printed. But its final suggestions were not made the subject of action in either branch. A writer of the day said, with equal truth and severity, "It was not noticed in Congress, where ability was wanting, or labor refused, to understand it." As Mr. Adams was one of the candidates in the approaching presidential election, party spirit was inclined to treat with silence and neglect labors which it realized could not fail to command admiration and approval. In England the merits of this report were more justly appreciated. In 1834, Col. Pasley, royal engineer, in a learned work on measures and money, acknowledged the benefits he had derived from "an official report upon weights and measures, published in 1821, by a distinguished American statesman, John Quincy Adams. This author," he adds, "has thrown more light into the history of our old English weights and measures *than all former writers on the subject*; and his views of historical facts, even when occasionally in opposition to the reports of our own parliamentary committees, appear to me most correct. For my own part, I do not think I could have seen my way into the history of English weights and measures in the feudal ages without his guidance."

In the summer of 1821 Mr. Adams was apprized that rumors, very unfavorable to his reputation, even for integrity, had been industriously circulated in the Western country. It had been stated that he had made a proposition at Ghent to grant to the British the right to navigate the Mississippi, in return for the Newfoundland fisheries, and that it was in that section represented as a high misdemeanor. Mr. Adams said, that a proposition to confirm both those rights as they had stood before the war, and as stipulated by the treaty of 1783, had been offered to the British commissioners, not by him, but by the whole American mission, every one of whom had subscribed to it. The proposition was not made by him, but by Mr. Gallatin, who knew it would be nothing to the British but a mere naked right, of which they could not make any use. It was accordingly promptly rejected by the British commissioners, and made the ground of a counter proposition of renouncing the right they had, under the treaty of 1783, of navigating that river, on condition of our renouncing the old article on the fisheries. Mr. Adams at once declared that, if it was acceded to, he would never sign the treaty; and it was promptly rejected by the American commissioners. When he was again told that he would be accused in the Western States of the proposition to confirm the British rights as they stood before the war, he replied, that he had no doubt it would be so; for Mr. Clay had already, in one of his speeches in Congress, represented that this proposition had been made by a *majority* of the Ghent commissioners, he being in the minority, without acknowledging *that he had himself signed the note by which the offer was made*, and without disclosing how lightly the concession was estimated by the British commissioners, and how promptly they rejected it.

Accordingly, on the 18th of April, 1822, John Floyd, of Virginia, who, both in that state and in Congress, was active in seeking and scattering malign imputations concerning the political course of Mr. Adams, called, in the House of Representatives, for a letter, written by Jonathan Russell, in 1814, to Mr. Monroe, then Secretary of State, and, as he stated, deposited in that office.

This call of Floyd was the springing of the mine for a long-meditated explosion. On searching the records of state, no such letter could be found. Mr. Russell immediately volunteered a copy, and deposited it in that office. This letter was addressed to James Monroe, then Secretary of State, and was dated Paris, 11th of February, 1815. It was a letter of seven folio sheets of paper, and amounted, said Mr. Adams, to little less than a denunciation of a majority of the Ghent commissioners for proposing the article recognizing the fishery, and the British right to navigate the Mississippi,—a proposition in which Mr. Russell had concurred. He wrote this letter at Paris, where all the commissioners then were, without ever communicating it to Mr. Adams, or letting him know he had any intention of writing such a letter. It was a most elaborate, disingenuous, and sophistical argument against principles in which Mr. Russell himself concurred, and against the joint letters of the 14th December, 1814, to which he signed his name. His motives, Mr. Adams considered, for writing then to a Virginian Secretary of State, under a Virginian President, were, apparently, at once to recommend himself to their sectional prejudices about the Mississippi, and to injure him in their esteem and favor, for future effect; and that his motive for now abetting Floyd, in his call for these papers as a public document, was to diminish the popularity of Mr. Adams in the Western States.

With these views of the purposes of Floyd and Russell, Mr. Adams immediately endeavored to obtain the original letter, of which Mr. Russell had now deposited in the Secretary of State's office a paper purporting to be a copy. The original he ascertained was still in the possession of Mr. Monroe, who had received it soon after its date; but, as it was marked "private" by Mr. Russell, he considered it confidential, and did not place it in the office of the Secretary of State. On ascertaining these facts, Mr. Adams claimed the original letter from Mr. Monroe, believing, from internal evidence, that the duplicate, instead of being a true copy of the original, had been in some respects adapted to present effect. Mr. Monroe declined to listen to the repeated remonstrances of Mr. Adams, and continued to maintain that he could not, with honor, make the original letter public. He did not consent until he was called upon for it by a vote of the House of Representatives, proposed by the friends of Mr. Adams, and resisted by Floyd and his party. The original letter being thus obtained, Mr. Adams prepared and published a severe and scrutinizing examination of its facts and suggestions, of the motives which prompted those who had brought it before the public, and of the discrepancies between the original and the alleged copy which Mr. Russell had volunteered to place in the office of the Secretary of State. Mr. Russell replied through the newspapers; on which reply Mr. Adams bestowed a searching and caustic analysis, commenting with great severity on his language and conduct.

The whole of this controversy was published immediately in an octavo pamphlet, including important documents relative to the subject and to the transactions of the commissioners at Ghent, by means of which Mr. Adams vindicates himself and his colleagues from the charges brought against them. This elaborate and powerful defence, on which the strength and character of his mind are deeply impressed, was regarded as triumphant.[9]

Mr. Gallatin also published a pamphlet, generally corroborative of the statements of Mr. Adams; an example which Mr. Clay, another of the Ghent commissioners, being at that time a prominent competitor with Mr. Adams for the Presidency, did not see fit to follow. But, as total silence on his part might be construed to his disadvantage, he published in the newspapers a letter, dated the 15th of November, 1822, in which he intimated that there were some errors, both as to matter of fact and opinion, in the letter of Mr. Adams, as well as in that of Mr. Gallatin; and declared that he would at some future period, more propitious to calm and dispassionate consideration, and when there could be no misrepresentation of motives, lay before the public his own narrative of these transactions.

Mr. Adams, on the 18th of the ensuing December, in a communication to the *National Intelligencer*, expressed the pleasure it would have given him, had Mr. Clay thought it advisable to have specified the errors he had intimated, to have rectified them by acknowledgment. He added, that whenever Mr. Clay's accepted time to publish his promised narrative should come, he would be ready, if living, to acknowledge indicated errors, and vindicate contested truth. But, lest it might be postponed until both should be summoned to account for all their errors before a higher tribunal than that of their country, he felt called upon to say that what he had written and published concerning this controversy would, in every particular essential or important to the interest of the nation, or to the character of Mr. Clay, be found to abide unshaken the test of human scrutiny, of talents, and of time.

41

In July, 1822, a plan for an independent newspaper was proposed to Mr. Adams by some members of Congress, and the necessity of such a paper was urged upon him with great earnestness. He replied: "An independent newspaper is very necessary to make truth known to the people; but an editor really independent must have a heart of oak, nerves of iron, and a soul of adamant, to carry it through. His first attempt will bring a hornet's nest about his head; and, if they do not sting him to death or to blindness, he will have to pursue his march with them continually swarming over him, and be beset on all sides with obloquy and slander."

In August, 1822, paragraphs from newspapers, laudatory of other candidates, and depreciatory of Mr. Adams, were shown to him, on which he remarked, "The thing is not new. From the nature of our institutions, competitors for public favor and their respective partisans seek success by slander of each other. I disdain the ignoble warfare, and neither wage it myself or encourage it in my friends. But, from appearances, they will decide the election to the Presidency."

In December, 1822, Alexander Smyth, also a representative of one of the districts of Virginia, followed the example of Mr. Floyd, and, in an address to his constituents, took occasion to introduce malign imputations upon the political course of Mr. Adams. To this end, having ransacked the journals of the Senate of the United States at the time when Mr. Adams was a member, he undertook to attribute to him base motives for the votes he had given, particularly such as would be likely most to affect his popularity in Virginia. Mr. Adams immediately caused to be printed and published an address to the freeholders of Smyth's district; the nature and spirit of which reply will be shown by the following extracts:

"Friends and Fellow-Citizens: By these titles I presume to address you, though personally known to few of you, because my character has been arraigned before you by your representative in Congress, in a printed handbill, soliciting your suffrages for reëlection, who seems to have considered his first claim to the continuance of your favor to consist in the bitterness with which he could censure me. I shall never solicit your suffrages, nor those of your representatives, for anything. But I value your good opinion, and wish to show you that I do not deserve to lose it."—"I come to repel the charges of General Smyth, but neither for the purpose of moving you to withhold your suffrages from him, nor induce the General himself to reconsider his opinion concerning me."—"As to his opinions, you will permit me to be indifferent to the opinions of a man capable of forming his judgment of character from such premises as he has alleged in support of his estimate of mine."—"His mode of proof is this: He has ransacked the journals of the Senate during the five years I had the honor of a seat in that body,—a period the expiration of which is nearly fifteen years distant,—and wherever he has found in the list of yeas and nays my name recorded to a vote which he disapproves, he has imputed it, without knowing any of the grounds on which it was given, to the worst of motives, for the purpose of ascribing them to me. Is this fair? Is this candid? Is this just? Where is the man who ever served in a legislative capacity in your councils whose character could stand a test like this?"

Mr. Adams then proceeds to reply to all the charges brought against him by Alexander Smyth, analyzing and explaining every vote which he had made the subject of animadversion fully and successfully. The close of his defence is as follows:

"Fellow-Citizens: I have explained to you the reasons and real motives of all the votes which your representative, General Alexander Smyth, has laid to my charge, in a printed address to you, and to which unusual publicity has been given in the newspapers. I am aware that, in presenting myself before you to give this explanation, my conduct may again be attributed to unworthy motives. The best actions may be, and have been, and will be, traced to impure sources, by those to whom troubled waters are a delight. If, in many cases, when the characters of public men are canvassed, however severely, it is their duty to suffer and be silent, there are others, in my belief many others, wherein their duty to their country, as well as to themselves and their children, is to stand forth the guardians and protectors of their own honest fame. Had your representative, in asking again for your votes, contented himself with declaring to you his intentions concerning me, you never would have heard from me in answer to him. But when he imputes to me a character and disposition unworthy of any public man, and adduces in proof mere naked votes upon questions of great public interest, all given under the solemn sense of duty, impressed by an oath to support the constitution, and by the sacred obligations of a public trust, to defend myself against charges so groundless and unprovoked is, in my judgment, a duty of respect to you, no less than a duty of self-vindication to me. I declare to you that not one of the votes which General Smyth has culled from an arduous service of five years in the Senate of the Union, to stigmatize them in the face of the country, was given from any of the passions or motives to which he ascribes them; that I never gave a vote either in hostility to the administration of Mr. Jefferson, or in disregard to republican principles, or in aversion to republican patriots, or in favor of the slave-trade, or in denial of due protection to commerce. I will add, that, having often differed in judgment upon particular measures with many of the best and wisest men of this Union of all parties, I have never lost sight either of the candor due to them in the estimate of their motives, or of the diffidence with which it was my duty to maintain the result of my own opinions in opposition to theirs."

In 1823, as the Presidential election approached, the influences to control and secure the interests predominating in the different sections of the country became more active. Crawford, of Georgia, Calhoun, of South Carolina, Adams, of Massachusetts, and Clay, of Kentucky, were the most prominent candidates. In December, Barbour, of Virginia, was superseded, as Speaker of the House of Representatives, by Clay, of Kentucky; an event ominous to the hopes of Crawford, and to that resistance to the tariff, and to internal improvements, which was regarded as dependent on his success. The question whether a Congressional caucus, by the instrumentality of which Jefferson, Madison, and Monroe, had obtained the Presidency, should be again held to nominate a candidate for that office, was the next cause of political excitement. The Southern party, whose hopes rested on the success of Crawford, were clamorous for a caucus. The friends of the other candidates were either lukewarm or hostile to that expedient. Pennsylvania, whose general policy favored a protective tariff and public improvements, hesitated. In 1816 she had manifested an opposition to that plan of Congressional influence, and in 1823 a majority of her representatives declined attending any partial meeting of members of Congress that might attempt a nomination. But the Democracy of that state, ever subservient to the views of the Southern aristocracy, held meetings at Philadelphia, and elsewhere, recommending a Congressional caucus. This motion would have been probably adopted, had not the Legislature of Alabama, about this time, nominated Andrew Jackson for the Presidency, and accompanied their resolutions in his favor with a recommendation to their representatives to use their best exertions to prevent a Congressional nomination of a President. The popularity of Jackson, and the obvious importance to his success of the policy recommended by Alabama, fixed the wavering counsels of Pennsylvania, so that only three representatives from that state attended the Congressional caucus, which was soon after called, and which consisted of *only sixty members*, out of *two hundred and sixty-one*, the whole number of the House of Representatives; of which Virginia and New York, under the lead of Mr. Van Buren, constituted nearly one half. Notwithstanding this meagre assemblage, Mr. Crawford was nominated for the Presidency, under a confident expectation that the influence of the caucus would be conclusive with the people, and the candidate and policy of Virginia would be confirmed in ascendency. But the days of Congressional caucuses were now numbered. The people took the nomination of President into their own hands, and the insolent assumption of members of Congress to dictate their choice in respect of this office was henceforth rebuked.

While these intrigues were progressing, Mr. Adams was zealously and laboriously fulfilling his duties as Secretary of State, neither endeavoring himself, nor exciting his friends, to counteract these political movements, one of the chief objects of which was to defeat his chance for the Presidency.

The course of Mr. Adams relative to the application of the Greeks, then struggling for independence, for the aid and countenance of the United States, next brought him into opposition to the prevailing tendency of the popular feeling of the time. A letter was addressed to him, as Secretary of State, by Andrew Luriottis, envoy of the provisional government of the Greeks, at London, entreating that political and commercial relations might be established between the United States and Greece, and proposing to enter upon discussions which might lead to advantageous treaties between the two countries. Mr. Rush, the American minister in London, enclosed this letter to Mr. Adams, and recommended the subject to the favorable attention of our government. Mr. Adams, after expressing the sympathy of the American administration in the cause of Greek freedom and independence, and their best wishes for its success, proceeded to state that their duties precluded their taking part in the war, peace with all the world being the settled policy of the United States; but that if, in the progress of events, the Greeks should establish and organize an independent government, the United States would welcome them, and form with them such diplomatic and commercial relations as were suitable to their respective relations. Mr. Adams also wrote a letter to Mr. Rush, requesting him to explain to Mr. Luriottis that the executive of the United States sympathized with the Greek cause, and would render the Greeks any service consistent with neutrality; but that assistance given by the application of the public force or revenue would involve them in a war with the Sublime Porte, or perhaps with the Barbary powers; that such aid could not be given without an act of Congress, and that the policy of the United States was essentially pacific.

The popular feeling in favor of granting aid to the Greeks soon began to be general and intense. Balls were held and benefits given to raise funds for their relief, and sermons and orations delivered in their behalf, in many parts of the United States. "On this subject," Mr. Adams remarked, "there are two sources of eloquence: the one, with reference to sentiment and enthusiasm; the other, to action. For the Greeks all is enthusiasm. As for action, there is seldom an agreement, and after discussion the subject is apt to be left precisely where it was. Nothing definite, nothing practical, is proposed." The United States were at peace with the Sublime Porte, and he did not think slightly of a war with Turkey. He had not much esteem for that enthusiasm for the Greeks which evaporated in words.

In the ensuing session, on the 9th of January, 1824, Mr. Webster, in the Senate of the United States, proposed a resolve "that provision ought to be made by law for defraying the expense incident to the appointment of an agent or commissioner to Greece, whenever the President shall deem it expedient to make such appointment;" supporting it by a speech adapted to catch the popular tide, then at the full, and, in fact, doing nothing with the appearance of doing something. A member of Congress consulted Mr. Adams on an amendment he proposed to make to the project of Mr. Webster, as specified in his resolve, it being then under consideration in the House of Representatives. Mr. Adams replied, it was immaterial what form the resolution might assume; the objection to it would be the same in every form. It was, in his opinion, the intermeddling of the legislature with the duties of the executive; it was the adoption of Clay's South American system; seizing upon the popular feeling of the moment to embarrass the administration. A few days afterwards, Mr. Adams took occasion to state his reasons to Mr. Webster for being averse to his resolution.

Notwithstanding the Virginia doctrine, that the constitution does not authorize the application of public moneys to internal improvement, was one of the hinges on which the selection of candidates in the Southern States turned, Mr. Adams did not refrain from openly expressing his own opinion. In a letter to a gentleman in Maryland, dated January, 1824, he stated that "Congress does possess the power of appropriating money for public improvements. Roads and canals are among the most essential means of improving the condition of nations; and a people which should deliberately, by the organization of its authorized power, deprive itself of the faculty of multiplying its own blessings, would be as wise as a Creator who should undertake to constitute a human being without a heart."[10]

While the election of President was pending, and the event uncertain, a member of Congress from Ohio told Mr. Adams there were sanguine hopes of his success; on which he remarked: "We know so little of that in futurity which is best for ourselves, that whether I ought to wish for success is among the greatest uncertainties of the election. Were it possible to look with philosophical indifference to the event, that is the temper of mind to which I should aspire. But who can hold a firebrand in his hand by thinking of the frosty Caucasus? To suffer without feeling is not in human nature; and when I consider that to me alone, of all the candidates before the nation, failure of success would be equivalent to a vote of censure by the nation upon my past services, I cannot dissemble to myself that I have more at stake in the result than any other individual. Yet a man qualified for the duties of chief magistrate of ten millions of people should be a man proof alike to prosperous and adverse fortune. If I am able to bear success, I must be tempered to endure defeat. He who is equal to the task of serving a nation as her chief ruler must possess resources of a power to serve her, even against her own will. This I would impress indelibly on my own mind; and for a practical realization of which, in its proper result, I look for wisdom and strength from above."

At the close of the year 1824, Mr. Adams responded to a like intimation: "You will be disappointed. To me both alternatives are distressing in prospect. The most formidable is that of success. All the danger is on the pinnacle. The humiliation of failure will be so much more than compensated by the safety in which it will leave me, that I ought to regard it as a consummation devoutly to be wished."

At this period an apprehension being expressed to him that if he was elected Federalists would be excluded from office, he said, he should exclude no person for political opinion, or on account of personal opposition to him; but that his great object would be to break up the remnant of all party distinctions, and to bring the whole people together, in point of sentiment, as much as possible; and that he should turn no one out of office on account of his conduct or opinions in the approaching election.

The result of this electioneering conflict was, that, by the returns of the electoral colleges of the several states, it appeared that none of the candidates had the requisite constitutional majority; the whole number of votes being two hundred and sixty-one—of which Andrew Jackson had ninety-nine, John Quincy Adams eighty-four, William H. Crawford forty-one, and Henry Clay thirty-seven. For the office of Vice-President, John C. Calhoun had one hundred and eighty votes, and was elected.

This result had not been generally anticipated by the friends of Mr. Adams. His political course had been, for sixteen years, identified with the policy of the leading statesmen of the Southern States, and had been acceptable to that section of the Union. It had therefore been hoped that, with regard to him, the general and inherent antipathy to a Northern President, which there existed, would have been weakened, if not subdued. His diplomatic talents had been successfully exercised in carrying into effect Mr. Madison's views during the whole of that statesman's administration. He had been the pillar on which Mr. Monroe had, during both terms of his Presidency, leaned for support, if not for direction. It was, therefore, not without reason anticipated that at least a partial support would have been given to him in the region where the influences of Jefferson, Madison, and Monroe, were predominant. But, of the *eighty-four* votes cast for Mr. Adams, not one was given by either of the three great Southern slaveholding states. *Seventy-seven* were given to him by New England and New York. The other *seven* were cast by the Middle or recently admitted states.

The selection of President from the candidates now devolved on the House of Representatives, under the provisions of the constitution. But, again, Mr. Adams had the support of none of those slaveholding states, with the exception of Kentucky, and her delegates were equally divided between him and General Jackson. The decisive vote was, in effect, in the hands of Mr. Clay, then Speaker of the House, who cast it for Mr. Adams;[11] a responsibility he did not hesitate to assume, notwithstanding the equal division of the Kentucky delegation, and in defiance of a resolution passed by the Legislature of that state, declaring their preference for General Jackson.[12] On the final vote Andrew Jackson had *seven* votes, William H. Crawford *four*, and John Quincy Adams *thirteen*; who was, therefore, forthwith declared President of the United States for four years ensuing the 4th of March, 1825.

In the answer of Mr. Adams to the official notice of his election by the House of Representatives, after paying tribute to the talents and public services of his competitors, he declared that if, by refusal to accept the trust thus delegated to him, he could give immediate opportunity to the people to express, with a nearer approach to unanimity, the object of their preference, he would not hesitate to decline the momentous charge. But the constitution having, in case of such refusal, otherwise disposed of the resulting contingency, he declared his acceptance of the trust assigned to him by his country through her constitutional organs, confiding in the wisdom of the legislative councils for his guide, and relying above all on the direction of a superintending Providence.

CHAPTER VII.

ADMINISTRATION AS PRESIDENT.—POLICY.—RECOMMENDATIONS TO CONGRESS.— PRINCIPLES RELATIVE TO OFFICIAL APPOINTMENTS AND REMOVALS.—COURSE IN ELECTION CONTESTS.—TERMINATION OF HIS PRESIDENCY.

Those sectional, party, and personal influences, which at all times tend to throw a republic out of the path of duty and safety, were singularly active and powerful during the Presidency of Mr. Adams. They were peculiar and unavoidable. His administration, beyond all others, was assailed by an unprincipled and audacious rivalry. Its course and consequences belong to the history of the United States, and will be here no further stated, or made the subject of comment, than as they affect or throw light on his policy and character.

Immediately after his inauguration, Mr. Adams appointed Henry Clay, of Kentucky, Secretary of State; Richard Rush, of Pennsylvania, Secretary of the Treasury; James Barbour, of Virginia, Secretary of War; Samuel L. Southard, of New Jersey, Secretary of the Navy; John McLean, of Ohio, Postmaster-General; and William Wirt, of Virginia, Attorney-General. The election of Mr. Adams to the Presidency depended on the vote of Henry Clay, who recognized and voluntarily assumed the responsibility. By voting for General Jackson, he would have coïncided with the majority of popular voices; but, actuated, as he declared, by an irrepressible sense of public duty, in open disregard of instructions from the dominant party in Kentucky, he dared to expose himself to the coming storm, the violence of which he anticipated, and soon experienced. In a letter to Mr. F. Brooke, dated 28th of January, 1825, which was soon published,[13] he thus expressed his views: "As a friend to liberty and the permanence of our institutions, I cannot consent, in this early stage of their existence, by contributing to the election of a military chieftain, to give the strongest guaranty that this republic will march in the fatal road which has conducted every other republic to ruin." In a letter dated the 26th of March, 1825, addressed to the people of his Congressional district, in Kentucky, Mr. Clay more fully illustrated the motives for his vote: "I did not believe General Jackson so competent to discharge the various intricate and complex duties of the office of chief magistrate as his competitor. If he has exhibited, either in the councils of the Union, or in those of his own state or territory, the qualities of a statesman, the evidence of the fact has escaped my observation."—"It would be as painful as it is unnecessary to recapitulate some of the incidents, which must be fresh in your recollection, of his public life, but I was greatly deceived in my judgment if they proved him to be endowed with that prudence, temper, and discretion, which are necessary for civil administration."—"In his elevation, too, I thought I perceived the establishment of a fearful precedent."—"Undoubtedly there are other and many dangers to public liberty, besides that which proceeds from military idolatry; but I have yet to acquire the knowledge of it, if there be one more pernicious or more frequent. Of Mr. Adams it is but truth and justice to say that he is highly gifted, profoundly learned, and long and greatly experienced in public affairs, at home and abroad. Intimately conversant with the rise and progress of every negotiation with foreign powers, pending or concluded; personally acquainted with the capacity and attainments of most of the public men of this country whom it might be proper to employ in the public service; extensively possessed of much of that valuable kind of information which is to be acquired neither from books nor tradition, but which is the fruit of largely participating in public affairs; discreet and sagacious, he will enter upon the duties of the office with great advantages."[14]

General Jackson was deeply mortified and irritated by Mr. Clay's preference of Mr. Adams, and still more by his avowal of the motives on which it was founded. In a letter to Samuel Swartwout, dated the 23d of February, 1825,[15] by whom it was immediately published, he complained bitterly of the term "military chieftain," which Mr. Clay, in his letter to Mr. Brooke, had applied to him; and, utterly disregarding the rights and duties which the provisions of the constitution had conferred and imposed on Mr. Clay, he assumed that he was himself entitled, by the plurality of votes he had received, to be regarded as the object indicated by "the supremacy of the people's will." Treating the objections as personal, and as ominously bearing on his future political prospects, after insinuating that there had been "art or management to entice a representative in Congress from a conscientious responsibility to his own or the wishes of his constituents," he declared his intention "to appeal from this opprobrium and censure to the judgment of an enlightened, patriotic, uncorrupted people."

Not content with uttering these general insinuations against Mr. Clay and Mr. Adams, he immediately put into circulation among his friends and partisans an unqualified statement to the effect that Mr. Adams had obtained the Presidency by means of a corrupt bargain with Henry Clay, on the condition that he should be elevated to the office of Secretary of State. To this calumny Jackson gave his name and authority, asserting that he possessed evidence of its truth; and, although Mr. Clay and his friends publicly denied the charge, and challenged proof of it, two years elapsed before they could compel him to produce his evidence. This, when adduced, proved utterly groundless, and the charge false; the whole being but the creation of an irritated and disappointed mind. Though detected and exposed, the calumny had the effect for which it was calculated. Jackson's numerous partisans and friends made it the source of an uninterrupted stream of abuse upon Mr. Adams, through his whole administration.

The Legislature of Tennessee immediately responded to General Jackson's appeal to the people, by nominating him as their candidate for the office of President, at the next election; a distinction which he joyfully accepted, and on that account immediately resigned his seat in the Senate of the United States.

Thus, before Mr. Adams had made any development of his policy as President, an opposition to him and his administration was publicly organized by his chief competitor, under the authority of one of the states of the Union, which manifested itself in party bitterness, and animosity to every act and proposition having any bearing on his political prospects. The appointment of Henry Clay to the office of Secretary of State was seized upon as unequivocal proof of Jackson's allegation; yet it was impossible to designate any leading politician who had such just, unequivocal, and high pretensions to that station, or one more popular, especially at the South and the West. Mr. Clay had been a prominent candidate for the Presidency in opposition to Mr. Adams. His talents were unquestionable, and a long career in public life rendered him more conspicuous and suitable for the office than any other statesman of the period. These qualifications weighed nothing in the scale of popular opinion and prejudice. The strength of opposition, based on the calumny circulated by Jackson, became apparent on every question which could be construed to affect the popularity of Mr. Adams; especially with regard to those measures which were obviously near his heart, and which tended to give a permanent and effective character to his administration.

In his inaugural address, on the 4th of March, 1825, after enumerating the duties of the people and their rulers, he proceeded to intimate the views which characterized his policy: "There remains one effort of magnanimity, one sacrifice of prejudice and passion, to be made by individuals, throughout the nation, who have heretofore followed the standard of political party. It is that of discarding every remnant of rancor against each other, of embracing as countrymen and friends, and of yielding to talents and virtue alone that confidence which, in times of contention for principle, was bestowed only on those who bore the badge of party communion."

His thoughts on this subject were again expressed in May, 1825: "The custom-house officers throughout the Union, in all probability, were opposed to my election. They are all now in my power; and I have been urged very earnestly, and from various quarters, to sweep away my opponents, and provide for my friends with their places. I can justify the refusal to adopt this policy only by the steadiness and consistency of my adhesion to my own. If I depart from this in any one instance, I shall be called upon by my friends to do the same in many. An invidious and inquisitorial scrutiny into the personal disposition of public officers will creep through the whole Union, and the most sordid and selfish passions will be kindled into activity, to distort the conduct and misrepresent the feelings of men, whose places may become the prize of slander upon them."

He made but two removals, both from unquestionable causes; and, in his new appointments, he was scrupulous in selecting candidates whose talents were adapted to the public service. It was averred, in the spirit of complaint or disappointment, that he often conferred offices on men who immediately coincided with the opponents and became

47

calumniators of his administration. He was soon made to realize the impracticability of disregarding the old lines of party. On being informed, by some of his friends in the Southern States, that the objections to the appointment of Federalists were insuperable, and would everywhere affect the popularity of his administration, he observed: "On such appointments all the wormwood and gall of the old party hatred ooze out. Not a vacancy to any office occurs but there is a distinguished Federalist started and pushed home as a candidate to fill it, always well qualified, sometimes in an eminent degree, and yet so obnoxious to the Republican party, that they cannot be appointed without exciting a vehement clamor against him and the administration. It becomes thus impossible to fill any vacancy in appointment without offending one half of the community—the Federalists, if their associate is overlooked; the Republicans, if he be preferred. To this disposition justice must sometimes make resistance, and policy must often yield."

The intention of Mr. Adams, avowed and invariably pursued, to make integrity and qualification the only criterions of appointment to office,—to remove no incumbent on account of political hostility, and to appoint no one from the sole consideration of political adherence,—diminished the power of the administration. The most active members of party, who follow for reward, either of place or station, were discouraged, and preferred to continue their allegiance to those from whom pay was certain, rather than to transfer it to an administration whose continuance, from the well-known influences on which political power in this country depends, was dubious, and probably short-lived. These consequences were familiar to the mind of Mr. Adams; but his spirit was of a temper which chose rather to fall in upholding the constitution of his country on its true and pure principles, than to become the abettor of corruption, and participator in its wages, for the sake of power. The firmness of these principles was put to frequent trial during his Presidency, but his resolution never wavered.

The confiding spirit in which he conducted his intercourse with his cabinet was thus stated by himself in November, 1825: "I have given the draft of my annual message to the members of the administration, who are to meet and examine it by themselves, and then discuss the result with me. I have adopted this mode of scrutinizing the message because I wish to have the benefit of every objection that can be made by every member of the administration. But it has never been practised before, and I am not sure that it will be a safe precedent to follow. In England the message or speech is delivered by a person under no responsibility for its contents; but here, where he who delivers it is alone responsible, and those who advise have no responsibility at all, there may be some danger in placing the composition of it under the control of cabinet members, by giving it up to discussion entirely among themselves."

His first message to Congress contained the following special recommendations: "The maturing into a permanent and regular system the application of all the superfluous revenues of the Union to internal improvement." "The establishment of a uniform standard of weights and measures, which had been a duty expressly enjoined on Congress by the constitution of the United States." "The establishment of a naval school of instruction for the formation of scientific and accomplished officers; the want of which is felt with a daily and increasing aggravation." "The establishment of a national university, which had been more than once earnestly recommended to Congress by Washington, and for which he had made express provision in his will." "Connected with a university, or separated from it, the erection of an astronomical observatory, with provision for the support of an astronomer." Every one of these recommendations was obviously intimately associated with the progress and character of the nation, and independent of all personal or party influences. Yet they were treated with utter neglect, or, after having been permitted to pass through the forms of commitment and report, were suffered to lie unnoticed on the tables of both houses, or to be lost by indefinite postponement.

The firmness of Mr. Adams, and his independence of personal considerations, were constantly manifested. Thus, in November, 1825, when he was urged by some of his influential friends to put into his message *something soothing to South Carolina*, he replied: "South Carolina has put it out of my power. She persists in a law[16] which a judge of the United States has declared to be in direct violation of the constitution of the United States, and

48

which the Attorney-General of the United States has also declared to be an infringement of the rights of foreign nations; against which the British government has repeatedly remonstrated, and upon which we have promised them that the cause of complaint should be removed;—a promise which the obstinate adherence of the government of South Carolina to their law has disenabled us from fulfilling. The Governor of South Carolina has not even answered the letter from the Department of State, transmitting to them the complaint of the British government against this law. In this state of things, for me to say anything gratifying to the feelings of the South Carolinians on this subject, would be to abandon the ground taken by the administration of Mr. Monroe, and disable us from taking hereafter measures concerning the law, which we may be compelled to take. To be silent is not to interfere with any state rights, and renounces no right of ourselves or others."

The same trait of character is evidenced by his persisting in recommending the application of the superfluous revenue to internal improvements, notwithstanding he well knew its unpopularity in Virginia, where it was denounced as realizing the prophecy of Patrick Henry, that "the Federal government would be a magnificent government." After delivering his first message, he was told, by a leading and influential member of Congress from Virginia, that "excitement against the general government was great and universal in that state; that opinions there had been before divided, but that now the whole state would move in one solid column." And the same member read to him letters from Jefferson and Madison, denouncing the doctrines of the message in the most emphatic terms.

A letter from distinguished friends of De Witt Clinton, stating that his adherents predominated in the Legislature of New York, and recommending a course to conciliate their influence, was shown to Mr. Adams in 1826. On this suggestion he remarked: "A conciliatory course, so far as may be compatible with self-respect, is proper and necessary towards all; but, in the protracted agony of character and reputation which it is the will of a superior power I should pass through, it is my duty to link myself to the fortunes of no man. In the balance of politics it is seldom wise to make one scale preponderate by weights taken from another. Neutrality towards parties is the proper policy of a President in office."

When officially informed that a senator from Georgia threatened that, unless the lands of the Creek Indians, claimed by that state as within its boundaries, were ceded, her weight would be thrown for General Jackson, Mr. Adams replied, "that we ought not to yield to Georgia, because we could not do so without gross injustice; and that, as to her being driven to support General Jackson, he felt little care about that. He had no more confidence in the one party than the other."

A similar reply was made to an influential New York politician, who told him that the friends of De Witt Clinton would probably support the administration, but that Van Buren and his bucktails would be inveterate in their opposition. "I consider it," said he, "a lottery-ticket whether either of those parties would support the administration."

The opposition to the election, and subsequently to the administration of Mr. Adams, in the South, had its origin and support, as we have seen, first, in the fact that he was (with the exception of his father) the only President who had not been a slaveholder; and, next, in the fixed determination, in that section of the Union, to keep the Presidency, if possible, in the hands of an individual belonging to that class. If, from circumstances, this should be no longer practicable, then their policy would be to select a candidate who had no sympathy for the slave, and whose subserviency to the supremacy of Southern interests was unquestionable. The attempt to extinguish slavery in Missouri, although it had resulted in what was called the Missouri compromise, had created towards all who were not slaveholders a feverish jealousy in the South, which descended on Mr. Adams with double violence because his free spirit was known. This was not diminished by the fact that he had, neither in act nor language, ever transcended the provisions of the constitution, but had, in every instance, fully recognized its obligations.

In February, 1826, two resolutions, which had been adopted in executive session, were brought to Mr. Adams. The first declared "that the expediency of the Panama mission ought to be debated in Senate with open doors, unless the publication of the documents, to which it would be necessary to refer in debate, would prejudice existing negotiations. The second was a respectful request to the President of the United States to inform the Senate whether such objection exists to the publication of all or any part of those documents; and, if so, to specify to what part it applies."

"These resolutions," said Mr. Adams, "are the fruit of the ingenuity of Martin Van Buren, and bear the impress of his character. The resolution to debate an executive nomination with open doors is without example; and the thirty-sixth rule of the Senate is explicit and unqualified, that all documents communicated in confidence by the President to the Senate shall be kept secret by the members. The request to me to specify the particular documents the publication of which would affect negotiations was delicate and ensnaring. The limitation was not of papers the publication of which might be injurious, but merely of such as would affect existing negotiations; and, this being necessarily a matter of opinion, if I should specify passages in the document as of such a character, any senator might make it a question for discussion in the Senate, and they might finally publish the whole, under color of entertaining an opinion different from mine upon the probable effect of the publication. Besides, should the precedent once be established of opening the doors of the Senate in the midst of a debate upon executive business, there would be no prospect of ever keeping them shut again. I answered the resolution of the Senate by a message stating that all the communications I had made on this subject had been confidential; and that, believing it important to the public interest that the confidence between the Executive and the Senate should continue unimpaired, I should leave to themselves the determination of a question, upon the motives of which, not being informed, I was not competent to decide."

When the intrigues which embarrassed and disturbed the Presidency of Mr. Adams were in full vigor, his spirit and strength of character were conspicuously manifested. In April, 1827, whilst the state elections were pending, letters were shown to him complaining that the administration did not support its friends, and intimating that time and money must be sacrificed to his success. Mr. Adams remarked: "I have observed the tendency of our elections to venality, and shall not encourage it. There is much money expended by the adversaries of the administration, and it runs chiefly in the channels of the press. They work by slander to vitiate the public spirit, and pay for defamation, to receive their reward in votes."

At the beginning of the third year of his term of office the currents of party began to run strongly towards the approaching struggle for the Presidency. Mr. Adams, writing concerning the aspects of the time, remarked. "General politics and electioneering topics appear to be the only material of interest and of discourse to men in the public service. There are in several states, at this time, and Maryland is one of them, meetings and counter meetings, committees of correspondence, delegations, and addresses, for and against the administration; and thousands of persons are occupied with little else than to work up the passions of the people preparatory to the presidential election, still more than eighteen months distant."

Complaints were constantly made that the administration neglected its friends, and gave offices to its enemies. Applications for appointments, especially for clerkships, in the departments, were continual, and were often made to Mr. Adams himself. He always refused to interfere directly, or by influence, unless his opinion was sought by the heads of the departments themselves, saying that to them the selection and responsibility properly belonged. "One of the heaviest burdens of my station," he observed, "is to hear applications for office, often urged, accompanied with the cry of distress, almost every day in the year, sometimes several times in the day, and having it scarcely ever in my power to administer the desired relief."

In May, 1827, Mr. Adams wrote to a friend: "Mr. Van Buren paid me a visit this morning. He is on his return from a tour through Virginia, North and South Carolina, and Georgia, with C. C. Cambreling, since the close of the last session of Congress. They are generally understood to be electioneering; and Van Buren is now the great manager for Jackson, as he was, before the last election, for Mr. Crawford. He is now acting over the part in the Union which Aaron Burr performed in 1799. Van Buren, however, has improved, in the art of electioneering, upon Burr, as the State of New York has grown in relative strength and importance in the Union. Van Buren has now every prospect of success in his present movements, and he will avoid the rock on which Burr afterwards split." These general conclusions, formed on observation and knowledge of character, projects, and movements, time has proved to be just. At this day there can be no doubt that, during a tour through the Southern section of the Union, in April and May, 1827, by Van Buren and Cambreling, one a senator, the other a representative in Congress from New York, an alliance was formed between the former and Jackson, having for its object to supersede Mr. Adams and to elevate themselves in succession to the Presidency. The result is illustrative of the means and the arts by which ambition shapes the destinies of republics, by pampering the passions and prejudices of the multitude, by casting malign suggestions on laborious merit, effective talent, and faithful services.

In June, 1827, some of the friends of Mr. Adams urged him to attend the celebration at the opening of the Pennsylvania Canal, to meet the German farmers, and speak to them in their own language. He replied: "I am highly obliged to my friends for their good opinion; but this mode of electioneering is suited neither to my taste nor my principles. I think it equally unsuitable to my personal character, and to the station in which I am placed."

As the year drew towards the close, Van Buren, who had increased his influence by union with De Witt Clinton, triumphed throughout the State of New York. "The consequences," said Mr. Adams, "are decisive on the next presidential election; but the principles on which my administration has been conducted cannot be overthrown. A session of Congress of unexampled violence and fury is anticipated by its friends. My own mind is made up for it. I have only to ask that as my day is so may my strength be."

A letter from Thomas Mann Randolph, on the opinions of Mr. Jefferson relative to the last presidential election, which had been recently published in Ohio, was at this time shown to Mr. Adams, and it was proposed to him to publish a letter to his father from Mr. Jefferson, on that subject; which he declined, saying: "The letter is not here, but if it were I would not publish it. I possess it only as executor to my father; and, it having been confidential, the executors of Mr. Jefferson have undoubtedly a copy of it, and, as depositaries of his confidence, are the only persons who can, with propriety, authorize its publication." He added: "The divulging private and confidential letters is one of the worst features of electioneering practised among us. Though often tempted and provoked to it, I have constantly refrained from it."

At this period Mr. Rush read to Mr. Adams his report on the finances, in which he largely discussed the policy of encouraging and protecting domestic manufactures. "It will, of course," said Mr. Adams, "be roughly handled in Congress and out of it; but the policy it recommends will outlive the blast of faction, and abide the test of time."

At the opening of the Twentieth Congress, in December, 1827, the election of Andrew Stevenson, of Virginia, a man decidedly hostile to the administration, as Speaker of the House of Representatives, manifested that the opposition had now gained a majority in both houses of Congress; a state of affairs which had never before occurred under the government of the United States.

Mr. Adams, being informed that it was Mr. Clay's intention to issue another pamphlet in refutation of the charge of bargaining and corruption, which General Jackson and his partisans under his authority had brought against them both, remarked: "They have been already amply refuted; but, in the excitement of contested elections, and of party spirit, judgment becomes the slave of the will. Men of intelligence, talent, and even of integrity upon other occasions, surrender themselves to their passions, believe anything, with and without, and even against reason, according as it suits their own wishes."

Mr. Clay and his friends were not disposed to permit a calumny so opprobrious to pass without disproof; yet during two years they could only oppose to it a general denial; but, in March, 1827, a letter from Mr. Carter Beverly, a friend of General Jackson, came into their possession, by which it appeared that Jackson, before a large company, in Beverly's presence, had declared that, "concerning the election of Mr. Adams to the Presidency, Mr. Clay's friends made a proposition to his friends, that if they would promise for *him* not to put Mr. Adams into the seat of Secretary of State, Mr. Clay and his friends would *in one hour* make him the President;"[17] —a proposition which, Jackson said, he indignantly rejected. No sooner was this statement made known to Mr. Clay, than he pronounced it "a gross fabrication, of a calumnious character, put forth for the double purpose of injuring his public character and propping up the cause of General Jackson; and that, for himself and his friends, he defied the substantiation of the charge before any fair tribunal whatever." This compelled General Jackson, in self-defence, to come before the public; and in a letter to Carter Beverly, dated the 5th of June, 1827, he made specific charges against Mr. Clay and Mr. Adams. He stated that early in January, 1825, a member of Congress, of high respectability, informed him that there was a great intrigue going on, which it was right he should know; that the friends of Mr. Adams had made overtures to the friends of Mr. Clay, that if they would unite in the election of Mr. Adams, Mr. Clay should be Secretary of State; that the friends of Mr. Adams were urging, as a reason to induce the friends of Mr. Clay to accede to their proposition, that if he (Gen. Jackson) was elected President, Mr. Adams would be continued Secretary of State [*Innuendo*, there would be no room for Kentucky]; that the friends of Mr. Clay stated, that the West did not wish to separate from the West, and if he would say, or permit any of his confidential friends to say, that, in case he was elected President, Mr. Adams should not be continued Secretary of State, by a complete union of Mr. Clay and his friends they would put an end to the presidential contest in one hour; and that this respectable member of Congress declared that *he was of opinion it was right to fight such intriguers with their own weapons*. To which General Jackson replied, that he would never step into the presidential chair by such means of bargain and corruption; and added, that the second day after this communication and reply, it was announced in the newspapers that Mr. Clay had come out openly and avowedly in favor of Mr. Adams.[18]

To this accusation Mr. Clay, in a letter to the public, dated the 4th of July, 1827, made "a direct, unqualified, and indignant denial," and called on General Jackson "to substantiate his charges by satisfactory evidence." General Jackson immediately gave to the public the name of James Buchanan, of Pennsylvania, as "the respectable member of Congress" who made to him this communication and proposition. This declaration compelled Mr. Buchanan to come before the public; who accordingly, in a letter dated the 8th of August, 1827,[19] published to the world what he declared to be "*the only conversation which he ever held with General Jackson*," in which he stated to him that, having heard a rumor that he intended, in case of his election, to appoint Mr. Adams Secretary of State, and thinking such an appointment would "cool the ardor of his friends," he called on him, and informed him of the rumor, and asked him whether he had ever intimated such intention; that Jackson replied he had not, and that, if elected President, he would enter upon the office untrammelled; and that this was substantially the whole conversation. Mr. Buchanan added, that he did not call upon General Jackson as the agent of Mr. Clay, or his friends, which he was not; and that he was incapable of entertaining the opinion Jackson had charged him with, that "*it was right to fight such intriguers with their own weapons*," and that he thought that Jackson "could not have received this impression until after Mr. Clay and his friends had actually elected Mr. Adams President, and Mr. Adams had appointed Mr. Clay Secretary of State."

A more full, direct, and conclusive contradiction of every fact asserted by General Jackson is impossible. Yet it had no effect upon his prospects or policy. His partisans continued to propagate the calumny, and profess their belief in it; and he gave encouragement to this course by maintaining a scrupulous silence on Mr. Buchanan's contradiction. Mr. Clay, speaking on this point, observed: "After Mr. Buchanan's statement appeared, there were many persons who believed that General Jackson's magnanimity would immediately prompt him to retract his charge. I did not participate in that just expectation, and therefore felt no disappointment that it was not realized."[20]

The calumny had done its work. It had been, for more than two years, cankering the public mind. General Jackson realized that it was an efficient means of victory, and was not disposed to diminish its power. His partisans, as Mr. Adams anticipated, had "surrendered themselves to their passions, and believed, without evidence and against evidence, as suited their own wishes."

The inveteracy of opposition to the administration of Mr. Adams was systematic, violent, and unprincipled. Party spirit determined that it should be prostrated. It was stated publicly that "a highly-respected member of Congress, of General Jackson's party, had declared that it was to be put down though it be as pure as the angels which stand at the right hand of the throne of God." No respect was paid, no regard had, for either faithful services or acknowledged integrity. An administration conducted on the most elevated and consistent principles, as far above party and selfish motives as it is possible for human beings to attain, was destined to be sacrificed. General Jackson entered upon his civil career in the spirit of a military chieftain. He knew well how to collect round his standard those intriguers in the free states who were content to adopt his badge, and ride into power in his train. Of the slave states he was sure, from both affinity and policy.

Mr. Clay, in his address to the public in December, 1827, thus represents the spirit of General Jackson's party at that period:|21| "The rancor of party spirit spares nothing. It penetrates and pervades everywhere. It does not scruple to violate the sanctity of social and private intercourse. It substitutes for facts dark surmises and malevolent insinuations. It misrepresents, and holds up in false and insidious lights, incidents perfectly harmless in themselves, of ordinary occurrence, or of mere common civility."

During these agitations Mr. Adams was diligently watching over the great interests of the country, and assiduously fulfilling the duties of his station, and no further interesting himself in the struggles of party than when compelled to notice them by their virulence, or by the earnestness of political friends. A member of the Senate having asked him how the interdiction of commerce by our vessels with the British colonies could be counteracted, "My opinion is," he replied, "that there should be an act of Congress totally interdicting the trade with all her colonies, both in the West Indies and North America; but the same act should provide for reopening the trade, upon terms of reciprocity, whenever Great Britain should be disposed to assent to them."

Early in 1828 Mr. Adams was informed that the question of Free-masonry was the conclusive criterion on which the elections in the western parts of the State of New York would turn; and that it was industriously circulated that he was a Free-mason. If the assertion was denied, offers had been made to produce extracts from the books of the lodge to which he belonged. He was, therefore, requested publicly to deny being a Mason. He replied, that he was not, and never had been, a Free-mason; but that, if he should publicly deny it, he would not be surprised if a forged extract from some imaginary lodge should be produced to counteract his statement. Such are the morals of electioneering!

On the subject of the Indians in the State of Georgia Mr. Adams said: "Our engagements with them and among ourselves, in relation to the lands lying within that state, are inconsistent. We have contracted with the State of Georgia to extinguish the title to the Indian lands lying within that state, and at the same time have stipulated with the Creeks and Cherokees that they should hold their lands forever. We have talked about benevolence and humanity, and preached them into civilization; but none of this benevolence is felt when the rights of the Indians come into collision with the interests of the white man. The Cherokees have now been making a written constitution; but this *imperium in imperio* is impracticable; and, in the instance of the New York Indians removed to Green Bay, and of the Cherokees removed to the Territory of Arkansas, we have scarce given them time to build their wigwams before we are called upon by our own people to drive them out again. My own opinion is that the most benevolent course towards them would be to give them the rights and subject them to the duties of citizens, as a part of our own people. But even this the people of the states within which they are situated would not permit."

In January, 1828, Mr. Adams received a letter from his friends in Pennsylvania, proposing a subscription for the purchase and setting up a German newspaper in support of the administration, and inquiring if he would permit his son, John Adams, to contribute to that object. He replied that, on full consideration of the transaction, he deemed it his duty to decline; that how far the employment of money to promote the success of the election might be proper in others, it was not for him to determine; he could only lament the necessity, if it existed; but to apply money himself for the promotion of his own election he thought incorrect in principle, and had invariably avoided it. He knew that others were less scrupulous, and that it had been done by one individual to the pecuniary embarrassment of his whole life. He had been solicited to adopt a like course, but had uniformly declined, not from pecuniary considerations, but because he could not approve of the thing.

In January, 1828, Mr. Floyd, of Virginia, who had taken upon himself the inglorious office of hunting up and disseminating malign aspersions against President Adams, brought before the House of Representatives statements concerning his accounts, which had been long before settled at the treasury of the United States; and, after recapitulating the number of the public offices he had held, and swelling to the utmost the amount he had received out of the public treasury, terminated his censorious attack with the mean sneer that he did not complain, since every man should make his own living, if he can. To this, Mr. Everett, of Massachusetts, replied, with truth and dignity, that whatever Mr. Adams had received, be it great or small, was sanctioned by other administrations, with which Mr. Adams had nothing to do, either in establishing the office fixing the compensations, or seeking the employment. For a third of a century passed in the service of his country, neither he, nor his friends for him, with his knowledge nor without his knowledge, ever solicited any public office or employment; and that, taking into consideration the number of years passed by him in the public service, and the variety and importance of the missions with which he had been intrusted in whole or in part, no foreign minister had ever received less than Mr. Adams, while many have received more. These statements he supported by many minute, accurate, and unanswerable details. In a like spirit Mr. Sargent, of Philadelphia, reprobated and refuted the calumnies uttered against the administration relative to these accounts.

In January, 1828, Mr. Chilton, of Kentucky, introduced a resolution into the House of Representatives, declaring the necessity of retrenchments, to save money and pay off the national debt; and proposing reductions not only in executive contingencies, but also in those of the two houses. This movement disconcerted the party to which Mr. Chilton belonged. They were disposed to point the battery against the administration, but charges of abusive applications of the public moneys by the past as well as the present administration, and both houses of Congress, did not suit party purposes. Randolph, of Virginia, Ingham, of Pennsylvania, and McDuffie, of South Carolina, accordingly strove, by amendments, to narrow down the discussion so as to make it bear upon Mr. Adams or Mr. Clay, and to give countenance to every slander with which the newspapers were teeming against them, but deprecating all general investigations.

Being repeatedly asked concerning his rule of conduct relative to appointments to office, Mr. Adams answered: "My system has been, and continues to be, to nominate for reäppointment all officers, for a term of years, whose commissions expire, unless official or moral misconduct is charged and substantiated against them. This does not suit the Falstaff friends 'who follow for the reward;' and I am importuned to serve my friends, and reproached for neglecting them, because I will not dismiss, or drop from executive favor, officers faithful and able, because they are my political opponents, to provide for my own partisans. This I will not do."

In February, 1828, Mr. Wright, of Ohio, defended Mr. Adams and his administration, on the subject of his votes in the Senate on the acquisition of Louisiana, on the Mississippi and fishery question at Ghent, on an expression in his message to Congress in December, 1825, and other charges and falsehoods which the friends of General Jackson were publishing against him in newspapers, handbills, and stump speeches, throughout the Union.

Mr. Adams was earnestly entreated by his friends to reply to a pamphlet by Samuel D. Ingham, of which many thousands had been franked by members of Congress to their constituents. He refused to do it, saying, "'The slanders and falsehoods of that pamphlet have already been abundantly refuted in the speeches of Jonathan Roberts, Edward Everett, and John C. Wright."

In the committee on retrenchments, Mr. Wickliffe and Mr. Ingham were extremely busy in search of charges against the administration, and asserted that there was a large item of secret services, vouched only by the certificate of Mr. Adams. A member of Congress informed him of their proceedings, and asked, if there should be any clamorers on that subject, whether he would have any objection to make a communication with regard to it. Mr. Adams replied: "Certainly. The secret was enjoined on me by the constitution and the law, and I shall not divulge it. It might be alleged as probable—and such was the fact—that, although the accounts had been but lately settled, the expenditures had been incurred and the payment authorized by the direction of the late President Monroe."

As the electioneering struggle was progressing, Mr. Adams, being asked to advance money in aid of his own election, replied: "The Presidency of the United States is not an office to be either sought or declined. To pay money for securing it is, in my opinion, incorrect in principle. The practices of all parties are tending to render elections altogether venal, and I am not disposed to countenance them."

On the subject of personal interviews with the President, he thus expressed himself: "I have never denied access to me as President to any one, of any color; and, in my opinion of the duties of that office, it never ought to be denied. Place-hunters are not pleasant visitors, or correspondents, and they consume an enormous disproportion of time. To this personal importunity the President ought not to be subjected; but it is, perhaps, not possible to relieve him from it, without excluding him from interviews with the people more, perhaps, than comports with the nature of our institutions."

In Kentucky the Senate of the state constituted itself into an inquisition on a charge against Mr. Adams of corruption, sent for persons and papers, and invited *ex parte* depositions and garbled statements, where the parties inculpated had no opportunity of being heard, and where the testimony given and the testimony suppressed were alike adapted to promote groundless slanders.

In South Carolina movements were made towards civil war and the dissolution of the Union, for the purpose of carrying the election by intimidation, or, if they should fail in that, of laying the foundation of a future forcible resistance, to break down or overawe the administration after the event.

Evidences of the vehement party war stimulated and personally waged by General Jackson against Mr. Adams might be easily multiplied; but enough has been stated to vindicate the character of his administration and the judgment of Henry Clay. By daring to exercise his constitutional rights, by taking the responsibility of preferring Mr. Adams to General Jackson, Mr. Clay postponed for four years an administration characteristic of its leader, violent, intriguing, headstrong, and corrupt. After the passions and interests of the present day have passed away, his vote on that occasion will be regarded by posterity as his choicest and purest title to their remembrance.

To aid the adversaries of Mr. Adams, and to awaken against him in the Northern States, where his strength lay, the dormant passions of former times, the name and influence of Mr. Jefferson were brought into the field. In December, 1825, a letter had been drawn from him, by William B. Giles, a devoted partisan of Jackson, and given to the public with appropriate commentaries and asperities. In this letter Mr. Jefferson, after acknowledging that "his memory was so broken, or gone, as to be almost a blank," undertook to relate a conversation he had with Mr. Adams in 1808, and connected it with facts with which it had no relation, and which occurred several years afterwards, while Mr. Adams was in Europe. These mistakes, in the opinion of Mr. Adams, required explanations. He, therefore, gave a full statement of the facts, so far as he was concerned, and of the communications he had made in 1808 to Mr. Jefferson. These explanations had the tendency which Mr. Giles and the authors of the scheme intended; but the controversies which ensued are not within the scope of this memoir. Feelings and passions, which had slept for almost twenty years, were awakened. Correspondences ensued, in which the policy and events of a former period were discussed with earnestness and warmth. But the ultimate object, for which the broken and incoherent recollections of Mr. Jefferson's old age were brought before the public, was not attained. Those who differed from the opinions of Mr. Adams, and had condemned his political course in former times, although their sentiments remained unchanged, were satisfied with the principles and ability he evinced in his present high station, and indicated no inclination to aid the projects of his opponents. The embers of former animosity were indeed uncovered, but in the Eastern States, where the friends of Mr. Adams were most numerous, no disposition was evinced to favor the elevation of General Jackson to the Presidency.

In other sections of the Union a combination of influences tended to defeat the reëlection of Mr. Adams. In Virginia William B. Giles engaged in giving publicity to violent and inflammatory papers against his administration; Thomas H. Benton, of Missouri, strenuously endeavored to destroy his popularity in the West; while Martin Van Buren, the leader of the party which then controlled New York, also devoted his efforts to secure Jackson's ascendency.

When Mr. Adams was informed that Mr. Clay's final and full vindication of himself against the aspersions of General Jackson had appeared from the press, he said: "It is unnecessary. Enough has already been said to put down that infamous slander, which has been more than once publicly branded as falsehood. The conspiracy will, however, probably succeed. When suspicions have been kindled into popular delusion, truth, reason, and justice, speak to the ears of adders. The sacrifice must be consummated. There will then be a reäction in public opinion. It may not be rapid, but it will be certain."

By one of those party arrangements which ever have shaped, and to human view forever will decide, the destinies of this republic,—a coalition being effected between the leading influences of the slave states and those of New York and Pennsylvania,—Andrew Jackson and John C. Calhoun, both slaveholders, were respectively elected President and Vice-President of the United States.

CHAPTER VIII.

PURSUITS OF MR. ADAMS IN RETIREMENT.—ELECTED TO CONGRESS.—PARTIES AND THEIR PROCEEDINGS.—HIS COURSE IN RESPECT OF THEM.—HIS OWN ADMINISTRATION AND THAT OF HIS SUCCESSOR COMPARED.—REPORT ON MANUFACTURES AND THE BANK OF THE UNITED STATES.—REFUSAL TO VOTE, AND CONSEQUENT PROCEEDINGS.—SPEECH AND REPORT ON THE MODIFICATION OF THE TARIFF AND SOUTH CAROLINA NULLIFICATION.

On the 4th of March, 1829, Andrew Jackson was inaugurated President of the United States, and Mr. Adams retired, as he then thought forever, from public life. His active, energetic spirit required neither indulgence nor rest, and he immediately directed his attention to those philosophical, literary, and religious researches, in which he took unceasing delight. The works of Cicero became the object of study, analysis, and criticism. Commentaries on that master-mind of antiquity were among his daily labors. The translation of the Psalms of David into English verse was a frequent exercise; and his study of the Scriptures was accompanied by critical remarks, pursued in the spirit of free inquiry, chastened by a solemn reference to their origin, and influence on the conduct and hopes of human life. His favorite science, astronomy, led to the frequent observation of the planets and stars; and his attention was also turned to agriculture and horticulture. He collected and planted the seeds of forest trees, and kept a record of their development, and, in the summer season, labored two or three hours daily in his garden. With these pursuits were combined sketches preparatory to a full biography of his father, which he then contemplated as one of his chief future employments.

From the subjects to which the labors of his life had been principally devoted his thoughts could not be wholly withdrawn. As early as the 27th of April, 1829, a citizen of Washington spoke to him with great severity on the condition of public affairs, and of the scandals in circulation concerning them; stating that removals from office were continuing with great perseverance; that the custom-houses in Boston, New York, Philadelphia, Portsmouth in New Hampshire, and New Orleans, had been swept clear; that violent partisans of Jackson were exclusively appointed, and that every editor of a scurrilous newspaper had been provided for.

Again, in June of the same year Mr. Adams wrote: "Mr. Van Buren is now Secretary of State. He is the manager by whom the present administration has been brought into power. He has played over again the game of Aaron Burr in 1800, with the addition of political inconsistency, in transferring his allegiance from Crawford to Jackson. He sold the State of New York to them both. The first bargain failed by the result of the choice of electors in the Legislature. The second was barely accomplished by the system of party management established in that state; and Van Buren is now enjoying his reward."

On the abolition of slavery, Mr. Adams observed: "It is the only part of European democracy which will find no favor in the United States. It may aggravate the condition of slaves in the South, but the result of the Missouri question, and the attitude of parties, have silenced most of the declaimers on that subject. This state of things is not to continue forever. It is possible that the danger of the abolition doctrines, when brought home to

56

Southern statesmen, may teach them the value of the Union, as the only thing which can maintain their system of slavery."

On the course and feelings of Mr. Jefferson on this subject, Mr. Adams thus expressed himself: "His love of liberty was sincere and ardent, but confined to himself, like that of most of his fellow-slaveholders. He was above that execrable sophistry of the South Carolina nullifiers, which would make of slavery the corner-stone of the temple of liberty. He saw the gross inconsistency between the principles of the Declaration of Independence and the fact of negro slavery; and he could not, or would not, prostitute the faculties of his mind to the vindication of that slavery, which, from his soul, he abhorred. But Jefferson had not the spirit of martyrdom. He would have introduced a flaming denunciation of slavery into the Declaration of Independence, but the discretion of his colleagues struck it out. He did insert a most eloquent and impassioned argument against it in his Notes on Virginia; but, on that very account, the book was published almost against his will. He projected a plan of a general emancipation, in his revision of the Virginia laws, but finally presented a plan leaving slavery precisely where it was; and, in his Memoir, he leaves a posthumous warning to the planters that they must, at no distant day, emancipate their slaves, or that worse will follow; but he withheld the publication of his prophecy till he should himself be in the grave."

Mr. Adams was not long permitted to remain in retirement. In October, 1830, he was nominated, in the newspapers, to represent in Congress the district of Massachusetts in which he resided. When asked if he would consent to be a candidate, he replied, in the spirit which had governed his whole life, never to seek and never to decline public service: "It must first be seen whether the people of the district will invite me to represent them. I shall not ask their votes. I wish them to act their pleasure." In the ensuing November he was elected Representative of the twelfth Congressional district of Massachusetts.

On the 3d of January, 1831, Mr. Adams thus remarked on the resolutions of the Legislature of Georgia setting at defiance the Supreme Court of the United States: "They are published and approved in the *Telegraph*, the administration newspaper at Washington. By extending the laws of Georgia over the country and people of the Cherokees, the constitution, laws, and treaties, of the United States, were *quoad hoc* set aside. They were chaff before the wind. In pursuance of these laws of Georgia, a Cherokee Indian is prosecuted for the murder of another Indian, before a state court of Georgia, tried by a jury of white men, and sentenced to death. He applies to a chief justice of the Court of the United States, who issues an injunction to the Governor and executive officers of Georgia, upon the appeal to the laws and treaties of the United States. The Governor of Georgia refuses obedience to the injunction, and the Legislature pass resolutions that they will not appear to answer before the Supreme Court of the United States. The constitution, the laws, and treaties, of the United States, are prostrate in the State of Georgia. Is there any remedy for this state of things? None; because the State of Georgia is in league with the Executive of the United States, who will not take care that the laws be faithfully executed. A majority of both houses of Congress sustain this neglect and violation of duty. There is no harmony in the government of the Union. The arm refuses its office. 'The whole head is sick, and the whole heart faint.' This example of the State of Georgia will be imitated by other states, and with regard to other national interests,—perhaps the tariff, more probably the public lands. As the Executive and Legislature now fail to sustain the Judiciary, it is not improbable cases may arise in which the Judiciary may fail to sustain them. The Union is in the most imminent danger of dissolution from the old, inherent vice of confederacies, anarchy in the members. To this end one third of the people is perverted, one third slumbers, and the rest wring their hands, with unavailing lamentations, in the foresight of evils they cannot avert."

On the 4th of July, 1831, Mr. Adams delivered an oration before the inhabitants of the town of Quincy, in which he controverted the doctrine of Blackstone, the great commentator upon the laws of England, who maintained "that there is, and must be, in all forms of government, however they began, and by what right soever they subsist, a supreme, irresistible, absolute, uncontrolled authority, in which the *jura summi imperii*, or *the rights of sovereignty*, reside." "It is not true," Mr. Adams remarks, "that there *must* reside in all governments an absolute, uncontrolled, irresistible, and despotic power; nor is such a power absolutely essential to sovereignty. The direct converse of the proposition is true. Uncontrollable power exists in no government upon earth. The sternest despotisms, in every region and every age of the world, *are and have been* under perpetual control; compelled, as Burke expresses it, to truckle and huckster. Unlimited power belongs not to the nature of man, and rotten will be the foundation of every government leaning upon such a maxim for its support. Least of all can it be predicated of any government professing to be founded upon an original compact. The pretence of an absolute, irresistible, despotic power, existing in every government *somewhere*, is incompatible with the first principle of natural right."

This proposition Mr. Adams proceeds fully to illustrate, and thus to apply: "This political sophism of identity between *sovereign* and *despotic* power has led, and continues to lead, into many vagaries, some of the statists of this our happy but disputatious Union. It seizes upon the brain of a heated politician, sometimes in one state, sometimes in another, and its natural offspring is the doctrine of nullification; that is, the *sovereign* power of any one state of the confederacy to nullify any act of the whole twenty-four states which the *sovereign* state shall please to consider as unconstitutional. Stripped of the sophistical argumentation in which this doctrine has been habited, its naked nature is an effort to organize insurrection against the laws of the United States; to interpose the arm of state sovereignty between rebellion and the halter, and to rescue the traitor from the gibbet. Although conducted under the auspices of state sovereignty, it would not the less be levying war against the Union; but, as a state cannot be punished for treason, nullification cases herself in the complete steel of sovereign power." "The citizen of the nullifying state becomes a traitor to his country by obedience to the law of his state,—a traitor to his state by obedience to the law of his country. The scaffold and the battle-field stream alternately with the blood of their victims. The event of a conflict in arms between the Union and one of its members, whether terminating in victory or defeat, would be but an alternative of calamity to all."

Mr. Adams took his seat in the House of Representatives in December, 1831, and immediately announced to his constituents that he should hold himself bound in allegiance to no party, whether sectional or political. Ten years afterwards he had occasion to explain to his fellow-citizens his policy and feelings at this period. "I thought this independence of party was a duty imposed upon me by my peculiar position. I had spent the greatest part of my life in the service of the whole nation, and had been honored by their highest trust; my duty of fidelity, of affection, and of gratitude, to the whole, was not merely inseparable from, but identical with, that which was due from me to my own commonwealth. The internal conflict between slavery and freedom had been, and still was, scarcely perceptible in the national councils. The Missouri compromise had laid it asleep, it was hoped, forever. The development of the moral principle which pronounced slavery *a crime* of man against his brother-man had not yet reached the conscience of Christendom. England, earnestly and zealously occupied in rallying the physical, moral, and intellectual energies of the civilized world against the African slave-trade, had scarcely yet discovered that it was but an instrument, and in truth a mitigation, of the great, irremissible wrong of slavery. Her final policy, the extinction of slavery throughout the earth, was not yet disclosed. The Jackson project of dismembering Mexico for the acquisition of Texas, already organized and in full operation, was yet profoundly a secret. I entered Congress without one sentiment of discrimination between the interests of the North and the South; and my first act, as a member of the House, was, on presenting fifteen petitions from Pennsylvania for the abolition of slavery within the District of Columbia, to declare, while moving their reference to the committee of the District, that I was not prepared to support the measure myself, and that I should not. I was not then a sectional partisan, and I never have been."[22]

When Mr. Adams was entering this new field of labor, Mr. Clay asked him how he felt at turning boy again, and going into the House of Representatives; and observed that he would find his situation extremely laborious. Mr. Adams replied: "I well know this; but labor I shall not refuse so long as my hands, my eyes, and my brain, do not desert me."

To understand the position in which Mr. Adams was placed, on his taking his seat in the House of Representatives, it is important that some of the events which had occurred during his absence from public life should be briefly recapitulated. General Jackson had been two years President of the United States. The alliance which he had entered into with Mr. Van Buren for their mutual advancement, to which allusion has been made in a former chapter, had not resulted immediately as the high contracting parties probably intended. An obstacle to the advancement of Mr. Van Buren to the Vice-Presidency presented itself which was insurmountable. John C. Calhoun, of South Carolina, possessed an influence in the slave states which it was important to conciliate, and imprudent to set at defiance. The allies were, consequently, compelled to accede to his nomination as Vice-President, and Van Buren was forced to be content with the prospect of being appointed Secretary of State.

The elevation of Calhoun to the Vice-Presidency, there is reason to believe, could not have been acceptable to Jackson. It appears, by the documents published by Calhoun in connection with his account of his controversy with Jackson, that William H. Crawford had, as early as December, 1827, taken direct measures to render the friendship of Calhoun suspected by Jackson. On the 14th of that month he wrote a letter to Alfred Balch, at Nashville, with the express purpose of its being shown to Jackson, containing the following statement: "My opinions upon the next presidential election" (against Adams and in favor of Jackson) "are generally known. When Mr. Van Buren and Mr. Cambreling made me a visit, last April, I authorized them, upon every proper occasion, to make these opinions known. The vote of the State of Georgia will, as certainly as that of Tennessee, be given to General Jackson, in opposition to Mr. Adams. The only difficulty that this state has upon that subject is, that, if Jackson should be elected, Calhoun will come into power. I confess I am not apprehensive of such a result. For —— —— writes to me, Jackson ought to know, and if he does not he shall know, that, at the Calhoun caucus in Columbia, the term *military chieftain* was bandied about even more flippantly than it had been by Henry Clay, and that the family friends of Mr. Calhoun were most active in giving it currency; and I know, personally, that Calhoun favored Mr. Adams' pretensions until Mr. Clay declared for him. He well knew that Clay would not have declared for Adams without it was well understood that he, Calhoun, was to be put down if Adams could effect it. If he was not friendly to his election, why did he suffer his paper to be purchased up by Adams' printers, without making some stipulation in favor of Jackson? If you can ascertain that Calhoun will not be benefited by Jackson's election, you will do him a service by communicating the information to me. Make what use you please of this letter, and show it to whom you please."[23]

That these opinions of Crawford concerning Calhoun were communicated to Van Buren and Cambreling when they visited him, as he states, on their electioneering tour, in April, 1827, cannot be reasonably questioned: and that Crawford's letter to Balch was also communicated to Jackson can as little be doubted. That at this period Calhoun's want of political sympathy with Jackson was publicly known and talked about at Nashville, is apparent from Calhoun's address to the people of the United States in his controversy with Jackson, in which he bitterly complains: "I remained ignorant and unsuspicious of these secret movements against me till the spring of 1828, when vague rumors reached me that some attempts were making at Nashville to injure me."

Why statements made by such a high authority as Crawford, so well adapted to kindle the inflammatory temperament of Jackson, and at once so auspicious to the hopes of Van Buren and so ominous to those of Calhoun, were not immediately made the subject of action, can only be accounted for by the fact that Calhoun was at that time too strong in the affections of the South for them then to commence hostilities; for, in that case he would, as Crawford intimated, have "favored the pretensions of Adams," and possibly have defeated the plans of the alliance. Jackson, therefore, yielded, and allowed Calhoun to be run as a candidate for the Vice-Presidency on the same ticket with himself, and postponed any attempt to deprive him of his chance of succession until a more convenient opportunity. To this arrangement Van Buren also was compelled to submit, and, after Adams was superseded, and Jackson inaugurated President, he was appointed Secretary of State.[24]

In April, 1830, when the Legislatures of New York and Pennsylvania took incipient measures to nominate Jackson for a second term of office, the favorable moment arrived to bring his artillery to bear upon Calhoun. At this time two letters of Crawford were brought to the mind of General Jackson,—the one to Alfred Balch, already referred to; the other to John Forsyth, dated the 30th of April, 1830,[25] —in which Crawford expressly stated that

"Mr. Calhoun had made a proposition to the cabinet of Monroe for *punishing* him for his conduct in the Seminole war." Jackson, greatly excited, immediately, on the 12th of May, 1830, addressed a letter to Mr. Calhoun, declaring his great surprise at the information those letters contained, and inquiring whether he had moved or sustained any attempt seriously to affect him in Monroe's cabinet council. Calhoun replied, that he "could not recognize the right of General Jackson to call in question his conduct in the discharge of a high official duty, and under responsibility to his conscience and his country only." The anger of Jackson was not in the least assuaged by this reply, nor by the explanations which accompanied it. A correspondence ensued, which, with collateral and documentary evidence, occupied fifty-two pages of an octavo pamphlet; resulting in Jackson's declaration of his poignant mortification to see in Calhoun's letter, instead of a negative, an admission of the truth of Crawford's allegations. An irreconcilable alienation between Jackson and Calhoun was evinced in this correspondence; a state of feeling which for the time was concealed from the public, but was well known to their respective partisans, who understood that at the approaching election the influence of the former would be thrown into the scale of Van Buren. Jackson's intention of standing for the Presidency a second time was kept a profound secret until January, 1831. Under the supposition that he might decline, the partisans of Calhoun, Clay, and Van Buren, engaged in active measures to put them respectively into the field.

From the party movements during this uncertainty it was clearly perceived that, if Jackson was not again a candidate, a contest between Van Buren and Calhoun for the Presidency was unavoidable. Calhoun's chance of success was preëminent, for he would unite in his favor all the votes and influence of the South,—Van Buren not having then had an opportunity to evince his entire subserviency to the slaveholding power. Jackson, into whose heart Van Buren had wound himself, looked with little complacency on the probable success of Calhoun. Under these circumstances, he resolved to enter the lists himself as a candidate for the Presidency, and, by taking Van Buren with him for the Vice-Presidency, put him at once in the best position to become his successor. Van Buren coïncided in these views, and acquiesced in, if he did not originate, this measure. He foresaw that the popularity of Jackson would throw Calhoun out of the field, whether he was a candidate at the next ensuing election for the Presidency or Vice-Presidency. The time had now come to put an end to the hopes of Calhoun for the attainment of either of those high stations, by making public the animosity of Jackson; but this could not be done without a struggle. Branch, Ingham, and Berrien, all members of Jackson's cabinet, were known friends to Calhoun, and far from being well disposed to Van Buren. Under these circumstances, Jackson resolved to dissolve his cabinet, in which Van Buren himself held a place, and form another, better adapted to their united views. As a violent contest with the friends of Calhoun was anticipated, Van Buren, if he should continue Secretary of State, would be considered responsible for all Jackson's proceedings to frustrate Calhoun's aspirations for the Presidency, which might injuriously affect his popularity in the Southern States. Van Buren therefore retired upon a mission to England.

Such were the general views and policy of these allied aspirants to the two highest offices of state, which public documents now make apparent, when, in April, 1831, say the newspapers of the period, "an explosion took place in the cabinet at Washington, the announcement of which came upon the public like a clap of thunder in a cloudless day."[26] On the 7th of April, the Secretary of War, General Eaton, resigned, without giving any other reason than his own inclination, and that he deemed the moment favorable, as General Jackson's "course of policy had been advantageously commenced." On the 11th of April, Van Buren resigned the office of Secretary of State. So far as his motive could be discerned through the haze of ambiguous and diplomatic language, it was that his name had been connected with that distracting topic, the question of successorship, which rendered his continuance in the cabinet embarrassing, and might be injurious to the public service. The two other secretaries, Ingham and Branch, were kept in ignorance of these resignations until the 19th of April, when Jackson informed them that, to command public confidence and satisfy public opinion, he deemed it proper to select a cabinet of entirely new materials,[27] and therefore requested them to resign their respective offices. They accordingly tendered their resignations, which were accepted by the President, in a letter to

60

each, couched in language perfectly identical, in which he admits that the dismissed officers had faithfully performed their respective official duties, but intimates that the want of harmony in the cabinet "made its entire renovation requisite."[28] Branch and Ingham both denied any want of harmony in the cabinet, and the latter declared that "it had never been interrupted for a moment, nor been divided in a single instance by difference of opinion as to the measures of the government."[29] These contradictions, thus openly made, created intense curiosity, and public clamor for a full development of facts. Branch, in a letter dated May 31st, 1831, addressed to certain citizens of Bertie County, North Carolina, declared that "discord had been introduced into the ranks of the administration by the intrigues of selfish politicians."[30]

The Attorney-General, Mr. Berrien, did not resign until the 15th of June ensuing, nor until he also had been invited to do so by Jackson. He then declared that he resigned "simply on account of the President's will," and that he knew of no want of harmony in the cabinet which either had or ought to have impeded the operations of the administration.[31] In July, Mr. Ingham, on returning home, was received by a great cavalcade of his fellow-citizens, and was called upon for an explanation of "the extraordinary measure, the dissolution of the cabinet, which had shocked the public mind." He replied, that it was exclusively the act of the President, who alone could perfectly explain his own motives, and he deemed it improper for him to anticipate the explanation which the President must deem it his duty to make.[32] As Jackson made no explanation, Mr. Branch, after being repeatedly called upon in the public papers, authorized the publication of a letter he had addressed to Edmund B. Freeman, dated the 22d of August, 1831,[33] in which he gave a full statement of the overbearing language and conduct of Jackson, and unequivocally declared that the contemporaneous resignation of Eaton and Van Buren was a measure adopted for the purpose of getting rid of the three offensive members of the cabinet; that "their dismission had been stipulated for, and the reason was that Van Buren, having discovered that the three members of the cabinet (afterwards ejected) disdained to become tools to subserve his ambitious aspirings, had determined to leave them as little power to defeat his machinations as possible; and that he had become latterly almost the sole confidant and adviser of the President."

The details of this controversy belong to general history, and will be found in the documents of the period. Enough has been given to indicate the great influence Van Buren had acquired, for his own political advancement, by an unscrupulous subserviency to the overbearing violence of the President.

On this subject Mr. Adams observed: "Van Buren outwits Calhoun in the favor of Jackson. He brought the administration into power, and now enjoys the reward of his intrigues. Jackson rides rough-shod over the Senate, in relation to appointments; but they dare not oppose him." It was impossible, in view of these scenes of discord and mutual crimination, for Mr. Adams not to feel self-congratulation when he recollected the uninterrupted harmony which, during four years, had prevailed in his own cabinet. From without it had been assailed with calumny and malignant passions; but within was peace, quiet, mutual assistance and support. No jealousies disturbed the tranquillity of their meetings. No ambitious spirit had shaped measures to purposes of his own aggrandizement. Though silent, he could not fail, while contemplating the comparison, to realize the triumph history was preparing for himself and his administration. The contrast presented by its principles, when compared with those of his successor, must have been also a natural source of intense self-congratulation. Notwithstanding the warning voice of Henry Clay, a military chieftain had been placed in the chair of state. He entered it with the spirit of a conqueror, and conducted in it in the spirit of the camp. The gratification of his feelings, and the reward of his partisans, were apparently his chief objects. He dismissed from office, without trial, without charge, and without fault, faithful and able men. During the whole period of Mr. Adams' administration not an officer of the government, from Maine to Louisiana, was dismissed on account of his political opinions. Many well known to him as opposed to his reëlection, and actively employed in behalf of his competitor, were permitted to hold their places, though subject to his power of dismission. Not one was discharged from that cause. In the early part of his administration appointments were promiscuously made from all the parties in the previous canvass. This course was pursued until an opposition was organized which denounced all appointments from its ranks as being made for party purposes. Of *eighty* newspapers employed in publishing the laws during the four years of his Presidency, only *twelve* or *fifteen* were changed, some for geographical, others for local considerations. Some papers among the most influential in the opposition, but otherwise conducted with decorum, were retained. Of the entire number of changes, not more than four or five were made on account of their scurrilous character. During the same period *not more than five* members of Congress received official appointments to any office. Even these shocked General Jackson's patriotism, from their mischievous bearing on the purity of the national legislature, and the permanency of our republican institutions. Being then a candidate for the Presidency, in opposition to Mr. Adams, he deliberately declared to the Legislature of Tennessee his firm conviction that no member of Congress ought to be appointed to any office except a seat on the bench; and he added that he himself would conform to that rule. Notwithstanding this pledge, he appointed *eight* or *ten* members of Congress to office in the first four weeks of his Presidency. Mr. Clay publicly asserted his belief that within two months after Jackson had attained that high station more members of Congress had offices conferred on them "than were appointed by any one of his predecessors during their whole period of four or eight years." His proceedings evidenced that among this favorite class no office is too high or too low for desire and acceptance, from the head of a department to the most subordinate office under a collector. On editors of newspapers he bestowed unexampled patronage. Fifteen or twenty of those who had been most active in his favor during the preceding canvass,—the most abusive of his opponents, and the most fulsome in his own praise,—were immediately rewarded with place. Of all attempts, his were the boldest and the most successful ever made to render the press venal, and to corrupt this palladium of liberty.[34]Happily the times were not propitious to give immediate development to these principles of permanent power. But the degree of success of this first attempt of one man to constitute "*himself the state*" contains a solemn foreboding as to the possible future fate of our republic. For, although at this time the ambition of the individual was not fully gratified, enough was effected to encourage the reckless and aspiring. The seeds of corruption were thickly scattered. In that Presidency the doctrine was first promulgated, "*To the victors belong the spoils.*" From that day, subserviency to the chief of the prevailing party became the condition on which station and place were given or holden. In his hands was lodged the power of reward and punishment, to be exercised ruthlessly for party support and perpetuation; resulting, in the higher departments, in tame submission to the will of the chief, and, in the lower, in the adoption of the detestable maxim that *all is fair in politics*. The consequences are daily seen in the servility of office-holders and office-seekers; in forced contributions, during pending elections, for the continuance of the prevailing power, and afterwards in a heartless proscription of all not acceptable to the successful dynasty; in the excluding every one from office who has not the spirit to be a slave, and filling the heart of every true lover of his country with ominous conjectures concerning the fate of our institutions.

During the early periods of Jackson's administration, Mr. Adams, though in retirement, was neither unobserving nor silent concerning its proceedings. In January, 1830, in the course of a conversation with a senator from Louisiana on the politics and the intrigues then going on at Washington in relation to the next presidential election, he said: "There are three divisions of the administration party: one for General Jackson, whose friends wish his reëlection; one for Mr. Van Buren, and one for Calhoun. Van Buren sees he cannot eight years longer discharge the duties of the Department of State; and that he must succeed at the end of four years, or not at all. His friends insist that Jackson has given a pledge that he will not serve another term. Calhoun and his friends are equally impatient, and he is much disposed to declare himself against the leading measures of the present administration. But if Mr. Clay was brought forward by his friends as a candidate, it would close all the cracks of the administration party, and rivet them together."

In the beginning of February, Mr. Adams remarked: "All the members of Congress are full of rumors concerning the volcanic state of the administration. The President has determined to remove Branch, but was told that if he did the North Carolina senators would join the opposition, and all his nominations would be rejected. The administration is split up into a blue and green faction upon a point of morals; an explosion has been deferred, but is expected."

On the 26th of March, 1830, he again remarked: "There is a controversy between the *Telegraph*, Calhoun's paper here, and the *New York Courier*, Van Buren's paper, upon the question whether Jackson is or is not a candidate for reëlection as President,— the *Courier* insisting that he is, and the *Telegraph* declaring that it is premature to ask the question. Mr. Van Buren has got the start of Calhoun, in the merit of convincing General Jackson that the salvation of the country depends on his reëlection. This establishes his ascendency in the cabinet, and reduces Calhoun to the alternative of joining in the shout 'Hurra for Jackson!' or of being counted in opposition."

On the 28th of March, 1830, the question being still in agitation before the public whether Jackson, if a candidate, would be successful, Mr. Adams said: "Jackson will be a candidate, and have a fair chance of success. His personal popularity, founded solely on the battle of New Orleans, will carry him through the next election, as it did through the last. The vices of his administration are not such as affect the popular feeling. He will lose none of his popularity unless he should do something to raise a blister upon public sentiment, and of that there is no prospect. If he lives, therefore, and nothing external should happen to rouse new parties, he may be reëlected not only twice, but thrice."

In June, 1830, he again expressed his views on the policy and prospects of the administration. He said it was impossible to foresee what would be the fluctuations of popular opinion. Hitherto there were symptoms of changes of opinion among members of Congress, but none among the people. These could be indicated only by the elections. He had great doubts whether the majorities in the Legislatures of the free states would be changed by the approaching elections, and was far from certain that the next Legislature of Kentucky would nominate Mr. Clay in opposition to the reëlection of General Jackson. The whole strength of the present administration rested on Jackson's personal popularity, founded on his military services. He had surrendered the Indians to the states within the bounds of which they are located. This would confirm and strengthen his popularity in those states, especially as he had burdened the Union with the expense of removing and indemnifying the Indians. He had taken practical ground against internal improvements and domestic industry, which would strengthen him in all the Southern States. He had, as might have been expected, thrown all his weight into the slaveholding scale; and that interest is so compact, so consolidated, and so fervent in action, that there is every prospect it will overpower the discordant and loosely constructed interest of the free states. The cause of internal improvement will sink, and that of domestic industry will fall with or after it. There is at present a great probability that Jackson's policy will be supported by a majority of the people.

After a conversation with Oliver Wolcott, the successor of Alexander Hamilton as Secretary of the Treasury under Washington, who had been subsequently Governor of Connecticut, Mr. Adams remarked: "Mr. Wolcott views the prospects of the Union with great sagacity, and with hopes more sanguine than mine. He thinks the continuance of the Union will depend upon the heavy population of Pennsylvania, and that its gravitation will preserve the Union. He holds the South Carolina turbulence too much in contempt. The domineering spirit naturally springs from the institution of slavery; and when, as in South Carolina, the slaves are more numerous than their masters, the domineering spirit is wrought up to its highest pitch of intenseness. The South Carolinians are attempting to govern the Union as they govern their slaves, and there are too many indications that, abetted as they are by all the slave-driving interest of the Union, the free portion will cower before them, and truckle to their insolence. This is my apprehension."

While Jackson's nominations were pending before the Senate, a senator from New Hampshire said to Mr. Adams that he hoped the whole tribe of editors of newspapers would be rejected; for he thought it the most dangerous precedent that could be established, and, if now sanctioned by the Senate, he despaired of its being controlled hereafter; and added that he was almost discouraged concerning the permanency of our institutions. Mr. Adams replied, that his hopes were better, but that undoubtedly the giving offices to editors of newspapers was of all species of bribery the most dangerous.

From the time Mr. Adams took his seat in the House of Representatives, in December, 1831, till the period of his death, few of his contemporaries equalled and none exceeded him in punctuality of attendance. He was usually among the first members in his place in the morning, and the last to leave it. On every question of general interest he bestowed scrupulous attention, yielding to it the full strength of his mind, and his extensive knowledge of public affairs. A full history of the proceedings of Congress during this period alone can do justice to his devotion to the public service. In this memoir his views and course will no further be recorded than as they regard topics obviously nearest his heart, and in which his principles and character are developed with peculiar ability and power.

In December, 1831, on the distribution of the several parts of the President's message to committees, Mr. Adams was appointed chairman of that on manufactures. Against this position he immediately remonstrated, and solicited the Speaker to relieve him from it. He stated that the subject of manufactures was connected with details not familiar to him; that, during the long period of a life devoted to public service, his thoughts had been directed in a very different line. It was replied, that he could not be excused without a vote of the House; that the continuance of the Union might depend on the questions relative to the tariff; and that it was thought his influence would have great weight in reconciling the Eastern States to such modifications as he might sanction. He therefore yielded all personal considerations to the interests of his country, and accepted the appointment.

In the ensuing March, on being appointed on a committee to investigate the affairs of the United States Bank, Mr. Adams requested of the House to be excused from service on the Committee on Manufactures, giving the same reasons he had previously urged, and others resulting from the incompatibility of the two offices. An opposition was made by Cambreling, of New York, Barbour, of Virginia, and Drayton, of South Carolina, in speeches which were characterized by the newspapers of the times as "most extraordinary."[35]Cambreling said: "The present condition of the country and of the public mind demanded the intelligence, industry, and patriotism, for which Mr. Adams was distinguished. The authority of his name was of infinite importance." Mr. Barbour followed in a like strain. "The member from Massachusetts," said he, "with whom I have been associated in the Committee on Manufactures, has not only fulfilled all his duties with eminent ability, in the committee, but in a spirit and temper that demanded grateful acknowledgments, and excited the highest admiration." He concluded with an appeal to Mr. Adams, "as a patriot, a statesman, and philanthropist, as well as an American, feeling the full force of his duties, and touched by all their incentives to lofty action, to forbear his request." Mr. Drayton also, in a voice of eulogy, declared that, "Amidst all the rancor of political parties with which our country has been distracted, and from which, unhappily, we are not now exempt, it has always been admitted that no individual was more eminently endowed with those intellectual and moral qualities which entitle their possessor to the respect of the community, and to entire confidence in the purity of his motives, than Mr. Adams."

These politicians were the active and influential members of a party which had raised General Jackson to the President's chair. When laboring to displace Mr. Adams from that high station, that party had represented him as "neither a statesman nor a patriot; without talents; as a mere professor of rhetoric, capable of making a corrupt bargain for the sake of power, and of condescending to intrigue for the attainment of place and office." To hear the leaders of such a party now extolling him for integrity, diligence, and intelligence, upon whose continuance in office the hopes of the country and the continuance of the Union might depend, was a change in opinions and language which might well be attributed to the awakening of conscience to a sense of justice, and a desire for reparation of wrong, were it not that leaders of factions have never any other criterion of truth, or rule in the use of language, than adaptation to selfish and party purposes.

Equally uninfluenced by adulation and undeterred by abuse, on the 23d of May, 1832, as chairman of the Committee on Manufactures, by order of a majority, Mr. Adams reported a bill, which, in presenting it, he declared was not coïncident with the views of that majority, and that for parts he alone was responsible. After lauding the anticipated extinction of the public debt, he proceeded to show, by a laborious research into its history, that such extinction had always been contemplated, and that the policy of the government, from the earliest period of its existence, had concurred in the wisdom of this application of the revenue. He proceeded to expose and deprecate that Southern policy, which seized on this occasion "to reduce the revenues of the Union to the lowest point absolutely necessary to defray the ordinary charges and indispensable expenditures of the government;" a system which, by inevitable consequence and by avowed design, "left our shores to take care of themselves, our navy to perish by dry rot upon the stocks, our manufactures to wither under the blast of foreign competition;" and he urged, in opposition to these destructive doctrines, the duty of levying revenue enough for "common defence," and also to "protect manufactures," and supported his argument by a great array of facts; severely animadverting upon those politicians who glorified themselves on the prosperous state of the country, and yet labored to break down that "system of protection for domestic manufactures by which this prosperity had been chiefly produced." The duty of "defensive preparation and internal improvements" he maintained to be unquestionable, obligations resulting from the language and spirit of the constitution. The doctrine that the interests of the planter and the manufacturer were irreconcilable, and that duties for the protection of domestic industry operate to the injury of the Southern States, he analyzed, illustrated, and showed to be fallacious, "striking directly at the heart of the Union, and leading inevitably to its dissolution;" a result to which more than one distinguished and influential statesman of the South had affirmed that "his mind was made up." The doctrine that the interest of the South is identified with the foreign competitor of the Northern manufacturer, he denounced as in conflict with the whole history of our Revolutionary War, and a satire on our institutions. If it should prove true that these interests were so irreconcilable as to cause a separation, as some Southern statesmen contended, after such separation the same state of irreconcilable interests would continue, and "with redoubled aggravation," resulting in an inextinguishable or exterminating war between the brothers of this severed continent, which nothing but a foreign umpire could settle or adjust, and this not according to the interests of either of the parties, but his own. The consequences of such a state of things he displayed with great power and eloquence, and concluded with alluding "to that great, comprehensive, but peculiar Southern interest, which is now protected by the laws of the United States, but which, in case of severance of the Union, must produce consequences from which a statesman of either portion of it cannot but avert his eyes."

Contemporaneously with this report on manufactures, Mr. Adams, as one of the committee to examine and report on the books and proceedings of the Bank of the United States, submitted to the House of Representatives a report, signed only by himself and Mr. Watmough, of Pennsylvania, in which he declared his dissent from the report of the committee on that subject. After examining their proceedings with minuteness and searching severity, he asserted that they were without authority, and in flagrant violation of the rights of the bank, and of the principles on which the freedom of this people had been founded.

In February, 1832, Mr. Adams delivered a speech on the ratio of representation—on the duty of making the constituent body small, and the representatives numerous; contending that a large representation and a small constituency was a truly republican principle, and illustrating it from history, and from its tendency to give the distinguished men of the different states opportunities to become acquainted with each other.

In July ensuing, a vote censuring a member for words spoken in debate being on its passage in the House, Mr. Adams, when the roll was called, and his name announced, rose with characteristic spirit, and delivered a paper to the clerk, which contained the following words: "I ask to be excused from voting on the resolution, believing it to be unconstitutional, inasmuch as it assumes inferences of fact from words spoken by the member, without giving the words themselves, and the fact not being warranted, in my judgment, by the words he did use." A majority of the house, being disposed to put down, and, if possible, disgrace Mr. Adams, refused to excuse him. On his name being called, he again declined voting, and stated that he did not refuse to vote from any contumacy or disrespect to the house, but because he had a right to decline from conscientious motives, and that he desired to place his reasons for declining upon the journals of the house. A member observed that, if they put those reasons on the journal, they would spread on it their own condemnation; adding that, by going out of the house, Mr. Adams might easily have avoided voting. The latter replied, "I do not choose to shrink from my duty by such an expedient. It is not my right alone, but the rights of all the members, and of the people of the United States, which are concerned in this question, and I cannot evade it. I regret the state of things, but I must abide by the consequences, whatever they may be." A motion made to reconsider the vote refusing to excuse him was lost—yeas *fifty-nine*, nays *seventy-four*. The Speaker then read the rule by which every member is required to vote, and stated that it was the duty of every member to vote on one side or the other. The question then being repeated, when the clerk called the name of Mr. Adams, he gave no response, and remained in his seat. A member then rose, said it was an unprecedented case, and moved two resolutions. By the one, the facts being first stated, the course pursued by Mr. Adams was declared "a breach of one of the rules of the house." By the other, a committee was to be appointed for inquiring and reporting "what course ought to be adopted in a case so novel and important." The house then proceeded to pass the original vote of censure on the member, without repeating the name of Mr. Adams.

The next day the vote for a committee of inquiry on the subject caused a desultory and warm debate, during which Mr. Adams took occasion to say that the whole affair was a subject of great mortification to him. The proposed resolution, after naming him personally, and affirming that he had been guilty of a breach of the rules of the house, proposed that a committee of inquiry should be raised, to consider what was to be done in a case so novel and important. On this resolution, which the mover seemed to suppose would pass of course, Mr. Adams said, that he trusted opportunity would be given him to show the reasons which had prevented him from voting. Mr. Everett, of Massachusetts, then remonstrated with the majority of the house for attempting thus to censure a man, such as they knew Mr. Adams to be, than whom he was confident the whole house would bear him witness that there was not an individual on that floor more regular, more assiduous, or more laborious, in the discharge of his public duty. A motion was then made to lay the resolution on the table, which prevailed—yeas *eighty-nine*, nays *sixty-three*.

Thus ended a debate which severely tested the firmness of the spirit of Mr. Adams. Neither seduced by the number nor quailing under the threats and violence of his assailants, he maintained the rights of his public station, and with silent dignity set at defiance their overbearing attempts to terrify, until they abandoned their purpose in despair, awed by the majestic power of principle.

In December, 1832, when the South Carolina state convention was opposing the revenue laws with great violence, accompanied with threats of disunion, President Jackson, in his message to Congress, recommended a reduction of the revenue, and a qualified abandonment of the system of protection; and also that the public lands be no longer regarded as a source of revenue, and that they be sold to actual settlers at a price merely sufficient to reïmburse actual expenses and the costs arising under Indian compacts. "In this message," said Mr. Adams, "Jackson has cast away all the neutrality he heretofore maintained upon the conflicting opinions and interests of the different sections of the country, and surrenders the whole Union to the nullifiers of the South and the land speculators of the West. This I predicted nearly two years since, in a letter to Peter B. Porter."

In January, 1833, with regard to a member friendly to modifying the tariff according to the Southern policy, and who professed himself a radical, Mr. Adams remarked: "He has all the contracted prejudices of that political sect; his whole system of government is comprised in the maxim of leaving money in the pockets of the people. This is always the high road to popularity, and it is always travelled by those who have not resolution, intelligence, and energy, to attempt the exploration of any other."

On January 16th, 1833, President Jackson communicated, in a message, the ordinance of the convention of South Carolina nullifying the acts of Congress laying duties on the importation of foreign commodities, with the counteracting measures he proposed to pursue. On the 4th of February, on a bill for a modification of the tariff, Mr. Adams moved to strike out the enacting clause, thereby destroying the bill. In a speech characterized by the fearless spirit by which he was actuated, he declared his opinion that neither the bill then in discussion nor any other on the subject of the tariff ought to pass, until it was "known whether there was any measure by which a state could defeat the laws of the Union." The ordinance of South Carolina had been called a "pacific measure." It was just as much so as placing a pistol at the breast of a traveller and demanding his money was pacific. Until that weapon was removed there ought to be no modification of the tariff. Mr. Adams then entered at large into the duty of government to protect all the great interests of the citizens. But protection might be extended in different forms to different interests. The complaint was, that government took money out of the pockets of one portion of the community, to give it to another. In extending protection this must always be more or less the case. But, then, while the rights of one party were protected in this way, the rights of the other party were protected equally in another way. This he proceeded to illustrate. In the southern and southwestern parts of this Union there existed a certain interest, which he need not more particularly designate, which enjoyed, under the constitution and laws of the United States, an especial protection peculiar to itself. It was first protected by representation. There were on that floor upwards of twenty members who represented what in other states had no representation at all. It was not three days since a gentleman from Georgia said that the species of property now alluded to was "the machinery of the South." Now, that machinery had twenty odd representatives in that hall; representatives elected, not by that machinery, but by those who owned it. Was there such representation in any other portion of the Union? That machinery had ever been to the South, in fact, the ruling power of this government. Was this not protection? This very protection had taken millions and millions of money from the free laboring population of this country, and put it into the pockets of the owners of Southern machinery. He did not complain of this. He did not say that it was not all right. What he said was, that the South possessed a great interest protected by the constitution of the United States. He was for adhering to the bargain; but he did not wish to be understood as saying that he would agree to it if the bargain was now to be made over again.

This interest was protected by another provision in the constitution of the United States, by which "no person held to service or labor in one state, under the laws thereof, escaping into another, shall, in consequence of any law or regulation therein, be discharged from such service or labor, but shall be delivered up, on claim of the party to whom such service or labor may be due." What was this but protection to this machinery of the South? And let it be observed that a provision like this ran counter to all the tenor of legislation in the free states. It was contrary to all the notions and feelings of the people of the North to deliver a man up to any foreign authority, unless he had been guilty of some crime; and, but for such a clause in the compact, a Southern gentleman, who had lost an article of his machinery, would never recover him back from the free states.

The constitution contained another clause guaranteeing protection to the same interest. It guaranteed to every state in the Union a republican form of government, protection against invasion, and, on the application of the Legislature or Executive of any state, furnished them with protection against domestic violence. Now, everybody knew that where this machinery existed the state was more liable to domestic violence than elsewhere, because that machinery sometimes exerted a self-moving power. The call for this protection had very recently been made, and it had been answered, and the power of the Union had been exerted to insure the owners of this machinery from domestic violence.

On the 28th of the ensuing February, Mr. Adams, on the part of the minority of the Committee on Manufactures, made a report, signed by himself and Lewis Condit, of New Jersey, which was read and ordered to be printed by the House. In this report he took occasion to express his dissent from the doctrine of the message, which he asserted to be that in all countries generally, and especially in our own, the strongest and best part of our population—the basis of society, and the friends preëminently of freedom—are the "*wealthy landholders.*" This he controverted with a spirit at once suggestive and sarcastic, as new, incorrect, and incompatible with the foundation of our political institutions. He maintained that this assertion was not true even in that part of the Union where the cultivators of the soil are slaves; for, although there the landholders possess a large portion of the wealth of the community, they were far from constituting an equal proportion of its strength. Nor was it true in that portion of the Union where the cultivators of the soil earn their bread by the sweat of their brow, that they were *the best* part of society. They were as good as, but no better than, the other classes of the community. The doctrine is in opposition to the Declaration of Independence and the government of the Union, which are founded on a very different principle—the principle that all men are born equal, and with equal rights. It cannot be assumed as a foundation of national policy, and is of a most alarming and dangerous tendency, threatening the peace and directly tending to "the dissolution of the Union, by a complicated civil and servile war." He traced its consequences, present and future, in the proposition to give away the public lands, thereby withdrawing all aid from this source to objects of internal improvement; and in the destiny to which it consigns our manufacturing interests, and those of the handicraftsmen and the mechanics of our populous cities and flourishing towns, for the benefit of these wealthy landholders.

The insincerity of the message and the danger of its doctrines he elucidates with scrutinizing severity, exposing its fallacies, and showing that, by its recommendations, "a nation, consisting of ten millions of freemen, must be crippled in the exercise of their associated power, unmanned of all the energies applicable to the improvement of their own condition, by the doubts, scruples, or fanciful discontents, of a portion among themselves less in number than double the number in the single city of New York."

Its doctrine, which divides the people into the best and worst part of the population, is here denounced as "the never-failing source of tyranny and oppression, of civil strife, the shedding of brothers' blood, and the total extinction of freedom."

This report earnestly entreats the general government not to abdicate, by *non user*, the power vested in them of appropriating public money to great national objects of internal improvements, and declares the final result of the doctrine of abdicating powers arbitrarily designated as doubtful is but the degradation of the nation, the reducing itself to impotence, by chaining its own hands, fettering its own feet, and thus disabling itself from bettering its own condition. The impotence resulting from the inability to employ its own faculties for its own improvement, is the principle upon which the roving Tartar denies himself a permanent habitation, because to him the wandering shepherd is the best part of the population; upon which the American savage refuses to till the ground, because to him the hunter of the woods is the best part of the population. "Imperfect civilization, in all stages of human society, shackles itself with fanatical prejudices of exclusive favor to its own occupations; as the owner of a plantation with a hundred slaves believes the summit of human virtue to be attained only by independent farmers, cultivators of the soil."

Mr. Adams avers that the spirit of these recommendations indicates "a proposed revolution in the government of the Union, the avowed purpose of which is to reduce the general government to a simple machine. Simplicity," he adds, "is the essential characteristic in the condition of slavery. It is by the complication of the government alone that the freedom of mankind can be assured. If the people of these United States enjoy a greater share of liberty than any other nation upon earth, it is because, of all the governments upon earth, theirs is the most complicated." The simplicity which the message recommends is "an abdication of the power to do good; a divestment of all power in this confederate people to improve their own condition."

The recommendation of the message, that the public lands shall cease as soon as practicable to be a source of public revenue,—that they shall be sold at a reduced price to actual settlers, and the future disposition of them be surrendered to the states in which they lie,—Mr. Adams condemns as the giving away of the national domain, the property of the whole people, to individual adventurers; and as taking away the property of one portion of the citizens, and giving it to another, the plundered portion of the community being insultingly told that those on whom their lands are lavished are *the best part of the population*. Neither this, nor the surrender of them to the states in which they lie, can be done without prejudicing the claims of the United States, and of every particular state within which there are no public lands, and trampling under foot solemn engagements entered into before the adoption of the constitution. He reprobates thus giving away lands which were purchased by the blood and treasure of our revolutionary fathers and ourselves, which, if duly managed, might prove an inexhaustible fund for centuries to come. He maintains that the policy

68

indicated by this message regards the manufacturing interests of the country "as a victim to be sacrificed." This view leads him into an illustrative and powerful argument on the duty of protection to domestic industry, in which are set forth its nature, limitations, and impressive obligations.

In this report the absurd doctrines of nullification and secession are canvassed, and it is shown that they never can be carried out in practice but by a dissolution of the Union. The encouragement given by the policy of the administration to the unjust claims and groundless pretensions of South Carolina is exposed. The assumed irreconcilableness of the interests of the great masses of population which geographically divide the Union, of which one part is entirely free, and the other consists of masters and slaves, which is the foundation of those doctrines, is denied, and the question declared to be only capable of being determined by experiment under the compact formed by the constitution of the United States. The nature of that compact is analyzed, as well as the effect of that representation of property which it grants to the slaveholding states, and which has secured to them "the entire control of the national policy, and, almost without exception, the possession of the highest executive office of the Union." The causes and modes of operation by which this has been attained Mr. Adams illustrates to this effect: The Northern and wholly free states conceded that, while in the popular branch of the Legislature they themselves should have a representation proportioned only to their numbers, the slaveholders of the South should, in addition to their proportional numbers, have a representation for three fifths of their living property—their machinery; while the citizens of the free states have no addition to their number of representatives on account of their property; nor have their looms and manufactories, or their owners in their behalf, a single representative. The consequent disproportion of numbers of the slaveholding representation in the House of Representatives has secured the absolute control of the general policy of the government, and especially of the fiscal system, the revenues and expenditures of the nation. Thus, while the free states are represented only according to their numbers, the slaveholders are represented also for their property. The equivalent for this privilege provided by the constitution is that the slaveholders shall bear a heavier burden of all direct taxation. But, by the ascendency which their excess of representation gives them in the enactment of laws, they have invariably in time of peace excluded all direct taxation, and thereby enjoyed their excess of representation without any equivalent whatever. This is, in substance, an evasion of the bilateral provision in the constitution. It gives an operation entirely one-sided. It is a privilege of the Southern and slaveholding section of the Union, without any equivalent whatever to the Northern and North-western freemen. Always united in the purpose of regulating the affairs of the whole Union by the standard of the slaveholding interest, the disproportionate numbers of this section in the electoral colleges have enabled them, in ten out of twelve quadriennial elections, to confer the chief magistracy on one of their own citizens. Their suffrages at every election have been almost exclusively confined to a candidate of their own caste. Availing themselves of the divisions which, from the nature of man, always prevail in communities entirely free, they have sought and found out auxiliaries in other quarters of the Union, by associating the passions of parties and the ambition of individuals with their own purposes to establish and maintain throughout the confederated nation the slaveholders' policy. The office of Vice-President—a station of high dignity, but of little other than contingent power—has been usually, by their indulgence, conceded to a citizen of the other section; but even this political courtesy was superseded at the election before the last (1829), and both the offices of President and Vice-President of the United States were, by the preponderancy of slaveholding votes, bestowed upon citizens of two adjoining slaveholding states. "At this moment (1833) the President of the United States, the President of the Senate, the Speaker of the House of Representatives, and the Chief Justice of the United States, are all citizens of this favored portion of this united republic."

Mr. Adams, regarding "the ground assumed by the South Carolina convention for usurping the sovereign and limitless power of the people of that state to dictate the laws of the Union, and prostrate the legislative, executive, and judicial authority of the United States, as destitute of foundation as the forms and substance of their proceedings are arrogant, overbearing, tyrannical, and oppressive," declared his belief "that one particle of compromise with that usurped power, or of concession to its pretensions, would be a heavy calamity to the people of the whole Union, and to none more than to the people of South Carolina themselves; that such concession would be a dereliction by Congress of their highest duties to their country, and directly lead to the final and irretrievable dissolution of the Union."

CHAPTER IX.

INFLUENCE OF MILITARY SUCCESS.—POLICY OF THE ADMINISTRATION.—MR. ADAMS' SPEECH ON THE REMOVAL OF THE DEPOSITS FROM THE BANK OF THE UNITED STATES.—HIS OPINIONS ON FREEMASONRY AND TEMPERANCE SOCIETIES.—EULOGY ON WILLIAM WIRT.—ORATION ON THE LIFE AND CHARACTER OF LAFAYETTE.—HIS COURSE ON ABOLITION PETITIONS.—ON INTERFERENCE WITH THE INSTITUTION OF SLAVERY.—ON THE POLICY RELATIVE TO THE PUBLIC LANDS.—SPEECH ON DISTRIBUTING RATIONS TO FUGITIVES FROM INDIAN HOSTILITIES.—ON WAR WITH MEXICO.—EULOGY ON JAMES MADISON.— HIS COURSE ON A PETITION PURPORTING TO BE FROM SLAVES.—FIRST REPORT ON JAMES SMITHSON'S BEQUEST.

On the 4th of March, 1833, Andrew Jackson was inaugurated President of the United States a second time. Of two hundred and eighty-eight votes, the whole number cast by the electors, he had received two hundred and nineteen, Henry Clay being the chief opposing candidate. Martin Van Buren, having been elected Vice-President by one hundred and eighty-nine votes, was inaugurated on the same day. The coalition formed in 1827 by Jackson with Van Buren had thus fulfilled its purpose. Jackson's triumph was complete; he had superseded Adams, defeated Clay, crushed Calhoun, and placed Van Buren in the most auspicious position to be his successor in the President's chair.

The infatuating influence of military success over the human mind, and the readiness with which intelligent and well-disposed men, living under a constitution of limited powers, while dazzled by its splendor, endure and encourage acts of despotic power, is at once instructive and suggestive. Violations of constitutional duty, known and voluntarily acquiesced in by a whole people, subservient to the will of a popular chieftain, may, and probably will, in time, change their constitution, and destroy their liberties.

When Mr. Adams said that "Jackson rode roughshod over the Senate of the United States," he only characterized the spirit by which he controlled every branch and department of the government. In every movement Jackson had displayed an arbitrary will, determined on success, regardless of the means, and had applied without reserve the corrupting temptation of office to members of Congress. He had rewarded subserviency by appointments, and punished the want of it by removal; had insolently called Calhoun to account for his official language in the cabinet of Monroe, and dismissed three members of his own, acknowledged to have been unexceptionable in the discharge of their official duties, because they would not submit to regulate the social intercourse of their families by his dictation. These and many other instances of his overbearing character in civil affairs had become subjects of severe public animadversion, without apparently shaking the submissive confidence of the citizens of the United States. Their votes on his second election indicated an unequivocal increase of popular favor; the admirer of arbitrary power exulted; the lover of constitutional liberty mourned. The friends of despotism in the Old World, ignorant of the real stamina of his popularity, regarded it as unquestionable evidence of the all-powerful influence of military achievement in the New. But the infatuation which had been the exciting cause of General Jackson's first election to the Presidency would soon have evaporated under the multiplied evidences of an ill-regulated will, had it not been encouraged and supported by a local interest which predominated in the councils of the nation. With no desire to establish arbitrary power in the person of the chief magistrate of the Union, the slave-holders of the South instinctively perceived the identity of Jackson's interests with their own, and gave zeal and intensity to his support. The acquisition of the province of Texas, and its introduction into the Union as a slave state, with the prospective design of forming out of its territories four or five slave states, was a project in which they knew Jackson's heart was deeply engaged, and for the advancement of which he had peculiar qualifications.

Such was the true basis of that extraordinary show of popularity which Jackson's second election as President indicated. Accordingly, his first measures were directed to the acquisition of Texas. These, as Mr. Adams said at the time, "were kept profoundly secret," but at this day they are clear and evident. The Florida treaty was accepted with approbation and joy by the government and people of the United States, under the administration of Mr. Monroe. But the extension of its boundaries to the Colorado, which had been hoped for during the negotiation of that treaty between Mr. Adams and Onis, was not attained. Afterwards, during the Presidency of Mr. Adams, when every engine in the South and West was set at work to depreciate his character, and destroy his popularity, John Floyd, of Virginia, in an address to his constituents, attributed the relinquishment of our claim to Texas to him, and said he had thus deprived the South of acquiring two or more slave states. The same charge was brought against him by Thomas H. Benton, of Missouri, who afterwards, when apprized of the facts, openly acknowledged, in the Senate of the United States, that it was unjust, and an error. The calumny had the effect for which it was fabricated; for Mr. Adams, out of respect for those through whose constitutional influence he had abandoned that claim, disdained to defend himself by publishing the truth.

The facts were, that slavery not being then permitted in Mexico, and the project of introducing it, by the annexation of Texas, not being yet developed, Mr. Adams deemed the extension of the territory of the United States to the Colorado so important, that when Onis absolutely refused to accede, he declined further negotiation, declaring that he would not renew it on any other ground. He did not yield until those deeply interested in obtaining Florida had, by their urgency, persuaded him to treat on the condition of not including Texas. Although desirous, from general considerations of national interest and policy, to obtain that province, it was well known that he would not engage in any conspiracy to wrest it from Mexico. His character and firmness in that respect lessened his popularity in the Southern States, and excited an inordinate zeal for Jackson.

Accordingly, Mr. Poinsett, of South Carolina, minister of the United States in Mexico, immediately after the inauguration of President Jackson, in 1829, being apprized of his views and policy, took measures to carry them into effect. Under pretence of negotiating for the purchase of Texas, he remained in Mexico, and so mingled with the parties which at the time distracted that republic as to become obnoxious to its government. The Legislature passed a vote to expel him from their territories, and issued a remonstrance intimating apprehensions of his assassination if he continued there; charging him expressly with being concerned in establishing "some of those secret societies which will figure in the history of the misfortunes of Mexico." It might have been expected that a foreign minister would have repelled such an accusation with indignation. Poinsett, on the contrary, in a letter[36] addressed to the public, admitted that he had been instrumental in establishing *five* such secret societies, but asserted that they were only lodges of Freemasons,—merely philanthropic institutions, which had nothing to do with politics. For the truth of these assertions he appealed to his own personal character, and to the character of the members of the secret societies, who, he declared, had been his intimate friends for more than three years, vouching himself for their patriotism and private virtues. Even this authentication did not create implicit belief in the minds of those to whom it was addressed.

During these proceedings of Poinsett in Mexico the newspapers in the United States announced that the American government were taking proper steps for the acquisition of Texas. Intimations were also circulated of the sum Poinsett had been authorized to offer for it; and, to make sure of its ultimate attainment, in the summer and autumn of 1829 emigrants from the United States were encouraged by the American government to settle in Texas. To the Southern States the acquisition of that province was desirable, to open a new area for slavery. In open defiance, therefore, of a formal decree about this time issued by the rulers of Mexico prohibiting slavery in Texas, the emigrants to that province took their slaves with them; for they knew that the object of the American government was not so much territory as a slave state, and that upon their effecting this result their admission into the Union would depend. Such was the policy commenced and pursued during the first term of Jackson's administration. It was the conviction of this which led Mr. Adams publicly to declare that, though "profoundly a secret as it respected the public, it was then in successful progress;"

and to make it a topic of severe animadversion and warning, combined with language of prophecy, which events soon expanded into history. Every movement of Jackson was in unison with the policy and imbued with the spirit of the slaveholders. He manifested animosity to the protection of manufactures, and to internal improvement by his veto of the bill for the Maysville Turnpike, and to the Bank of the United States by his veto of the bill for extending its charter; and, after violently denouncing the spirit of nullification, he publicly succumbed to it by proposing a modification of the tariff, in obedience to its demands. But the most flagrant, act, and beyond all others characteristic of his indomitable tenacity of will, overleaping all the limitations of precedent and the constitution, was his removal, on his own responsibility, of the deposits from the Bank of the United States. After ascertaining that Duane, the Secretary of the Treasury, would not be his tool in that service, he, in the language of that officer, "concentrating in himself the power to judge and execute, to absorb the discretion given to the Secretary of the Treasury, and to nullify the law itself," proceeded at once to remove him, and to raise Roger B. Taney from the office of Attorney-General to that of Secretary of the Treasury, for the sole object of availing himself of an instrument subservient to his purposes.

In his annual message, at the opening of the session, Jackson announced to Congress that the Secretary of the Treasury had, by his orders, removed the public moneys from the Bank of the United States, and deposited them in certain state banks.

The spirit of Mr. Adams kindled at this usurpation, and he gave eloquent utterance to his indignation. Among the remonstrances to Congress against this act of President Jackson, one from the Legislature of Massachusetts was sent to him for presentation. In his attempt to fulfil this duty he was defeated three several times by the address of the Speaker of the House, and finally deprived of the opportunity by the previous question. He immediately published the speech he had intended to deliver, minutely scrutinizing the President's usurpation of power. The removal of the deposits, and the contract with the state banks to receive those deposits, he asserts were both unlawful; and the measure itself neither lawful nor just—an arbitrary act, without law and against law. He then proceeds to analyze the whole series of documents adduced by the Secretary of the Treasury, and by the Committee of Ways and Means in his aid, as *precedents* to justify the removal of the deposits, and concludes a lucid and laborious argument with, "I have thus proved, to the very rigor of mathematical demonstration, that the Committee of Ways and Means, to bolster up the lawless act of the Secretary of the Treasury, in transferring public moneys from their lawful places of deposit to others, in one of which, at least, the Secretary had an interest of private profit to himself, have ransacked all the records of the Treasury, from its first institution in July, 1775, to this day, in vain. From the whole mass of vouchers, to authenticate the lawful disposal of the public moneys, which that department can furnish, the committee have gathered fifty pages of documents, which they would pass off as *precedents* for this flagrant violation of the laws, and not one of them will answer their purpose. One of them alone bears a partial resemblance to the act of the present secretary; and that one the very document adduced by the committee themselves pronounces and proves to be unlawful."

After some remarks upon the office of Secretary of the Treasury, and the legal restraints upon it, he proceeds: "I believe both the spirit and the letter of this law to have been violated by the present Secretary of the Treasury when he transferred the public funds from the Bank of the United States to the Union Bank of Baltimore, he himself being a stockholder therein. And so thorough is my conviction of this principle, and so corrupting and pernicious do I deem the example which he has thereby set to future Committees of Ways and Means, to cite as *precedents* for yet ranker rottenness, that, if there were a prospect of his remaining in office longer than till the close of the present session of the Senate, I should deem it an indispensable, albeit a painful, duty of my station, to take the sense of this house on the question. And, sir, if, after this explicit declaration by me, the chairman of the Committee of Ways and Means has not yet slaked his thirst for *precedents*, he may gratify it by offering a fifth resolution, in addition to the four reported by the committee, as thus: Resolved, that the thanks of this house be given to Roger B. Taney, Secretary of the Treasury, for his pure and DISINTERESTED patriotism in transferring the use of the public funds from the Bank of the United States, where they were profitable to the people, to the Union Bank of Baltimore, where they were profitable to himself."

He then proceeds to show, in a severe and searching examination of the proceedings of this secretary, that the transfers were utterly unwarrantable; that he *tampered* with the public moneys to sustain the staggering credit of selected depositaries, and "scatter it abroad among swarms of rapacious political partisans." After stating and answering all the charges brought by the Secretary of the Treasury against the Bank of the United States, and showing their falsehood or futility, he declares all the proceedings of the directors of the bank to have been within the pale of action warranted by the laws of the land; and, so long as they do this, "a charge of dishonesty or corruption against them, uttered by the President of the United States, or by the Secretary of the Treasury, is neither more nor less than slander, emitted under the protection of official station, against private citizens. This is both ungenerous and unjust. It is the abuse of the shelter of official station to circulate calumny with impunity."

Mr. Adams next examines and severely reprobates the declaration of the President of the United States, that, "if the last Congress had continued in session one week longer, the bank would, by corrupt means, have procured a re-charter by majorities of two thirds in both houses of Congress;" and declares the imputation as unjust as it was dishonorable to all the parties implicated in it. He did not believe there was *one* member in the last Congress, who voted against re-chartering of the bank, who could have been induced to change his vote by corrupt means, had the president and directors of the bank been base enough to attempt the use of them. "That the imputation is cruelly ungenerous towards the friends of the administration in this house, is," said Mr. Adams, "my deliberate opinion; and now, when we reflect that this defamatory and disgraceful suspicion, harbored or professed against his own friends, supporters, and adherents, was the real and efficient *cause* (to call it reason would be to *shame* the term), that it was the real *motive* for the removal of the deposits during the recess of Congress, and only two months before its meeting, what can we do but hide our heads with *shame*? Sir, one of the duties of the President of the United States—a duty as sacred as that to which he is bound by his official oath—is that of maintaining unsullied the honor of his country. But how could the President of the United States assert, in the presence of any foreigner, a claim to honorable principle or moral virtue, as attributes belonging to his countrymen, when he is the first to cast the indelible stigma upon them? '*Vale, venalis civitas, mox peritura, si emptorem invenias,*' was the prophetic curse of Jugurtha upon Rome, in the days of her deep corruption. If the imputations of the President of the United States upon his own partisans and supporters were true, our country would already have found a purchaser."

"That this was the true and efficient *cause*," Mr. Adams proceeds, "of that removal, is evident, not only by the positive testimony of Mr. Duane, but from the utter futility of the reasons assigned by Mr. Taney. Mr. Duane states that, on the second day after he entered upon his duties as Secretary of the Treasury, the President himself declared to him his determination to cause the public deposits to be removed before the meeting of Congress. He said that the matter under consideration was of vast consequence to the country; that, unless the bank was broken down, it would break us down; that, if the last Congress had remained a week longer in session, two thirds would have been secured for the bank by corrupt means; and that the like result might be apprehended the next Congress; that such a state bank agency must be put in operation, before the meeting of Congress, as would show that the United States Bank was not necessary, and thus some members would have no excuse for voting for it. 'My suggestions,' added Mr. Duane, 'as to an inquiry by Congress, as in 1832, or a recourse to the judiciary, the President repelled, saying that it would be idle to depend upon either; referring, as to the judiciary, to the decisions already made as indications of what would be the effect of an appeal to them in future.'

"These, then," continued Mr. Adams, "were the effective *reasons* of the President for requiring the removal of the deposits *before* the meeting of Congress. The corruptibility of Congress itself, and the foregone decisions of the Supreme Court of the United States, were alike despised and degraded. The executive will was substituted in the place of both. These reasons had been urged, without success, on one Secretary of the Treasury, Louis McLane. He had been promoted out of office, and they were now pressed upon the judgment and pliability of another. He, too, was found refractory, and displaced. A third, more accommodating, was found in the person of Mr. Taney. To *him* the reasons of the President were all-sufficient, and he adopted them without reserve. They were all summed up in one,—'*Sic volo, sic jubeo, stet pro* RATIONE *voluntas.*'

"It is to be regretted that the Secretary of the Treasury did not feel himself at liberty to assign this reason. In my humble opinion it ought to have stood in front of all the rest. There is an air of conscious shamefacedness in the suppression of that which was so glaringly notorious; and something of an appearance of trifling, if not of mockery, in presenting a long array of reasons, omitting that which lies at the foundation of them all.

"The will of the President of the United States was the reason paramount to all others for the removal, by the Secretary of the Treasury, of the deposits from the Bank of the United States. It was part of his system of simplifying the machine of government, to which it was admirably adapted. It placed the whole revenue of the Union at any time at his disposal, for any purpose to which he might see fit to apply it. In vain had the laws cautiously stationed the Register, the Comptroller, the Treasurer, as checks upon the Secretary of the Treasury, so that the most trifling sum in the treasury should never be accessible to any one or any two men. With a removal of the deposits and a transfer draft, millions on millions may be transferred, by the stroke of the pen of a supple and submissive Secretary of the Treasury, from place to place, at home and abroad, wherever any purpose, personal or political, may thereby be promoted.

"To this final object of simplifying the machine two other maxims have been proclaimed as auxiliary fundamental principles of this administration. First, that the contest for place and power, in this country, is a state of war, and all the emoluments of office are the spoils of victory. The other, that it is the invariable rule of the President to reward his friends and punish his enemies."

In the course of the years 1832 and 1833, Freemasonry having become mingled with the politics of the period, Mr. Adams openly avowed his hostility to the institution, and addressed a series of letters to William L. Stone, an editor of one of the New York papers, and another to Edward Livingston, one of its high officers, and a third to the Anti-masonic Convention of the State of New York, in which his views, opinions, and objections to that craft, are stated and developed with his usual laborious, acute, and searching pathos and power.

In October, 1833, Mr. Adams was applied to by one of his friends for minutes of the principal measures of Mr. Monroe's administration, while he was Secretary of State, and also of his own, as President of the United States, to be used in his defence in a pending election. "I cannot reconcile myself," said Mr. Adams, "to write anything for my own election, not even for the refutation of the basest calumnies. In all my election contests, therefore, my character is at the mercy of the basest slanderer; and slander is so effective a power in all our elections, that the friends of the candidates for the highest offices use it without scruple. I know by experience the power of party spirit upon the people. Party triumphs over party, and the people are all enrolled in one party or another. The people can only act by the machinery of party."

About this time there was an attempt in Norfolk County to get up a Temperance Society, and a wish was expressed to him that he would take a lead in forming it. He declined from an unwillingness to shackle himself with obligations to control his individual, family, and domestic arrangements; from an apprehension that the temperance societies, in their well-intended zeal, were already manifesting a tendency to encroach on personal freedom; and also from an opinion that the cause was so well sustained by public approbation and applause that it needed not the aid of his special exertions, beyond that of his own example.

On the 12th of December, 1833, Mr. Clay sent a message to the President of the United States, asking a copy of his written communication to his cabinet, made on the 18th of September, about the removal of the deposits from the United States Bank; to which the President replied by a flat refusal. Mr. Adams remarked: "There is a tone of insolence and insult in his intercourse with both houses of Congress, especially since his reëlection, which never was witnessed between the Executive and Legislature before. The domineering tone has heretofore been usually on the side of the legislative bodies to the Executive, and Clay has not been sparing in the use of it. He is now paid in his own coin."

An intelligent foreigner, in relating a visit to Mr. Adams, in 1834, thus describes his powers of conversation: "He spoke with infinite ease, drawing upon his vast resources with the certainty of one who has his lecture before him ready written. He maintained the conversation nearly four hours, steadily, in one continuous stream of light. His subjects were the architecture of the middle ages, the stained glass of that period, sculpture, embracing monuments particularly. Milton, Shakspeare, Shenstone, Pope, Byron, and Southey, were in turn remarked upon. He gave Pope a wonderfully high character, and remarked that one of his chief beauties was the skill exhibited in varying the cæsural pause, quoting from various parts of his author to illustrate his remarks. He said little on the politics of the country, but spoke at considerable length of Sheridan and Burke, both of whom he had heard, and described with graphic effect. Junius, he said, was a bad man, but maintained that as a writer he had never been equalled."[37]

In March, 1834, Mr. Polk, of Tennessee, having indulged in an idolizing glorification of General Jackson, with some coarse invectives against Mr. Adams, the latter rose and said: "I shall not reply to the gentleman from Tennessee; and I give notice, once for all, that, whenever any admirer of the President of the United States shall think fit to pay his court to him in this house, either by a flaming panegyric upon him, or by a rancorous invective on me, he shall never elicit one word of reply from me.

'No; let the candied tongue lick absurd pomp,
And crook the pregnant hinges of the knee,
Where THRIFT may follow fawning.'"

On the 20th of February, 1834, Mr. Adams attended the funeral of Mr. Wirt, on which event he thus uttered his feelings: "For the rest of the day I was unable to attend to anything. I could think of nothing but William Wirt,—of his fine talents, of his amiable and admirable character; the twelve years during which we had been in close official relation together;[38] the scene when he went with me to the capitol; his warm and honest sympathy with me in my trials when President of the United States; my interview with him in January, 1831, and his faithful devotion to the memory of Monroe. These recollections were oppressive to my feelings. I thought some public testimonial from me to his memory was due at this time. But Mr. Wirt was no partisan of the present administration. He had been a formal and dreaded opponent to the reëlection of Andrew Jackson; and so sure is anything I say or do to meet insuperable obstruction, that I could not imagine anything I could offer with the remotest prospect of success. I finally concluded to ask of the house, tomorrow morning, to have it entered upon the journal of this day that the adjournment was that the Speaker and members might be able to attend the funeral of William Wirt. I wrote a short address, to be delivered at the meeting of the house."

It appears, by the journal of the house, that, on the 21st of February, 1834, Mr. Adams, of Massachusetts, addressed the chair as follows:[39]

"MR. SPEAKER: A rule of this house directs that the Speaker shall examine and correct the journal before it is read. I therefore now rise, not to make a motion, nor to offer a resolution, but to ask the unanimous consent of the house to address to you a few words with a view to an addition which I wish to be made to the journal, of the adjournment of the house yesterday.

"The Speaker, I presume, would not feel himself authorized to make the addition in the journal which I propose, without the unanimous consent of the house; and I therefore now propose it before the reading of the journal.

"I ask that, after the statement of the adjournment of the house, there be added to the journal words importing that it was to give the Speaker and members of the house an opportunity of attending the funeral obsequies of William Wirt.

"At the adjournment of the house on Wednesday I did not know what the arrangements were, or would be, for that mournful ceremony. Had I known them, I should have moved a postponed adjournment, which would have enabled us to join in the duty of paying the last tribute of respect to the remains of a man who was an ornament of his country and of human nature.

"The customs of this and of the other house of Congress warrant the suspension of their daily labors in the public service, for the attendance upon funeral rites, only in the case of the decease of their own members. To extend the usage further might be attended with inconvenience as a precedent; nor should I have felt myself warranted in asking it upon any common occasion.

"Mr. Wirt had never been a member of either house of Congress. But if his form in marble, or his portrait upon canvas, were placed within these walls, a suitable inscription for it would be that of the statue of Molière in the hall of the French Academy: 'Nothing was wanting to his glory; he was wanting to ours.'

"Mr. Wirt had never been a member of Congress; but, for a period of twelve years, during two successive administrations of the national government, he had been the official and confidential adviser, upon all questions of law, of the Presidents of the United States; and he had discharged the duties of that station entirely to the satisfaction of those officers and of the country. No member of this house needs to be reminded how important are the duties of the Attorney-General of the United States; nor risk I contradiction in affirming that they were never more ably or more faithfully discharged than by Mr. Wirt.

"If a mind stored with all the learning appropriate to the profession of the law, and decorated with all the elegance of classical literature; if a spirit imbued with the sensibilities of a lofty patriotism, and chastened by the meditations of a profound philosophy; if a brilliant imagination, a discerning intellect, a sound judgment, an indefatigable capacity, and vigorous energy of application, vivified with an ease and rapidity of elocution, copious without redundance, and select without affectation; if all these, united with a sportive vein of humor, an inoffensive temper, and an angelic purity of heart;—if all these, in their combination, are the qualities suitable for an Attorney-General of the United States, in him they were all eminently combined.

"But it is not my purpose to pronounce his eulogy. That pleasing task has been assigned to abler hands, and to a more suitable occasion. He will there be presented in other, though not less interesting lights. As the penetrating delineator of manners and character in the British Spy; as the biographer of Patrick Henry, dedicated to the young men of your native commonwealth; as the friend and delight of the social circle; as the husband and father in the bosom of a happy, but now most afflicted family;—in all these characters I have known, admired, and loved him; and now witnessing, from the very windows of this hall, the last act of piety and affection over his remains, I have felt as if this house could scarcely fulfil its high and honorable duties to the country which he had served, without some slight, be it but a transient, notice of his decease. The addition which I propose to the journal of yesterday's adjournment would be such a notice. It would give his name an honorable place on the recorded annals of his country, in a manner equally simple and expressive. I will only add that, while I feel it incumbent upon me to make this proposal, I am sensible that it is not a fit subject for debate; and, if objected to, I desire you to consider it as withdrawn."

Mr. Adams proceeds: "When the question of agreeing to the proposed addition was put by the Speaker, Joel K. Mann, of Pennsylvania, precisely the rankest Jackson man in the house, said 'No.' There was a general call upon him, from all quarters of the house, to withdraw his objection; but he refused. Blair, of South Carolina, rose, and asked if the manifest sense of the house could be defeated by one objection. The Speaker said I had requested that my proposal should be considered as withdrawn if an objection should be made, but the house was competent to give the instruction, upon motion made. I was then called upon by perhaps two thirds of the house,—'Move, move, move,'—and said, I had hoped the proposal would have obtained the unanimous assent of the house, and as only one objection had been made, which did not appear to be sustained by the general sense of the house, I would make the motion that the addition I had proposed should be made on the journal. The Speaker took the question, and nine tenths, at least, of the members present answered 'Ay.' There were three or four who answered 'No.' But no division of the house was asked."

In a debate in the House of Representatives, on the 30th of April, 1834, on striking out the appropriation for the salaries of certain foreign ministers, in the course of his remarks, Warren R. Davis, of South Carolina, turning with great feeling towards Mr. Adams, said: "Well do I remember the enthusiastic zeal with which we reproached the administration of that gentleman, and the ardor and vehemence with which we labored to bring in another. For the share I had in those transactions,—and it was not a small one,—*I hope God will forgive me, for I never shall forgive myself.*"

In December, 1834, Mr. Adams, at the unanimous request of both houses of Congress, delivered an oration on the life, character, and services, of Gilbert Motier de Lafayette. The House of Representatives ordered fifty thousand copies to be published at the national expense, and the Senate ten thousand. Mr. Clay said that, in proposing the latter number, he was governed by the extraordinary vote of the house; but that, "if he were to be guided by his opinion of the great talents of the orator, and the extraordinary merit of the oration, he felt he should be unable to specify any number."

In January, 1835, Mr. Adams, on presenting a petition of one hundred and seven women of his Congressional district, praying for the abolition of slavery in the District of Columbia, moved its reference to a select committee, with instructions; but stated that, if the house chose to refer it to the Committee on the District of Columbia, he should be satisfied. All he wished was that it should be referred to some committee. He begged those members who could command a majority of the house, and who, like himself, were unwilling to make the abolition question a stumbling-block, to take a course which should treat petitions with respect. He wished a report. It would be easy to show that such petitions relative to the District of Columbia ought not to be granted. He believed the true course to be to let error be tolerated; to grant freedom of speech and freedom of the press, and apply reason to put it down. On the contrary, it was contended by Southern men that Congress had a right not to receive petitions, especially if produced to create excitement, and wound the feelings of Southern members. Mr. Adams advocated the right of petition. If the language was disrespectful, that objection might be stated on the journal. He knew that it was difficult to use language on this subject which slaveholders would not deem disrespectful. Congress had declared the slave-trade, when carried on out of the United States *piracy*. He was opposed to that act, because he did not think it proper that this traffic without our boundaries should be called piracy, while there was no constitutional right to interdict it within our borders. It was carried on in sight of the windows of the capitol. He deemed it a fundamental principle that Congress had no right to take away or abridge the constitutional right of petition.

The petition was received, its commitment refused by the house, and it was laid on the table.

About this time Mr. Adams remarked: "There is something extraordinary in the present condition of parties throughout the Union. Slavery and democracy—especially a democracy founded, as ours is, on the rights of man—would seem to be incompatible with each other; and yet, at this time, the democracy of the country is supported chiefly, if not entirely, by slavery. There is a small, enthusiastic party preaching the abolition of slavery upon the principles of extreme democracy. But the democratic spirit and the popular feeling are everywhere against them."

In August, 1835, Mr. Adams was invited to deliver an address before the American Institute of New York. After expressing his good wishes for the prosperity of the institution, and of their cause, he stated, in reply, that the general considerations which dictated the policy of sustaining and cherishing the manufacturing interests were obvious, and had been presented by Judge Baldwin, Mr. J. P. Kennedy, and Mr. Everett, with eloquence and ability, in addresses on three preceding years. If he should deliver the address requested, it would be expected that he would present the subject under new and different views. His own opinion was that one great difficulty under which the manufacturing interest of the country labors is a political combination of the South and the West against it. The slaveholders of the South have bought the coöperation of the Western country by the bribe of the Western lands, abandoning to the new Western States their own proportion of this public property, and aiding them in the design of grasping all the lands in their own hands. Thomas H. Benton was the author of this system, which he brought forward as a substitute for the American system of Mr. Clay, and to supplant the latter as the leading statesman of the West. Mr. Clay, by his tariff compromise with Mr. Calhoun, abandoned his own American system. At the

77

same time he brought forward a plan for distributing among all the states of the Union the proceeds of the sales of the public lands. His bill for that purpose passed both houses of Congress, but was vetoed by President Jackson, who, in his annual message of December, 1832, formally recommended that all the public lands should be gratuitously given away to individual adventurers, and to the states in which the lands are situated. "Now," said Mr. Adams, "if, at this time, on the eve of a presidential election, I should, in a public address to the American Institute, disclose the state of things, and comment upon it as I should feel it my duty to do, it would probably produce a great excitement and irritation; would be charged with having a political bearing, and subject me to the imputation of tampering with the election."

On the 25th of May, 1836, Mr. Adams delivered, in the House of Representatives, a speech on certain resolutions for distributing rations from the public stores to the distressed fugitives from Indian hostilities in the States of Alabama and Georgia. "It is," said he, "I believe, the first example of a system of gratuitous donations to our own countrymen, infinitely more formidable in its consequences as a precedent, than from anything appearing on its face. I shall, nevertheless, vote for it." "It is one of a class of legislative enactments with which we are already becoming familiar, and which, I greatly fear, will ere long grow voluminous. I shall take the liberty to denominate them *the scalping-knife and tomahawk laws.* They are all urged through by the terror of those instruments of death, under the most affecting and pathetic appeals, from the constituents of the sufferers, to all the tender and benevolent sympathies of our nature. It is impossible for me to withhold from those appeals a responsive and yielding voice." He had voted, he said, for millions after millions, and would again and again vote for drafts from the public chest for the same purpose, should they be necessary, until the treasury itself should be drained.

In seeking for a principle to justify his vote, he could find it nowhere but in the war power and its limitation, as expressed in the constitution of the United States by the words "*the common defence and general welfare.*" The war power was in this respect different from the peace power. The former was derived from, and regulated by, the laws and usages of nations. The latter was limited by regulations, and restricted by provisions, prescribed within the constitution itself. All the powers incident to war were, by necessary implication, conferred on the government of the United States. This was the power which authorized the house to pass this resolution. There was no other. "It is upon this principle," said Mr. Adams, "that I shall vote for this resolution, and *did vote against* the vote reported by the slavery committee, 'that Congress possess no constitutional authority to interfere with the institution of slavery.' I do not admit that there is, even among the peace powers of Congress, no such authority; but in many ways Congress not only have the authority, but are bound to interfere with the institution of slavery in the states." Of this he cites many instances, and asks if, in case of a servile insurrection, Congress would not have power to interfere, and to supply money from the funds of the whole Union to suppress it.

In this speech Mr. Adams exposes the effects of the slave influence in the United States, by the measures taken to bring about a war with Mexico. 1. By the proposal that she should cede to us a territory large enough to constitute nine states equal in extent to Kentucky. 2. By making this proposition at a time when swarms of land-jobbers from the United States were covering these Mexican territories with slaves, in defiance of the laws of Mexico by which slavery had been abolished throughout that republic. 3. By the authority given to General Gaines to invade the Mexican republic, and which had brought on the war then raging, which was for the reëstablishment of slavery in territories where it had been abolished. It was a war, on the part of the United States, of conquest, and for the extension of slavery. Mr. Adams then foretold, what subsequent events proved, that the war then commencing would be, on the part of the United States, "a war of aggression, conquest, and for the reëstablishment of slavery where it has been abolished. In that war the banners of *freedom* will be the banners of Mexico, and your banners—I blush to speak the word—will be the banners of slavery."

The nature of that war, its dangers, and its consequences, Mr. Adams proceeded to analyze, and to show the probability of an interference on the part of Great Britain, who "will probably ask you a perplexing question—by what authority you, with freedom, independence, and democracy, on your lips, are waging a war of extermination, to forge new manacles and fetters instead of those which are falling from the hands and feet of men? She will carry emancipation and abolition with her in every fold of her flag; while your stars, as they increase in numbers, will be overcast by the murky vapors of oppression, and the only portion of your banners visible to the eye will be the blood-stained stripes of the taskmaster."

"Mr. Chairman," continued Mr. Adams, "are you ready for all these wars? A Mexican war; a war with Great Britain, if not with France; a general Indian war; a servile war; and, as an inevitable consequence of them all, a civil war;—for it must ultimately terminate in a war of colors, as well as of races. And do you imagine that while, with your eyes open, you are wilfully kindling these wars, and then closing your eyes and blindly rushing into them,—do you imagine that, while in the very nature of things your own Southern and South-western States must be the Flanders of these complicated wars, the battle-field upon which the last great conflict must be fought between slavery and emancipation,—do you imagine that your Congress will have no constitutional authority to interfere with the institution of slavery, *in any way*, in the states of this confederacy? Sir, they must and will interfere with it, perhaps to sustain it by war, perhaps to abolish it by treaties of peace; and they will not only possess the constitutional power so to interfere, but they will be bound in duty to do it by the express provisions of the constitution itself.

"From the instant that your slaveholding states become the theatre of war, civil, servile, or foreign, from that instant the war powers of Congress extend to interference with the institution of slavery in every way by which it can be interfered with, from a claim of indemnity for slaves taken or destroyed, to the cession of the state burdened with slavery to a foreign power.

"Little reason have the inhabitants of Georgia and of Alabama to complain that the government of the United States has been remiss or neglectful in protecting them from Indian hostilities. The fact is directly the reverse. The people of Alabama and Georgia are now suffering the recoil of their own unlawful weapons. Georgia, sir, Georgia, by trampling upon the faith of our national treaties with the Indian tribes, and by subjecting them to her state laws, first set the example of that policy which is now in the process of consummation by this Indian war. In setting this example she bade defiance to the authority of the government of this nation. She nullified your laws; she set at naught your executive and judicial guardians of the common constitution of the land. To what extent she carried this policy, the dungeons of her prisons, and the records of the Supreme Judicial Court of the United States, can tell.

"To those prisons she committed inoffensive, innocent, pious ministers of the Gospel of truth, for carrying the light, the comforts, the consolations of that Gospel, to the hearts and minds of those unhappy Indians. A solemn decision of the Supreme Court of the United States pronounced that act a violation of your treaties and your laws. Georgia defied that decision. Your executive government never carried it into execution. The imprisoned missionaries of the Gospel were compelled to purchase their ransom from perpetual captivity by sacrificing their rights as freemen to the meekness of their principles as Christians: and you have sanctioned all these outrages upon justice, law, and humanity, by succumbing to the power and the policy of Georgia; by accommodating your legislation to her arbitrary will; by tearing to tatters your old treaties with the Indians, and by constraining them, under *peine forte et dure*, to the mockery of signing other treaties with you, which, at the first moment when it shall suit your purpose, you will again tear to tatters, and scatter to the four winds of heaven; till the Indian race shall be extinct upon this continent, and it shall become a problem, beyond the solution of antiquaries and historical societies, *what* the red man of the forest was.

"This, sir, is the remote and primitive cause of the present Indian war—your own injustice sanctioning and sustaining that of Georgia and Alabama. This system of policy was first introduced by the present administration of your national government. It is directly the reverse of that system which had been pursued by all the preceding administrations of this government under the present constitution. That system consisted in the most anxious and persevering efforts to civilize the Indians, to attach them to the soil upon which they lived, to enlighten their minds, to soften and humanize their hearts, to fix in permanency their habitations, and to turn them from the wandering and precarious pursuits of the hunter to the tillage of the ground, to the cultivation of corn and cotton, to the comforts of the fireside, to the delights of *home*. This was the system of Washington and of Jefferson, steadily pursued by all their successors, and to which all your treaties and all your laws of intercourse with the Indian tribes were accommodated. The whole system is now broken up, and instead of it you have adopted that of expelling, by force or by compact, all the Indian tribes from their own territories and dwellings to a region beyond the Mississippi, beyond the Missouri, beyond the Arkansas, bordering upon Mexico; and there you have deluded them with the hope that they will find a permanent abode, a final resting-place from your never-ending rapacity and persecution. There you have undertaken to lead the willing, and drive the reluctant, by fraud or by force, by treaty or by the sword and the rifle—all the remnants of the Seminoles, the Creeks, of the Cherokees and the Choctaws, and of how many other tribes I cannot now stop to enumerate. In the process of this violent and heartless operation you have met with all the resistance which men in so helpless a condition as that of the Indian tribes can make.

"Of the *immediate* causes of the war we are not yet fully informed; but I fear you will find them, like the remoter causes, all attributable to yourselves.

"It is in the last agonies of a people forcibly torn and driven from the soil which they had inherited from their fathers, and which your own example, and exhortations, and instructions, and treaties, had riveted more closely to their hearts—it is in the last convulsive struggles of their despair, that this war has originated; and, if it bring some portion of the retributive justice of Heaven upon our own people, it is our melancholy duty to mitigate, as far as the public resources of the national treasury will permit, the distresses of our own kindred and blood, suffering under the necessary consequences of our own wrong. I shall vote for the resolution."

This speech, perhaps one of the most suggestive and prophetic ever made, appears in none of the newspapers of the time, and was published by Mr. Adams from his own minutes and recollections.

In September, 1836, Mr. Adams, at the request of the Mayor, Aldermen, and Common Council of the city of Boston, delivered a eulogy on the life and character of James Madison.

On the 7th of January, 1837, Mr. Adams offered to present the petition of one hundred and fifty women for the abolition of slavery in the District of Columbia. Mr. Glascock, of Georgia, objected to its reception. Mr. Adams said that the proposition not to receive a petition was directly in the face of the constitution. He hoped the people of this country would be spared the mortification, the injustice, and the wrong, of a decision that such petitions should not be received. It was indeed true that all discussion, all freedom of speech, all freedom of the press, on this subject, had been, within the last twelve months, violently assailed in every form in which the liberties of the people could be attacked. He considered these attacks as outrages on the constitution of the country, and the freedom of the people, as far as they went. But the proposition that such petitions should not be received went one step further. He hoped it would not obtain the sanction of the house, which could always reject such petitions after they had been considered. Among the outrages inflicted on that portion of the people of this country whose aspirations were raised to the greatest improvement that could possibly be effected in the condition of the human race,— the total abolition of slavery on earth,—that of calumny was the most glaring. Their petitions were treated with contempt, and the petitioners themselves loaded with foul and infamous imputations, poured forth on a class of citizens as pure and virtuous as the inhabitants of any section of the United States.

Violent debates and great confusion in the house ensued; but when the question, "Shall the petition be received?" was put, it was decided in the affirmative—*one hundred and twenty-seven* ayes, *seventy-five* nays. Mr. Adams then moved that the petition should be referred to the Committee on the District of Columbia. This was superseded by a motion to lay it on the table, which passed in the affirmative—ayes *one hundred and fifty*, nays *fifty*.

80

On the 18th of January, 1837, the House of Representatives passed a resolution,—one hundred and thirty-nine ayes, sixty-nine nays,—"that all petitions relating to slavery, without being printed or referred, shall be laid on the table, and no action shall be had thereon."

On the 6th of February, 1837, Mr. Adams stated that he held in his hand a paper, on which, before presenting it, he desired to have the decision of the Speaker. It purported to come from slaves; and he wished to know if such a paper came within the order of the house respecting petitions. Great surprise and astonishment were expressed by the slaveholders in the house at such a proposition. One member pronounced it an infraction of decorum, that ought to be punished severely. Another said it was a violation of the dignity of the house, and ought to be taken and burnt. Waddy Thompson, of South Carolina, moved the following resolution: "Resolved, that the Honorable John Quincy Adams, by the attempt just made by him to introduce a petition purporting on its face to be from slaves, has been guilty of a gross disrespect to the house; and that he be instantly brought to the bar to receive the severe censure of the Speaker." Charles E. Haynes, of Georgia, moved "to strike out all after Resolved, and insert 'that John Quincy Adams, a representative from the State of Massachusetts, has rendered himself justly liable to the severest censure of this house, and is censured accordingly, for having attempted to present to the house the petition of slaves.'" Dixon H. Lewis, of Alabama, offered a modification of Waddy Thompson's resolution, which he accepted, "that John Quincy Adams, by his attempt to introduce into the house a petition from slaves, for the abolition of slavery in the District of Columbia, committed an outrage on the rights and feelings of a large portion of the people of this Union, and a flagrant contempt on the dignity of this house; and, by extending to slaves a privilege only belonging to freemen, directly invites the slave population to insurrection; and that the said member be forthwith called to the bar of this house, and be censured by the Speaker."

After violent debates and extreme excitement, Mr. Adams rose and said: "In regard to the resolutions now before the house, as they all concur in naming me, and charging me with high crimes and misdemeanors, and in calling me to the bar of the house to answer for my crimes, I have thought it my duty to remain silent until it should be the pleasure of the house to act on one or other of those resolutions. I suppose that, if I shall be brought to the bar of the house, I shall not be struck mute by the previous question, before I have an opportunity to say a word or two in my own defence. But, sir, to prevent further consumption of the time of the house, I deem it my duty to ask them to modify their resolution. It may be as severe as they propose, but I ask them to change the matter of fact a little, so that when I come to the bar of the house, I may not, by a single word, put an end to it. I did not present the petition, and I appeal to the Speaker to say that I did not. I said I had a paper purporting to be a petition from slaves. I did not say what the prayer of the petition was. I asked the Speaker whether he considered such a paper as included within the general order of the house that all petitions, memorials, resolutions, and papers, relating in any way to the subject of slavery, should be laid upon the table. I intended to take the decision of the Speaker before I went one step towards presenting, or offering to present, that petition. I stated distinctly to the Speaker that I should not send the paper to the table until the question was decided whether a paper from persons declaring themselves slaves was included within the order of the house. This is the *fact*."

It having been stated in one of the resolutions that the petition was for the abolition of slavery, Mr. Adams said the gentleman moving it "must amend his resolution; for, if the house should choose to read this petition, I can state to them they would find it something very much the reverse of that which the resolution states it to be; and that if the gentleman from Alabama still shall choose to bring me to the bar of the house, he must amend his resolution in a very important particular, for he probably will have to put into it that my crime has been for attempting to introduce the petition of slaves that slavery should not be abolished; and that the object of these slaves, who have sent this paper to me, is precisely that which he desires to accomplish, and that they are his auxiliaries, instead of being his opponents."

In respect of the allegation that he had introduced a petition for the abolition of slavery in the District of Columbia, Mr. Adams said: "It is well known to all the members of

81

this house—it is certainly known to all petitioners for the abolition of slavery in the District of Columbia—that, from the day I entered this house to the present moment, I have invariably here, and invariably elsewhere, declared my opinions to be adverse to the prayer of petitions that call for the abolition of slavery in the District of Columbia. But, sir, it is equally well known that, from the time I entered this house, down to the present day, I have felt it a sacred duty to present any petition, couched in respectful language, from any citizen of the United States, be its object what it may—be the prayer of it that in which I could concur, or that to which I was utterly opposed. I adhere to the right of petition; and let me say here that, let the petition be, as the gentleman from Virginia has stated, from free negroes, prostitutes, as he supposes,—for he says there is one put on this paper, and he infers that the rest are of the same description,—*that* has not altered my opinion at all. Where is your law which says that the mean, the low, and the degraded, shall be deprived of the right of petition, if their moral character is not good? Where, in the land of freemen, was the right of petition ever placed on the exclusive basis of morality and virtue? Petition is supplication—it is entreaty—it is prayer! And where is the degree of vice or immorality which shall deprive the citizen of the right to supplicate for a boon, or to pray for mercy? Where is such a law to be found? It does not belong to the most abject despotism. There is no absolute monarch on earth who is not compelled, by the constitution of his country, to receive the petitions of his people, whosoever they may be. The Sultan of Constantinople cannot walk the streets and refuse to receive petitions from the meanest and vilest in the land. This is the law even of despotism; and what does your law say? Does it say that, before presenting a petition, you shall look into it, and see whether it comes from the virtuous, and the great, and the mighty? No, sir; it says no such thing. The right of petition belongs to all; and so far from refusing to present a petition because it might come from those low in the estimation of the world, it would be an additional incentive, if such an incentive were wanting."

In the course of this debate Mr. Thompson, of South Carolina, said that the conduct of Mr. Adams was a proper subject of inquiry by the Grand Jury of the District of Columbia, and stated that such, in a like case, would be the proceedings under the law in South Carolina. Mr. Adams, in reply, exclaimed: "If this is true,—if a member is there made amenable to the Grand Jury for words spoken in debate,—I thank God I am not a citizen of South Carolina! Such a threat, when brought before the world, would excite nothing but contempt and amazement. What! are we from the Northern States to be indicted as felons and incendiaries, for presenting petitions not exactly agreeable to some members from the South, by a jury of twelve men, appointed by a marshal, his office at the pleasure of the President! If the gentleman from South Carolina, by bringing forward this resolution of censure, thinks to frighten me from my purpose, he has mistaken his man. I am not to be intimidated by him, nor by all the Grand Juries of the universe."

After a debate of excessive exacerbation, lasting for four days, only twenty votes could be found indirectly and remotely to censure. In the course of this discussion circumstances made it probable that the names appended to the petition were not the signatures of slaves, and that the whole was a forgery, and designed as a hoax upon him. On which suggestion Mr. Adams stated to the house that he now believed the paper to be a *forgery*, by a slaveholding master, for the purpose of daring him to present a petition purporting to be from slaves; that, having now reason to believe it a forgery, he should not present the petition, whatever might be the decision of the house. If he should present it at all, it would be to invoke the authority of the house to cause the author of it to be prosecuted for the forgery, if there were competent judicial tribunals, and he could obtain evidence to prove the fact. He did not consider a forgery committed to deter a member of Congress from the discharge of his duty as a *hoax*.[40]

In March, 1837, Mr. Adams addressed a series of letters to his constituents, transmitting his speech vindicating his course on the right of petition, and his proceedings on the subject of the presentation of a petition purporting to be from slaves. These letters were published in a pamphlet, and were at the time justly characterized as "a triumphant vindication of the right of petition, and a graphic delineation of the slavery spirit in Congress;" and it was further said of them, that, "apart from the interest excited by the subjects under discussion, and viewed only as literary productions, they may be ranked among the highest literary efforts of the author. Their sarcasm is Junius-like—cold, keen, unsparing." A few extracts may give an idea of the spirit and character of this publication.

Commenting on Mr. Thompson's resolution, as modified by Mr. Lewis (p. 249), Mr. Adams exclaims:

"My constituents! Reflect upon the purport of this resolution, which was immediately accepted by Mr. Thompson as a modification of his own, and as unhesitatingly received by the Speaker. He well knew I had made no attempt to introduce to the house a petition from slaves; and, if I had, he knew I should have done no more than exercise my right as a member of the house, and that the utmost extent of the power of the house would have been to refuse to receive the petition. The Speaker's duty was to reject instantly this resolution, and tell Mr. Lewis and Mr. Thompson that the first of his obligations was to protect the rights of speech of members of that house, which I had not in the slightest degree infringed. But the Speaker was a *master*.

"Observe, too, that in this resolution the notable discovery was first made that I had directly invited the slaves to insurrection; of which bright thought Mr. Thompson afterwards availed himself to threaten me with the Grand Jury of the District of Columbia, as an incendiary and felon. I pray you to remember this, not on my account, or from the suspicion that I could or shall ever be moved from my purpose by such menaces, but to give you *the measure* of slaveholding freedom of speech, of the press, of action, of thought! If such a question as I asked of the Speaker is a direct invitation of the slaves to insurrection, forfeiting all my rights as representative of the people, subjecting me to indictment by a grand jury, conviction by a petit jury, and to an infamous penitentiary cell, I ask you, not what freedom of speech is left to your representative in Congress, but what freedom of speech, of the press, and of thought, is left to yourselves.

"There is an express provision of the constitution that Congress shall pass no law *abridging* the right of petition; and here is a resolution declaring that a member ought to be considered as regardless of the feelings of the house, the rights of the South, and an enemy to the Union, *for presenting a petition*.

"Regardless of the feelings of the house! What have the feelings of the house to do with the free agency of a member in the discharge of his duty? One of the most sacred duties of a member is to present the petitions committed to his charge; a duty which he cannot refuse or neglect to perform without violating his oath to support the constitution of the United States. He is not, indeed, bound to present all petitions. If the language of the petition be disrespectful to the house, or to any of its members,—if the prayer of the petition be unjust, immoral, or unlawful,—if it be accompanied by any manifestation of intended violence or disorder on the part of the petitioners,—the duty of the member to present ceases, not from respect for the feelings of the house, but because those things themselves strike at the freedom of speech and action as well of the house as of its members. Neither of these can be in the least degree affected by the mere circumstance of the condition of the petitioner. Nor is there a shadow of reason why feelings of the house should be outraged by the presentation of a petition from slaves, any more than by petitions from soldiers in the army, seamen in the navy, or from the working-women in a manufactory.

"Regardless of the rights of the South! What are the rights of the South? What is the *South*? As a component portion of this Union, the population of the South consists of masters, of slaves, and of free persons, white and colored, without slaves. Of which of these classes would the rights be disregarded by the presentation of a petition from slaves? Surely not those of the slaves themselves, the suffering, the laborious, the *producing* classes. O, no! there would be no disregard of their rights in the presentation of a petition from them. The very essence of the crime consists in an alleged *undue* regard for their rights; in not denying them the rights of human nature; in not classing them with horses, and dogs, and cats. Neither could the rights of the free people without slaves, whether white, black, or colored, be disregarded by the presentation of a petition from slaves. Their rights could not be affected by it at all. The rights of the South, then, here mean the rights of the masters of slaves, which, to describe them by an inoffensive word, I will call the rights of *mastery*. These, by the constitution of the United States, are recognized, not directly, but by implication, and

83

protection is stipulated for them, by that instrument, to a certain extent. But they are rights incompatible with the inalienable rights of all mankind, as set forth in the Declaration of Independence—incompatible with the fundamental principles of the constitutions of all the free states of the Union; and therefore, when provided for in the constitution of the United States, are indicated by expressions which must receive the narrowest and most restricted construction, and never be enlarged by implication. There is, I repeat, not one word, not one syllable, in the constitution of the United States, which interdicts to Congress the reception of petitions from slaves; and as there is express interdiction to Congress to abridge by law the right of petition, that right, upon every principle of fair construction, is as much the right of the South as of the North—as much the right of the slave as of the master; and the presentation of a petition from slaves, for a legitimate object, respectful in language, and in its tone and character submissive to the decision which the house may pass upon it, far from degrading the rights of the South, is a mark of signal homage to those rights.

"An enemy to the Union for presenting a petition!—an enemy to the Union! I have shown that the presentation of petitions is one of the most imperious duties of a member of Congress. I trust I have shown that the right of petition, guaranteed to the people of the United States, without exception of slaves, express or implied, cannot be *abridged* by any act of both houses, with the approbation of the President of the United States; but this resolution, by the act of one branch of the Legislature, would effect an enormous abridgment of the right of petition, not only by denying it to full one sixth part of the whole people, but by declaring an enemy to the Union any member of the house who should present such a petition.

"When the resolution declaring that I had trifled with the house was under consideration, one of the most prominent allegations laid to my charge was that, by asking that question, I had intended indirectly to cast ridicule upon that resolution, and upon the house for adopting it. Nor was this entirely without foundation. I did not intend to cast ridicule upon the house, but to expose the absurdity of that resolution, against which I had protested as unconstitutional and unjust. But the characteristic peculiarity of this charge against me was, that, while some of the gentlemen of the South were urging the house to pass a vote of censure upon me, for a distant and conjectural inference of my intention to deride that resolution, others of them, in the same debate, and on the same day, were showering upon the same resolution direct expressions of unqualified contempt, without even being called to order. Like the saints in Hudibras,—

'The saints may do the same thing by
The Spirit in sincerity,
Which other men are prompted to,
And at the devil's instance do;
And yet the actions be contrary,
Just as the saints and wicked vary,'—

so it was with the gentlemen of the South. While Mr. Pickens could openly call the resolution of the 18th of January a miserable and contemptible resolution,—while Mr. Thompson could say it was only fit to be burnt by the hands of the hangman, without rebuke or reproof,—I was to be censured by the house for casting ridicule upon them by asking the question whether the resolution included petitions from slaves."

About this time Mr. Adams received an invitation to attend a public meeting at New York during the session of Congress. He replied: "I do not hold myself at liberty to absent myself from the house a single day. Such is my estimate of representative duty, confirmed by a positive rule of the house itself, not the less obligatory for being little observed."

In December, 1835, President Jackson transmitted to Congress a message relative to the bequest of four hundred thousand dollars, from James Smithson, of London, to the United States, for the purpose of establishing at Washington an institution "for the increase and diffusion of knowledge among men;" and submitted the subject to Congress for its consideration. A question was immediately raised whether Congress had power, in its legislative capacity, to accept such a bequest; and also whether, having the power, its acceptance was expedient. The message of the President was referred to a committee, of which Mr. Adams was appointed chairman. No subject could be better adapted to excite into action his public spirit than the hopes awakened for his country by the amount of this bequest, and the wisdom of the objects for which it was appropriated. The general tenor of the testator's will excited numerous private interests and passions with regard to the application of the fund. Mr. Adams immediately brought the whole strength and energy of his mind to give it a proper direction. Although some of his recommendations were slighted, and an object near his heart, an astronomical observatory, was resisted by party spirit, his zeal and perseverance effectually prevented the bequest from being diverted to local and temporary objects, and his general views relative to Mr. Smithson's design ultimately prevailed.

In January, 1836, Mr. Adams, as chairman of the committee, made a report, declaring that Congress was competent to accept the bequest, and that its acceptance was enjoined by considerations of the most imperious obligations, and suggesting some interesting reflections on the subject. The testator, he said, was a descendant in blood from the Percys and the Seymours,—two of the most illustrious names of the British islands;—the brother of the Duke of Northumberland, who, by the name of Percy, was known at the sanguinary opening scenes of our Revolutionary War, and fought as a British officer at Lexington and Bunker Hill, and was the bearer of the despatches, from the commander of the British forces to his government, announcing the event of that memorable day. "The suggestions which present themselves to the mind," Mr. Adams adds, "by the association of these historical recollections with the condition of the testator, derive additional interest from the nature of the bequest, the devotion of a large estate to an institution 'for the increase and diffusion of knowledge among men.'" The noble design of Mr. Smithson Mr. Adams thus proceeds to illustrate:

"Of all the foundations of establishments for pious or charitable uses, which ever signalized the spirit of the age, or the comprehensive beneficence of the founder, none can be named more deserving of the approbation of mankind than this. Should it be faithfully carried into effect, with an earnestness and sagacity of application, and a steady perseverance of pursuit, proportioned to the means furnished by the will of the founder, and to the greatness and simplicity of his design, as by himself declared, 'the increase and diffusion of knowledge among men,' it is no extravagance of anticipation to declare that his name will be hereafter enrolled among the eminent benefactors of mankind.

"The attainment of knowledge is the high and exclusive attribute of man, among the numberless myriads of animated beings, inhabitants of the terrestrial globe. On him alone is bestowed, by the bounty of the Creator of the universe, the power and the capacity of acquiring knowledge. Knowledge is the attribute of his nature which at once enables him to improve his condition upon earth, and to prepare him for the enjoyment of a happier existence hereafter. It is by this attribute that man discovers his own nature as the link between earth and heaven; as the partaker of an immortal spirit; as created for higher and more durable ends than the countless tribes of beings which people the earth, the ocean, and the air, alternately instinct with life, and melting into vapor, or mouldering into dust.

"To furnish the means of acquiring knowledge is, therefore, the greatest benefit that can be conferred upon mankind. It prolongs life itself, and enlarges the sphere of existence. The earth was given to man for cultivation—to the improvement of his own condition. Whoever increases his knowledge multiplies the uses to which he is enabled to turn the gift of his Creator to his own benefit, and partakes in some degree of that goodness which is the highest attribute of Omnipotence itself."

"If, then, the Smithsonian Institution, under the smile of an approving Providence, and by the faithful and permanent application of the means furnished by its founder to the purpose for which he has bestowed them, should prove effective to their promotion,—if they should contribute essentially *to the increase and diffusion of knowledge among men*,—to what higher or nobler object could this generous and splendid donation have been devoted?"

After further illustrating the renown of the name of Percy from the historical annals of England, Mr. Adams proceeds to urge other considerations, from among which we make the following extracts:

"It is, then, a high and solemn trust which the testator has committed to the United States of America; and its execution devolves upon their representatives in Congress duties of no ordinary importance. In adverting to the character of the trustee selected by the testator for the fulfilment of his intentions, it is deemed no indulgence of unreasonable pride to mark it as a signal manifestation of the moral effect of our political institutions upon the opinions and the consequent action of the wise and good of other regions and of distant climes, even upon that nation from whom we generally boast our descent."

The report continues:

"In the commission of every trust there is an implied tribute to the integrity and intelligence of the trustee, and there is also an implied call for the faithful exercise of those properties to the fulfilment of the purposes of the trust. The tribute and the call acquire additional force and energy when the trust is committed for performance after the decease of him by whom it is granted; when he no longer lives to constrain the effective fulfilment of his design. The magnitude of the trust, and the extent of confidence bestowed in the committal of it, do but enlarge and aggravate the pressure of the obligation which it carries with it. The weight of duty imposed is proportioned to the honor conferred by confidence without reserve. Your committee are fully persuaded, therefore, that, with a grateful sense of the honor conferred by the testator upon the political institutions of this Union, the Congress of the United States, in accepting the bequest, will feel, in all its power and plenitude, the obligation of responding to the confidence reposed by him, with all the fidelity, disinterestedness, and perseverance of exertion, which may carry into effective execution the noble purpose of an endowment for the increase and diffusion of knowledge among men."

The report concludes with recommending a bill, which passed in both branches, vesting authority in the President to take measures to prosecute, in the court of chancery in England, the right of the United States to this bequest.

CHAPTER X.

MARTIN VAN BUREN PRESIDENT OF THE UNITED STATES.—MR. ADAMS' SPEECH ON THE CLAIMS OF THE DEPOSIT BANKS.—HIS LETTER ON BOOKS FOR UNIVERSAL READING.—ORATION AT NEWBURYPORT.— SPEECH ON THE RIGHT OF PETITION.— LETTER TO THE MASSACHUSETTS ANTI-SLAVERY SOCIETY.—ADDRESS TO THE INHABITANTS OF HIS DISTRICT.—HIS VIEWS AS TO THE APPLICATION OF THE SMITHSONIAN FUND.—HIS INTEREST IN THE SCIENCE OF ASTRONOMY.—LETTER TO THE SECRETARY OF STATE ON AN ASTRONOMICAL OBSERVATORY.—LETTER ON THE ABOLITION OF SLAVERY IN THE DISTRICT OF COLUMBIA.— RESOLUTIONS FOR THE LIMITING OF HEREDITARY SLAVERY.—DISCOURSE BEFORE THE NEW YORK HISTORICAL SOCIETY.—ADDRESS ON THE SUBJECT OF EDUCATION.—REMARKS ON PHRENOLOGY.—ON THE LICENSE LAW OF MASSACHUSETTS.—HE ORGANIZES THE HOUSE OF REPRESENTATIVES.

On the 4th of March, 1837, Martin Van Buren succeeded to the Presidency of the United States. The undeviating zeal with which he had supported all the plans of Andrew Jackson, especially those for dismembering Mexico and annexing Texas to the Union as a slave state, had proved, to the satisfaction of the slaveholders, that reliance might be placed on a Northern man to carry into effect Southern policy.

On the 14th of October ensuing Mr. Adams delivered a speech, in the House of Representatives, on a bill for "adjusting the remaining claims upon the late deposit banks." When this bill was in discussion in a committee of the whole house, Mr. Adams asked the author of it (Mr. Cambreling, of New York) to what banks certain words, which he stated, were intended to apply. Cambreling replied that Mr. Adams could answer his own interrogatory by reading the bill himself. Mr. Adams then proceeded to state several other objections to the terms of the bill, and confessed that his faculties of comprehension did not permit him to understand its phraseology. Mr. Cambreling rose quickly, and remarked that, at so late a period of the session, the last working night, he could not waste his time in discussing nouns, pronouns, verbs, and adverbs, with the gentleman from Massachusetts. Mr. Adams replied: "Well, sir, as language is composed of nouns and pronouns, verbs and adverbs, when they are put together to constitute the law of the land the *meaning* of them may surely be demanded of the legislator, and those parts of speech may well be used for such a purpose. But, if such explanation be impossible, it certainly ought not to be expected that this house will consent to pass a law, composed of nouns and pronouns, verbs and adverbs, which the author of it himself does not understand."[41]

"On which," said Mr. Adams, "I took the floor, and, in a speech of upwards of two hours, exposed the true character of the bill, and of that to which it is a supplement, in all their iniquity and fraud. I made free use of the computations I had drawn from the reports of the Secretary of the Treasury, and minutely scrutinized the bill in all its parts, and denounced the bargain made in the face of the house by Cambreling and the members of the debtor states, procuring their votes for the postponement of the bill by promising them increased indulgence for their banks. Cambreling, who could not answer me, kept up a continual succession of interruptions and calls to order, in despite of which I went through, with constant attention from the house, and not a mark of impatience, except from Cambreling. When I finished, he moved to lay the bill aside, and take up the appropriation bill, which was done."

On this subject the editor of the *National Register* remarks: "Mr. Adams' speech upon nouns, pronouns, verbs, and adverbs, displays a degree of patient labor and research, which must convince both political friends and foes that neither time nor circumstances have impaired the strength or acuteness of his mind, or his zeal in behalf of what he deems to be the interests of the people. Familiar as we have been, for a series of years, with minute calculations and statistical details, the most powerful but least prized modes of exhibiting results, we have been surprised and delighted at the clearness and force with which every point is illustrated, and most warmly commend the speech to all who wish to understand the questions on which it treats."[42]

The name thus given, of "A Speech on Nouns and Pronouns, Verbs and Adverbs," was assumed by Mr. Adams, and adopted as its title.

On the 22d of June, 1838, Mr. Adams addressed a letter to certain young men of Baltimore, who had written to him a very respectful letter, asking his advice concerning the books or authors he would recommend. After a general expression of his sense of their confidence, and regret of his inability fully to recommend any list of books or authors worthy of the attention of all, he proceeds to speak of the *Bible* as almost the only book deserving such universal recommendation, and as the book, of all others, to be read at all ages and in all conditions of human life—to be read in small portions, one or two chapters every day, never to be intermitted unless by some overruling necessity. He then enters at large into the advantages of such a practice, and into the mode of conducting it, and proceeds to suggest other subsidiary studies in history, biography, and poetry, concluding with the advice of the serving-man to a young student, in Shakspeare—"Study what you most affect."[43]

On the 4th of July, 1837, Mr. Adams delivered at Newburyport, at the request of its inhabitants, an oration on the Declaration of Independence, the spirit of which may be discerned in the following extract:

"Our government is a complicated machine. We have twenty-six states, with governments administered by separate legislatures and executive chiefs, and represented by equal numbers in the general Senate of the nation. This organization is an anomaly in the history of the world. It is that which distinguishes us from all other nations, ancient and modern: from the simple monarchies and republics of Europe, and from the confederacies which have figured in any age upon the face of the globe. The seeds of this complicated machine were all sown in the Declaration of Independence; and their fruits can never be eradicated but by the dissolution of the Union. The calculators of the value of the Union, who would palm upon you, in the place of this sublime invention, a mere cluster of sovereign, confederated states, do but sow the wind to reap the whirlwind.

"One lamentable evidence of deep degeneracy from the spirit of the Declaration of Independence is the countenance which has been occasionally given, in various parts of the Union, to this doctrine; but it is consolatory to know that, whenever it has been distinctly disclosed to the people, it has been rejected by them with pointed reprobation. It has, indeed, presented itself in its most malignant form in that portion of the Union the civil institutions of which are most infected by the gangrene of slavery. The inconsistency of the institution of domestic slavery with the principles of the Declaration of Independence was seen and lamented by all the Southern patriots of the Revolution; by no one with deeper and more unalterable conviction than by the author of the Declaration himself. No insincerity or hypocrisy can fairly be laid to their charge. Never, from *their* lips, was heard one syllable of attempt to justify the institution of slavery. They universally considered it as a reproach fastened upon them by the unnatural step-mother country; and they saw that, before the principles of the Declaration of Independence, slavery, in common with every other mode of oppression, was destined sooner or later to be banished from the earth. Such was the undoubting conviction of Jefferson to his dying day. In the memoir of his life, written at the age of seventy-seven, he gave to his countrymen the solemn and emphatic warning that the day was not distant when they *must* hear and adopt the general emancipation of their slaves. 'Nothing is more certainly written,' said he, 'in the book of fate, than that these people are to be free.' My countrymen! it is written in a better volume than the book of fate; it is written in the laws of Nature and of Nature's God.

"We are told, indeed, by the learned doctors of the nullification school, that color operates as a forfeiture of the rights of human nature: that a dark skin turns a man into a chattel; that crispy hair transforms a human being into a four-footed beast. The master-priest informs you that slavery is consecrated and sanctified by the Holy Scriptures of the Old and New Testament: that Ham was the father of Canaan, and all his posterity were doomed, by his own father, to be hewers of wood and drawers of water to the descendants of Shem and Japhet: that the native Americans of African descent are the children of Ham, with the curse of Noah still fastened upon them; and the native Americans of European descent are children of Japhet, pure Anglo-Saxon blood, born to command, and to live by the sweat of another's brow. The master-philosopher teaches you that slavery is no curse, but a blessing! that Providence—Providence!—has so ordered it that this country should be inhabited by two races of men,—one born to wield the scourge, and the other to bear the record of its stripes upon his back; one to earn, through a toilsome life, the other's bread, and to feed him on a bed of roses; that slavery is the guardian and promoter of wisdom and virtue; that the slave, by laboring for another's enjoyment, learns disinterestedness and humility; that the master, nurtured, clothed, and sheltered, by another's toils, learns to be generous and grateful to the slave, and sometimes to feel for him as a father for his child; that, released from the necessity of supplying his own wants, he acquires opportunity of leisure to improve his mind, to purify his heart, to cultivate his taste; that he has time on his hands to plunge into the depths of philosophy, and to soar to the clear empyrean of seraphic morality. The master-statesman—ay, the statesman in the land of the Declaration of Independence, in the halls of national legislation, with the muse of history recording his words as they drop from his lips, with the colossal figure of American Liberty leaning on a column entwined with the emblem of eternity over his head, with the forms of Washington and Lafayette speaking to him from the canvas—turns to the image of the father of his country, and, forgetting that the last act of his life was to emancipate his slaves, to bolster up the cause of slavery says, '*That* man was a slaveholder.'

"My countrymen! these are the tenets of the modern nullification school. Can you wonder that they shrink from the light of free discussion—that they skulk from the grasp of freedom and of truth? Is there among you one who hears me, solicitous above all things for the preservation of the Union so truly dear to us—of that Union proclaimed in the Declaration of Independence—of that Union never to be divided by any act whatever—and who dreads that the discussion of the merits of slavery will endanger the continuance of the Union? Let him discard his terrors, and be assured that they are no other than the phantom fears of nullification; that, while doctrines like these are taught in her schools of philosophy, preached in her pulpits, and avowed in her legislative councils, the free, unrestrained discussion of the rights and wrongs of slavery, far from endangering the Union of these states, is the only condition upon which that Union can be preserved and perpetuated. What! are you to be told, with one breath, that the transcendent glory of this day consists in the proclamation that all lawful government is founded on the inalienable rights of man, and, with the next breath, that you must not whisper this truth to the winds, lest they should taint the atmosphere with freedom, and kindle the flame of insurrection? Are you to bless the earth beneath your feet because she spurns the footsteps of a slave, and then to choke the utterance of your voice lest the sound of liberty should be reëchoed from the palmetto-groves, mingled with the discordant notes of disunion? No! no! Freedom of speech is the only safety-valve which, under the high pressure of slavery, can preserve your political boiler from a fearful and fatal explosion. Let it be admitted that slavery is an institution of internal police, exclusively subject to the separate jurisdiction of the states where it is cherished as a blessing, or tolerated as an evil as yet irremediable. But let that slavery which intrenches herself within the walls of her own impregnable fortress not sally forth to conquest over the domain of freedom. Intrude not beyond the hallowed bounds of oppression; but, if you have by solemn compact doomed your ears to hear the distant clanking of the chain, let not the fetters of the slave be forged afresh upon your own soil; far less permit them to be riveted upon your own feet. Quench not the spirit of freedom. Let it go forth, not in panoply of fleshly wisdom, but with the promise of peace, and the voice of persuasion, clad in the whole armor of truth, conquering and to conquer."

In July, 1838, Mr. Adams published a speech "on the right of the people, men and women, to petition; on the freedom of speech and debate in the House of Representatives of the United States; on the resolutions of seven State Legislatures, and on the petitions of more than one hundred thousand petitioners, relative to the annexation of Texas to this Union;" the report of the Committee on Foreign Affairs on these subjects being under the consideration of the House. In this publication he states and analyzes the course of that "conspiracy for the dismemberment of Mexico, the reinstitution of slavery in the dismembered portion of that republic, and the acquisition, by purchase or by conquest, of the territory, to sustain, spread, and perpetuate, the *moral and religious blessing* of slavery in this Union;" and which he declares to be in the full tide of successful experiment. But a few only of the topics illustrated in this publication, which expanded into a pamphlet of one hundred and thirty octavo pages, can here be touched. It is, in fact, a history of the disgraceful proceedings by which that conspiracy effected its purpose.

Mr. Adams inquired of the committee whether they had given as much as five minutes' consideration to the resolutions of the Legislatures, and the very numerous petitions of individuals, which had been referred to them. One of the committee, Hugh S. Legaré, of South Carolina, answered, he had not read the papers, nor looked into one of them. Mr. Adams exclaimed, "I denounce, in the face of the country, the proceeding of the committee, in reporting upon papers referred to them, without looking into any one of them, as utterly incorrect. I assert, as a great general principle, that when resolutions from Legislatures of states, and petitions from a vast multitude of our fellow-citizens, on a subject of deep, vital importance to the country, are referred to a committee of this house, if that committee make up an opinion without looking into such resolutions and memorials, the committee betray their trust to their constituents and this house. I give this out to the nation."

A long and exciting debate, lasting from the 16th of June to the 7th of July, on the report of the committee relative to the annexation of Texas, ensued; the heat and violence of which were chiefly directed upon Mr. Adams.

One of the topics agitated during this debate arose upon a speech of Mr. Howard, of Maryland. Among the petitions against the annexation of Texas were many signed by women. On these Mr. Howard said, he always felt a regret when petitions thus signed were presented to the house, relating to political subjects. He thought these females could have a sufficient field for the exercise of their influence in the discharge of their duties to their fathers, their husbands, or their children, cheering the domestic circle, and shedding over it the mild radiance of the social virtues, instead of rushing into the fierce struggles of political life. He considered it *discreditable*, not only to their particular section of country, but also to the national character.

Mr. Adams immediately entered into a long and animated defence of the right of petition by women; in the course of which he asked "whether women, by petitioning this house in favor of suffering and distress, perform an office 'discreditable' to themselves, to the section of the country where they reside, and to this nation. The gentleman says that women have no right to petition Congress on political subjects. Why? Sir, what does the gentleman understand by 'political subjects'? Everything in which the house has an agency—everything which relates to peace and relates to war, or to any other of the great interests of society. Are women to have no opinions or actions on subjects relating to the general welfare? Where did the gentleman get this principle? Did he find it in sacred history—in the language of Miriam the prophetess, in one of the noblest and most sublime songs of triumph that ever met the human eye or ear? Did the gentleman never hear of Deborah, to whom the children of Israel came up for judgment? Has he forgotten the deed of Jael, who slew the dreaded enemy of her country? Has he forgotten Esther, who, by HER PETITION, saved her people and her country? Sir, I might go through the whole of the sacred history of the Jews to the advent of our Saviour, and find innumerable examples of women, who not only took an active part in the politics of their times, but who are held up with honor to posterity for doing so Our Saviour himself, while on earth, performed that most stupendous miracle, the raising of Lazarus from the dead, at *the petition of a woman*! To go from sacred history to profane, does the gentleman there find it 'discreditable' for women to take any interest or any part in political affairs? In the history of Greece, let him read and examine the character of Aspasia, in a country in which the character and conduct of women were more restricted than in any modern nation, save among the Turks. Has he forgotten that Spartan mother, who said to her son, when going out to battle, 'My son, come back to me *with* thy shield, or *upon* thy shield'? Does he not remember Clœlia and her hundred companions, who swam across the river, under a shower of darts, escaping from Porsenna? Has he forgotten Cornelia, the mother of the Gracchi, who declared that her children were her jewels? And why? Because they were the champions of freedom. Does he not remember Portia, the wife of Brutus and daughter of Cato, and in what terms she is represented in the history of Rome? Has he not read of Arria, who, under imperial despotism, when her husband was condemned to die by a tyrant, plunged the sword into her own bosom, and, handing it to her husband, said, 'Take it, Pætus, it does not hurt,' and expired?

"To come to a later period,—what says the history of our Anglo-Saxon ancestors? To say nothing of Boadicea, the British heroine in the time of the Cæsars, what name is more illustrious than that of Elizabeth? Or, if he will go to the Continent, will he not find the names of Maria Theresa of Hungary, the two Catharines of Russia, and of Isabella of Castile, the patroness of Columbus, the discoverer in substance of this hemisphere, for without her that discovery would not have been made? Did she bring 'discredit' on her sex by mingling in politics? To come nearer home,—what were the women of the United States in the struggle of the Revolution? Or what would the men have been but for the influence of the women of that day? Were they devoted*exclusively* to the duties and enjoyments of the fireside? Take, for example, the ladies of Philadelphia."

Mr. Adams here read a long extract from Judge Johnson's life of General Greene, relating that during the Revolutionary War a call came from General Washington stating that the troops were destitute of shirts, and of many indispensable articles of clothing. "And from whence," writes Judge Johnson, "did relief arrive, at last? From the heart where patriotism erects her favorite shrine, and from the hand which is seldom withdrawn when the soldier solicits. The ladies of Philadelphia immortalized themselves by commencing the generous work, and it was a work too grateful to the American fair not to be followed up with zeal and alacrity."

Mr. Adams then read a long quotation from Dr. Ramsay's history of South Carolina, "which speaks," said he, "trumpet-tongued, of the daring and intrepid spirit of patriotism burning in the bosoms of the ladies of that state." After reading an extract from this history, Mr. Adams thus comments upon it: "Politics, sir! 'rushing into the vortex of politics!'—glorying in being called rebel ladies; refusing to attend balls and entertainments, but crowding to the prison-ships! Mark this, and remember it was done with no small danger to their own persons, and to the safety of their families. But it manifested the spirit by which they were animated; and, sir, is that spirit to be charged here, in this hall where we are sitting, as being 'discreditable' to our country's name? Shall it be said that such conduct was a national reproach, because it was the conduct of women who left 'their domestic concerns, and rushed into the vortex of politics'? Sir, these women did more; they *petitioned*—yes, they petitioned—and that in a matter of politics. It was for the *life of Hayne*."

In connection with this eloquent defence of the right of women to interfere in politics, of which the above extracts are but an outline, Mr. Adams thus applies the result to the particular subject of controversy:

"The broad principle is *morally wrong, vicious,* and the very reverse of that which ought to prevail. Why does it follow that women are fitted for nothing but the cares of domestic life: for bearing children, and cooking the food of a family; devoting all their time to the domestic circle,—to promoting the immediate personal comfort of their husbands, brothers, and sons? Observe, sir, the point of departure between the chairman of the committee and myself. I admit that it is their duty to attend to these things. I subscribe fully to the elegant compliment passed by him upon those members of the female sex who devote their time to these duties. But I say that the correct principle is that women are not only justified, but exhibit the most exalted virtue, when they do depart from the domestic circle, and enter on the concerns of their country, of humanity, and of their God. The mere departure of woman from the duties of the domestic circle, far from being a reproach to her, is a virtue of the highest order, when it is done from purity of motive, by appropriate means, and towards a virtuous purpose. There is the true distinction. The motive must be pure, the means appropriate, and the purpose good; and I say that woman, by the discharge of such duties, has manifested a virtue which is even above the virtues of mankind, and approaches to a superior nature. That is the principle I maintain, and which the chairman of the committee has to refute, if he applies the position he has taken to the mothers, the sisters, and the daughters, of the men of my district who voted to send me here. Now, I aver further, that, in the instance to which his observation refers, namely, in the act of petitioning against the annexation of Texas to this Union, the motive was pure, the means appropriate, and the purpose virtuous, in the highest degree. As an evident proof of this, I recur to the particular petition from which this debate took its rise, namely, to the first petition I presented here against the annexation—a petition consisting of three lines, and signed by two hundred and thirty-eight women of Plymouth, a principal town in my own district. Their words are:

"'The undersigned, women of Plymouth (Mass.), thoroughly aware of the sinfulness of slavery, and the consequent impolicy and disastrous tendency of its extension in our country, do most respectfully remonstrate, with all our souls, against the annexation of Texas to the United States as a slaveholding territory.'

"These are the words of their memorial; and I say that, in presenting it here, their motive was pure, and of the highest order of purity. They petitioned under a conviction that the consequence of the annexation would be the advancement of that which is sin in the sight of God, namely, slavery. I say, further, that the means were appropriate, because it is Congress who must decide on the question; and therefore it is proper that they should petition Congress, if they wish to prevent the annexation. And I say, in the third place, that the end was virtuous, pure, and of the most exalted character, namely, to prevent the perpetuation and spread of slavery throughout America. I say, moreover, that I subscribe, in my own person, to every word the petition contains. I do believe slavery to be a sin before God; and that is the reason, and the only insurmountable reason, why we should refuse to annex Texas to this Union."

On the 28th July, 1838, to an invitation from the Massachusetts Anti-Slavery Society to attend their celebration of the anniversary of the day upon which slavery was abolished in the colonial possessions of Great Britain, Mr. Adams responded:

"It would give me pleasure to comply with this invitation; but my health is not very firm. My voice has been affected by the intense heat of the season; and a multiplicity of applications, from societies political and literary, to attend and address their meetings, have imposed upon me the necessity of pleading the privilege of my years, and declining them all.

"I rejoice that the defence of the cause of human freedom is falling into younger and more vigorous hands. That, in three-score years from the day of the Declaration of Independence, its self-evident truths should be yet struggling for existence against the degeneracy of an age pampered with prosperity, and languishing into servitude, is a melancholy truth, from which I should in vain attempt to shut my eyes. But the summons has gone forth. The youthful champions of the rights of human nature have buckled and are buckling on their armor; and the scourging overseer, and the lynching lawyer, and the servile sophist, and the faithless scribe, and the priestly parasite, will vanish before them like Satan touched by the spear of Ithuriel. I live in the faith and hope of the progressive advancement of Christian liberty, and expect to abide by the same in death. You have a glorious though arduous career before you; and it is among the consolations of my last days that I am able to cheer you in the pursuit, and exhort you to be steadfast and immovable in it. So shall you not fail, whatever may betide, to reap a rich reward in the blessing of him that is ready to perish, upon your soul."

In August, 1838, Mr. Adams addressed a letter to the inhabitants of his district, in which, after stating what had been done on the same subject by the Legislature of Massachusetts and other states, he proceeded to recapitulate the wrongs which had been done to the colored races of Africa on this continent, "which have indeed been of long standing, but which in these latter days have been aggravated beyond all measure. To repair the injustice of our fathers to these races had been, from the day of the Declaration of Independence, the conscience of the good and the counsel of the wise rulers of the land. Washington, by his own example in the testamentary disposal of his property,—Jefferson, by the unhesitating convictions of his own mind, by unanswerable argument and eloquent persuasion, addressed almost incessantly, throughout a long life, to the reason and feelings of his countrymen,—had done homage to the self-evident principles which the nation, at her birth, had been the first to proclaim. Emancipation, universal emancipation, was the lesson they had urged on their contemporaries, and held forth as transcendent and irremissible duties to their children of the present age. Instead of which, what have we seen? Communities of slaveholding braggarts, setting at defiance the laws of nature and nature's God, restoring slavery where it had been extinguished, and vainly dreaming to make it eternal; forming, in the sacred name of liberty, constitutions of government interdicting to the legislative authority itself that most blessed of human powers, the power of giving liberty to the slave! Governors of states urging upon their Legislatures to make the exercise of the freedom of speech to propagate the right of the slave to freedom felony, without benefit of clergy! Ministers of the gospel, like the priest in the parable of the Good Samaritan, coming and looking at the bleeding victim of the highway robber, and passing on the other side; or, baser still, perverting the pages of the sacred volume to turn into a code of slavery the very word of God! Philosophers, like the Sophists of ancient Greece, pulverized by the sober sense of Socrates, elaborating theories of *moral slavery* from the alembic of a sugar plantation, and vaporing about lofty sentiments and generous benevolence to be learnt from the hereditary bondage of man to man! Infuriated mobs, murdering the peaceful ministers of Christ for the purpose of extinguishing the light of a printing-press, and burning with unhallowed fire the hall of freedom, the orphan's school, and the church devoted to the worship of God! And, last of all, both houses of Congress turning a deaf ear to hundreds of thousands of petitioners, and quibbling away their duty to read, to listen, and consider, in doubtful disputations whether they shall receive, or, receiving, refuse to read or hear, the complaints and prayers of their fellow-citizens and fellow-men!"

Mr. Adams proceeds, in a like spirit of eloquent plainness, to denounce the violation of that beneficent change which both Washington and Jefferson had devised for the red man of the forest, and had assured to him by solemn treaties pledging the faith of the nation, and by laws interdicting by severe penalties the intrusion of the white man on his domain. "In contempt of those treaties," said he, "and in defiance of those laws, the sovereign State of Georgia had extended her jurisdiction over these Indian lands, and lavished, in lottery-tickets to her people, the growing harvests, the cultivated fields, and furnished dwellings, of the Cherokee, setting at naught the solemn adjudication of the Supreme Court of the United States, pronouncing this licensed robbery alike lawless and unconstitutional." He then proceeds, in a strain of severe animadversion, to reprobate the conduct of the Executive administration, in "truckling to these usurpations of Georgia;" and reviews that of Congress, in refusing "the petitions of fifteen thousand of these cheated and plundered people," when thousands of our own citizens joined in their supplications.

In this letter Mr. Adams states and explains the origin of the treaty of peace and alliance between Southern nullification and Northern pro-slavery, and the nature and consequences of that alliance. In the course of his illustrations on this subject he repels, with an irresistible power of argument, the attempt of the slaveholder to sow the seeds of discord among the freemen of the North. "The condition of master and slave is," he considered, "by the laws of nature and of God, a state of perpetual, inextinguishable war. The slaveholder, deeply conscious of this, soothes his soul by sophistical reasonings into a belief that this same war still exists in free communities between the capitalist and free labor." The fallacy and falsehood of this theory he analyzes and exposes, and proceeds to state and reason upon various measures of Congress connected with these topics, at great length, and with laborious elucidation.[44]

On the 27th of October, 1838, Mr. Adams addressed a letter to the district he represented in Congress, in which he touched on those points of national policy which most deeply affected his mind. Among many remarks worthy of anxious thought, which subsequent events have confirmed and are confirming, he traces the "smothering for nearly three years, in legislative halls, the right of petition and freedom of debate," to the influence of slavery, "which shrinks, and will shrink, from the eye of day. Northern subserviency to Southern dictation is the price paid by a Northern administration for Southern support. The people of the North still support by their suffrages the men who have truckled to Southern domination. I believe it impossible that this total subversion of every principle of liberty should be much longer submitted to by the people of the free states of this Union. But their fate is in their own hands. If they choose to be represented by slaves, they will find servility enough to represent and betray them. The suspension of the right of petition, the suppression of the freedom of debate, the thirst for the annexation of Texas, the war-whoop of two successive Presidents against Mexico, are all but varied symptoms of a deadly disease seated in the marrow of our bones, and that deadly disease is slavery."

When, in the latter part of June, 1838, news of the success of Mr. Rush in obtaining the Smithsonian bequest, and information that he had already received on account of it more than half a million of dollars, were announced to the public, Mr. Adams lost no time in endeavoring to give a right direction to the government on the subject. He immediately waited upon the President of the United States, and, in a conversation of two hours, explained the views he entertained in regard to the application of that fund, and entreated him to have a plan prepared, to recommend to Congress, for the foundation of the institution, at the commencement of the next session. "I suggested to him," said Mr. Adams, "the establishment of an Astronomical Observatory, with a salary for an astronomer and assistant, for nightly observations and periodical publications; annual courses of lectures upon the natural, moral, and political sciences. Above all, no jobbing, no sinecure, no monkish stalls for lazy idlers. I urged the deep responsibility of the nation to the world and to all posterity worthily to fulfil the great object of the testator. I only lamented my inability to communicate half the solicitude with which my heart is on this subject full, and the sluggishness with which I failed properly to pursue it." "Mr. Van Buren," Mr. Adams added, "received all this with complacency and apparent concurrence of opinion, seemed favorably disposed to my views and willing to do right, and asked me to name any person whom I thought might be usefully consulted."

The phenomena of the heavens were constantly observed and often recorded by Mr. Adams. Thus, on the 3d of October, 1838, he writes: "As the clock struck five this morning, I saw the planets Venus and Mercury in conjunction, Mercury being about two thirds of a sun's disk below and northward of Venus. Three quarters of an hour later Mercury was barely perceptible, and five minutes after could not be traced by my naked eye, Venus being for ten minutes longer visible. I ascertained, therefore, that, in the clear sky of this latitude, Mercury, at his greatest elongation from the sun, may be seen by a very imperfect naked eye, in the morning twilight, for the space of one hour. I observed, also, the rapidity of his movements, by the diminished distance between these planets since the day before yesterday."

In the following November he again writes: "To make observations on the movements of the heavenly bodies has been, for a great portion of my life, a pleasure of gratified curiosity, of ever-returning wonder, and of reverence for the great Creator and Mover of these innumerable worlds. There is something of awful enjoyment in observing the rising and the setting of the sun. That flashing beam of his first appearing upon the horizon; that sinking of the last ray beneath it; that perpetual revolution of the Great and Little Bear around the pole; that rising of the whole constellation of Orion from the horizon to the perpendicular position, and his ride through the heavens with his belt, his nebulous sword, and his four corner stars of the first magnitude, are sources of delight which never tire. Even the optical delusion, by which the motion of the earth from west to east appears to the eye as the movement of the whole firmament from east to west, swells the conception of magnificence to the incomprehensible infinite."

When one of his friends expressed a hope that we should hereafter know more of the brilliant stars around us, Mr. Adams replied: "I trust so. I cannot conceive of a world where the stars are not visible, and, if there is one, I trust I shall never be sent to it. Nothing conveys to my mind the idea of eternity so forcibly as the grand spectacle of the heavens in a clear night."

To a letter addressed to him by the Secretary of State, by direction of the President, requesting him to communicate the result of his reflections on the Smithsonian Institution, Mr. Adams made the following reply:

"QUINCY, *October 11, 1838.*

"SIR: I have reserved for a separate letter what I proposed to say in recommending the erection and establishment of an Astronomical Observatory at Washington, as one and the first application of the annual income from the Smithsonian bequest, because that, of all that I have to say, I deem it by far the most important; and because, having for many years believed that the national character of our country demanded of us the establishment of such an institution as a debt of honor to the cause of science and to the world of civilized man, I have hailed with cheering hope this opportunity of removing the greatest obstacle which has hitherto disappointed the earnest wishes that I have entertained of witnessing, before my own departure for another world, now near at hand, the disappearance of a stain upon our good name, in the neglect to provide the means of increasing and diffusing knowledge among men, by a systematic and scientific continued series of observations on the phenomena of the numberless worlds suspended over our heads—the sublimest of physical sciences, and that in which the field of future discovery is as unbounded as the universe itself. I allude to the continued and necessary *expense* of such an establishment.

"In my former letter I proposed that, to preserve entire and unimpaired the Smithsonian fund, as the principal of a perpetual annuity, the annual appropriations from its proceeds should be strictly confined to its annual income; that, assuming the amount of the fund to be five hundred thousand dollars, it should be so invested as to secure a permanent yearly income of thirty thousand; and that it should be committed to an incorporated board of trustees, with a secretary and treasurer, the only person of the board to receive a pecuniary compensation from the fund."

Mr. Adams then refers to a report made by C. F. Mercer, chairman of a committee of the House of Representatives, on the 18th of March, 1826 (during his own administration), relative to the expenses of an Observatory, for much valuable information, and thus proceeds:

"But, as it is desirable that the principal building, the Observatory itself, should be, for the purposes of observation, unsurpassed by any other edifice constructed for the same purposes, I would devote one year's interest from the fund to the construction of the buildings; a second and a third to constitute a fund, from the income of which the salaries of the astronomer, his assistants and attendants, should be paid; a fourth and fifth for the necessary instruments and books; a sixth and seventh for a fund, from the income of which the expense should be defrayed of publishing the ephemeris of observation, and a yearly nautical almanac. These appropriations may be so distributed as to apply a part of the appropriation of each year to each of those necessary expenditures; but for an establishment so complete as may do honor in all time alike to the testator and his trustees, the United States of America, I cannot reduce my estimate of the necessary expense below two hundred thousand dollars.

"My principles for this disposal of funds are these:

"1st. That the most complete establishment of an Astronomical Observatory in the world should be founded by the United States of America; the whole expense of which, both its first cost and its perpetual maintenance, should be amply provided for, without costing one dollar either to the people or to the *principal* sum of the Smithsonian bequest.

"2d. That, by providing from the income alone of the fund a supplementary fund, from the interest of which all the salaries shall be paid, and all the annual expenses of publication shall be defrayed, the fund itself would, instead of being impaired, accumulate with the lapse of years. I do most fervently wish that this principle might be made the fundamental law, now and hereafter, so far as may be practicable, of all the appropriations of the Smithsonian bequest.

"3d. That, by the establishment of an Observatory upon the largest and most liberal scale, and providing for the publication of a yearly nautical almanac, knowledge will be dispersed among men, the reputation of our country will rise to honor and reverence among the civilized nations of the earth, and our navigators and mariners on every ocean be no longer dependent on English or French observers or calculators for tables indispensable to conduct their path upon the deep."

Mr. Adams, about this period, expressed himself with deep dissatisfaction at the course pursued by the President relative to the Smithsonian bequest, combining the general expression of a disposition to aid his views with apparently a total indifference as to the expenditure of the money. "The subject," said he, "weighs deeply upon my mind. The private interests and sordid passions into which that fund has already fallen fill me with anxiety and apprehensions that it will be squandered upon cormorants, or wasted in electioneering bribery. Almost all the heads of department are indifferent to its application according to the testator's bequest; distinguished senators open or disguised enemies to the establishment of the institution in any form. The utter prostration of public spirit in the Senate, proved by the selfish project to apply it to the establishment of a university; the investment of the whole fund, more than half a million of dollars, in Arkansas and Michigan state stocks; the mean trick of filching ten thousand dollars, last winter, to pay for the charges of procuring it, are all so utterly discouraging that I despair of effecting anything for the honor of the country, or even to accomplish the purpose of the bequest, the increase and diffusion of knowledge among men. It is hard to toil through life for a great purpose, with a conviction that it will be in vain; but possibly seed now sown may bring forth some good fruits. In my report, in January, 1836, I laid down all the general principles on which the fund should have been accepted and administered. I was then wholly successful. My bill passed without opposition, and under its provisions the money was procured and deposited in the treasury in gold. If I cannot prevent the disgrace of the country by the failure of the testator's intention, I can leave a record to future time of what I have done, and what I would have done, to accomplish the great design, if executed well. And let not the supplication to the Author of Good be wanting."

In November, 1838, the anti-slavery party made the immediate abolition of slavery in the District of Columbia a test question, on which Mr. Adams remarked: "This is absurd, because notoriously impracticable. The house would refuse to consider the question two to one." Writing on the same subject, in December of the same year, "I doubt," said he, "if there are five members in the house who would vote to abolish slavery in the District of Columbia at this time. The conflict between the principle of liberty and the fact of slavery is coming gradually to an issue. Slavery has now the power, and falls into convulsions at the approach of freedom. That the fall of slavery is predetermined in the councils of Omnipotence I cannot doubt. It is a part of the great moral improvement in the condition of man attested by all the records of history. But the conflict will be terrible, and the progress of improvement retrograde, before its final progress to consummation."

In January, 1839, Mr. Adams, in presenting a large number of petitions for the abolition of slavery, asked leave to explain to the house his reasons for the course he had adopted in relation to petitions of this character. He asked it as a courtesy. He had received a mass of letters threatening him with assassination for this course. His real position was not understood by his country. The house having granted the leave, he proceeded to state that, although he had zealously advocated the right to petition for the abolition of slavery in the District of Columbia, he was not himself then, prepared to grant their prayer; that, if the question should be presented at once, he should vote against it. He knew not what change might be produced on his mind by a full and fair discussion, but he had not yet seen any reason to change his opinion, although he had read all that abolitionists themselves had written and published on the subject. He then presented the petitions, and moved appropriate resolutions.

On the 21st of February, 1839, Mr. Adams presented to the house several resolutions, proposing, in the form prescribed by the constitution of the United States, 1st. That after the 4th day of July, 1842, there shall be no hereditary slavery in the United States, and that every child born on and after that day, within the United States and their territories, shall be born free. 2d. That, with exception of Florida, there shall henceforth never be admitted into this Union any state the constitution of which shall tolerate within the same the existence of slavery. 3d That from and after the 4th of July, 1848, there shall be neither slavery nor slave-trade at the seat of government of the United States.

Mr. Adams proceeded to state that he had in his possession a paper, which he desired to present, and on which these resolutions were founded. It was a petition from John Jay, and forty-three most respectable citizens of the city of New York. Being here interrupted by violent cries of "Order!" he at that time refrained from further pressing the subject.

On the 30th of April, 1839, Mr. Adams delivered before the Historical Society of New York a discourse entitled "The Jubilee of the Constitution;" it being the fiftieth year after the inauguration of George Washington as President of the United States. Of all his occasional productions, this was, probably, the most labored. In it he traces the history of the constitution of the United States from the period antecedent to the American Revolution, through the events of that war, to the circumstances which led to its adoption, concluding with a solemn admonition to adhere to the principles of the Declaration of Independence, practically interwoven into the constitution of the United States.

In October, 1839, in an address to the inhabitants of Braintree, of which "Education" was the topic, he traces that of New England to the Christian religion, of which the Bible was the text-book and foundation, and the revelation of eternal life. He then illustrated the history of that religion by recapitulating the difficulties it had to encounter through ages of persecution; commented upon the ecclesiastical hierarchy established under Constantine, and the abuses arising from the policy of the Church of Rome, until their final exposure by Martin Luther, out of which emanated the Protestant faith. The display of learning, the power of reasoning, and the suggestive thoughts, in this occasional essay, exhibit the extent and depth of his studies of the sacred volume, to which, more than to any other, the strength of his mind had been devoted.

About this time was published in the newspapers a letter from Mr. Adams to Dr. Thomas Sewall, concerning his two letters on Phrenology, and giving his own opinion on that subject in the following characteristic language: "I have never been able to persuade myself to think of the *science of Phrenology* as a *serious* speculation. I have classed it with judicial astrology, with alchemy, and with *augury*; and, as Cicero says he wonders how two Roman augurs could have looked each other in the face without laughing, I have felt something of the same surprise that two learned phrenologists can meet without like temptation. But, as it has been said of Bishop Berkeley's anti-material system, that he has demonstrated, beyond the possibility of refutation, what no man in his senses can believe, so, without your assistance, I should never have been able to encounter the system of thirty-three or thirty-five faculties of the immortal soul all clustered on the blind side of the head. I thank you for furnishing me with argument to meet the doctors who pack up the five senses in thirty-five parcels of the brain. I hope your lectures will be successful in recalling the sober sense of the *material* philosophers to the dignity of an *imperishable* mind."

With an urgent request, contained in a letter dated the 28th of June, 1839, for his opinion on the constitutionality and expediency of the law, then recently sanctioned by two Legislatures of Massachusetts, called the license law, Mr. Adams declined complying, for reasons stated at length. He regarded the purpose of the law as "in the highest degree pure, patriotic, and benevolent." It had, however, given rise to two evils, which were already

96

manifested. "The first, a spirit of concerted and determined resistance to its execution. The second, a concerted effort to turn the dissatisfaction of the people with the law into a political engine against the administration of the state. There is no duty more impressive upon the Legislature than that of accommodating the exercise of its power to the spirit of those over whom it is to operate. Abstract right, deserving as it is of the profound reverence of every ruler over men, is yet not the principle which must guide and govern his conduct; and whoever undertakes to make it exclusively his guide will soon find in the community a resistance that will overrule him and his principles. The Supreme Ruler of the universe declares himself, in the holy Scriptures, that, in dealing with the prevarications of his chosen people, he sometimes gave them statutes which were *not good.*"

On the 2d December, 1839, at the opening of the Twenty-Sixth Congress, the clerk began to call the roll of the members, according to custom. When he came to New Jersey, he stated that five seats of the members from that state were contested, and that, not feeling himself authorized to decide the question, he should pass over those names, and proceed with the call. This gave rise to a general and violent debate on the steps to be pursued under such circumstances. It was declared by Mr. Adams that the proceeding of the clerk was evidently preconcerted to exclude the five members from New Jersey from voting at the organization of the house. Innumerable questions were raised, but the house could not agree upon the mode of proceeding, and from the 2d to the 5th it remained in a perfectly disorganized state, and in apparently inextricable confusion. The remainder of the scene is thus described, in the newspapers, by one apparently an eye-witness:

"Mr. Adams, from the opening of this scene of confusion and anarchy, had maintained a profound silence. He appeared to be engaged most of the time in writing. To a common observer he seemed to be reckless of everything around him. But nothing, not the slightest incident, escaped him.

"The fourth day of the struggle had now commenced. Mr. Hugh A. Garland, the clerk, was directed to call the roll again. He commenced with Maine, as usual in those days, and was proceeding towards Massachusetts. I turned and saw that Mr. Adams was ready to get the floor at the earliest moment possible. His eye was riveted on the clerk, his hands clasped the front edge of his desk, where he always placed them to assist him in rising. He looked, in the language of Otway, like a 'fowler eager for his prey,'

"'New Jersey!' ejaculated Mr. Hugh Garland, 'and—'

"Mr. Adams immediately sprang to the floor.

"'I rise to interrupt the clerk,' was his first exclamation.

"'Silence! Silence!' resounded through the hall. 'Hear him! Hear him! Hear what he has to say! Hear John Quincy Adams!' was vociferated on all sides.

"In an instant the most profound stillness reigned throughout the hall,—you might have heard a leaf of paper fall in any part of it,—and every eye was riveted on the venerable Nestor of Massachusetts—the purest of statesmen, and the noblest of men! He paused for a moment, and, having given Mr. Garland a withering look, he proceeded to address the multitude.

"'It was not my intention,' said he, 'to take any part in these extraordinary proceedings. I had hoped this house would succeed in organizing itself; that a speaker and clerk would be elected, and that the ordinary business of legislation would be progressed in. This is not the time or place to discuss the merits of conflicting claimants from New Jersey. That subject belongs to the House of Representatives, which, by the constitution, is made the ultimate arbiter of the qualifications of its members. But what a spectacle we here present! We degrade and disgrace our constituents and the country. We do not and cannot organize; and why? Because the clerk of this house—the mere clerk, whom we create, whom we employ, and whose existence depends upon our will—usurps the *throne*, and sets us, the representatives, the vicegerents of the whole American people, at defiance, and holds us in contempt! And what is this clerk of yours? Is he to suspend, by his mere negative, the functions of government, and put an end to this Congress? He refuses to call the roll! It is in your power to compel him to call it, if he will not do it voluntarily.' [Here he was interrupted by a member, who said that he was authorized to say that compulsion could not reach the clerk, who had avowed that he would resign rather than call the State of New Jersey.] 'Well,

97

sir, let him resign,' continued Mr. Adams, 'and we may possibly discover some way by which we can get along without the aid of his all-powerful talent, learning, and genius!

"'If we cannot organize in any other way,—if this clerk of yours will not consent to our discharging the trust confided to us by our constituents,—then let us imitate the example of the Virginia House of Burgesses, which, when the colonial Governor Dinwiddie ordered it to disperse, refused to obey the imperious and insulting mandate, and, like men—'

"The multitude could not contain or repress their enthusiasm any longer, but saluted the eloquent and indignant speaker, and interrupted him with loud and deafening cheers, which seemed to shake the capitol to its centre. The very genii of applause and enthusiasm seemed to float in the atmosphere of the hall, and every heart expanded with an indescribable feeling of pride and exultation. The turmoil, the darkness, the very 'chaos of anarchy,' which had for three successive days pervaded the American Congress, was dispelled by the magic, the talismanic eloquence, of a single man; and once more the wheels of government and legislation were put in motion.

"Having, by this powerful appeal, brought the yet unorganized assembly to a perception of its hazardous position, he submitted a motion requiring the acting clerk to call the roll. Accordingly Mr. Adams was interrupted by a burst of voices demanding, 'How shall the question be put?' 'Who will put the question?' The voice of Mr. Adams was heard above the tumult: 'I intend to put the question myself!' That word brought order out of chaos. There was the master mind.

"As soon as the multitude had recovered itself, and the excitement of irrepressible enthusiasm had abated, Mr. Richard Barnwell Rhett, of South Carolina, leaped upon one of the desks, waved his hand, and exclaimed: 'I move that the Honorable John Quincy Adams take the chair of the Speaker of the house, and officiate as presiding officer till the house be organized by the election of its constitutional officers. As many as are agreed to this will say Ay; those—'

"He had not an opportunity to complete the sentence, 'those who are not agreed will say No;' for one universal, deafening, thundering AY responded to the nomination.

"Hereupon it was moved and ordered that Lewis Williams, of North Carolina, and Richard Barnwell Rhett, conduct John Quincy Adams to the chair.

"Well did Mr. Wise, of Virginia, say: 'Sir, I regard it as the proudest hour of your life; and if, when you shall be gathered to your fathers, I were asked to select the words which, in my judgment, are best calculated to give at once the character of the man, I would inscribe upon your tomb this sentence: *I will put the question myself.*'"

CHAPTER XI.

SECOND REPORT ON THE SMITHSONIAN FUND.—HIS SPEECH ON A BILL FOR INSURING A MORE FAITHFUL EXECUTION OF THE LAWS RELATING TO THE COLLECTION OF DUTIES ON IMPORTS.—REMARKS ON THE ESTABLISHMENT OF AN EXTENSIVE SERIES OF MAGNETICAL AND METEOROLOGICAL OBSERVATIONS.—ON ITINERANT ELECTIONEERING.— ON ABUSES IN RESPECT OF THE NAVY FUND.—ON THE POLITICAL INFLUENCES OF THE TIME.—ON THE ORIGIN AND RESULTS OF THE FLORIDA WAR.—HIS DENUNCIATION OF DUELLING.—HIS ARGUMENT IN THE SUPREME COURT ON BEHALF OF AFRICANS CAPTURED IN THE AMISTAD.

On the 5th of March, 1840, Mr. Adams, as chairman of the select committee on the Smithsonian bequest, made a report, in which he recapitulated all the material facts which had previously occurred relative to the acceptance of this fund, and entered into the motives which prevailed with the former committee as to its disposal. It appeared from this report, which was accompanied by a publication of all the documents connected with the subject up to that period, that the fund had been received, and paid into the Treasury, and invested in state stocks, and that the President now invited the attention of Congress to the obligation devolving upon the United States to fulfil the object of the bequest. While this message was under consideration various projects for disposing of the funds had been presented by individuals, in memorials, concerning which the report states that they generally contemplated the establishment of a school, college, or university, proposing expenditures absorbing the whole in the erection of buildings, and leaving little or nothing for the improvement of future ages. "In most of these projects," says Mr. Adams, "there might be perceived purposes of personal accommodation and emolument to the projectors, more adapted to the promotion of their own interest than to the increase and diffusion of knowledge among men."

While these memorials and the subject of the disposal of the whole Smithson fund were before the select committee, a resolution came from the Senate appointing "a joint committee, consisting of seven members of the Senate, and such a number as the House of Representatives should appoint, to consider the expediency of providing an institution of learning, to be established at the city of Washington, for the application of the legacy bequeathed by James Smithson, of London, to the United States, in trust for that purpose." The House, out of courtesy to the Senate, concurred in their resolution, and added on their part the members of that of which Mr. Adams was chairman.

The propositions of the committee on the part of the House and that on the part of the Senate were so widely at variance, that it was found that no result could be obtained in which both committees would concur. It was finally agreed that the committee on the part of the House should report their project to the House for consideration. Mr. Adams, thereupon, as chairman, reported a series of resolutions, substantially of the following import: That the whole Smithson fund should be vested in a corporate body of trustees, to remain, under the pledge of the faith of the United States, undiminished and unimpaired, at an interest yielding annually six per cent., appropriated to the declared purpose of the founder, exclusively from the interest, and not in any part from the principal,—the first appropriation of interest to be applied for the erection of an astronomical observatory, and for the various objects incident to such an establishment;—that the education of youth had not for its object the *increase* and diffusion of knowledge among men, but the endowment of individuals with knowledge already acquired; and the Smithson fund should not be applied to the purpose of education, or to any school, college, university, or institution of education.

The chairman of the committee of the Senate, in their behalf, presented counter resolutions, disapproving the application of any part of the funds to the establishment of an astronomical observatory, and urging the appropriation of them to the establishment of a university. The bill prepared by the House is presented at large in this report, accompanied with the argument in its support, prepared by Mr. Adams with a strength and fulness to which no abstract can do justice. In this argument he illustrates the reasons for preserving the principal of the fund unimpaired, and confining all expenditures from it to the annual interest; also those which preclude any portion of it to be applied to any institution for education; showing, from the peculiar expressions of the testator, that it could not have been his intention that the fund should be applied in this manner. He then proceeds to set forth the reasons why the income of the fund should in the first instance be applied to an astronomical observatory, without intending to exclude any branch of human knowledge from its equitable share of this benefaction. The importance of this object he thus eloquently illustrates: "The express object of Mr. Smithson's bequest is the *diffusion of knowledge* among men. IT IS KNOWLEDGE, the source of all human wisdom, and of all beneficent power; knowledge, as far transcending the postulated lever of Archimedes as the universe transcends this speck of earth upon its face; knowledge, the attribute of Omnipotence, of which man alone, in the physical and material world, is permitted to anticipate."

Why astronomical science should be the object to which the income of this fund should be first applied he thus proceeds to set forth:

"The express object of an observatory is the increase of knowledge by new discovery. The physical relations between the firmament of heaven and the globe allotted by the Creator of all to be the abode of man are discoverable only by the organ of the eye. Many of these relations are indispensable to the existence of human life, and perhaps of the earth itself. Who, that can conceive the idea of a world without a sun, but must connect with it the extinction of light and heat, of all animal life, of all vegetation and production, leaving the lifeless clod of matter to return to the primitive state of chaos, or to be consumed by elemental fire? The influence of the moon—of the planets, our next-door neighbors of the solar system—of the fixed stars, scattered over the blue expanse in multitudes exceeding the power of human computation, and at distances of which imagination herself can form no distinct conception;—the influence of all these upon the globe which we inhabit, and upon the condition of man, its dying and deathless inhabitant, is great and mysterious, and, in the search for final causes, to a great degree inscrutable to his finite and limited faculties. The extent to which they are discoverable is and must remain unknown; but, to the vigilance of a sleepless eye, to the toil of a tireless hand, and to the meditations of a thinking, combining, and analyzing mind, secrets are successively revealed, not only of the deepest import to the welfare of man in his earthly career, but which seem to lift him from the earth to the threshold of his eternal abode; to lead him blindfold up to the council-chamber of Omnipotence, and there, stripping the bandage from his eyes, bid him look undazzled at the throne of God.

"In the history of the human species, so far as it is known to us, astronomical observation was one of the first objects of pursuit for the acquisition of knowledge. In the first chapter of the sacred volume we are told that, in the process of creation, 'God said, Let there be lights in the firmament of the heavens to divide the day from the night; and let them be for signs, and for seasons, and for days, and for years.' By the special appointment, then, of the Creator, they were made the standards for the measurement of time upon earth. They were made for more: not only for seasons, for days, and for years, but for SIGNS. Signs of what? It may be that the word, in this passage, has reference to the signs of the Egyptian zodiac, to mark the succession of solar months; or it may indicate a more latent connection between the heavens and the earth, of the nature of judicial astrology. These relations are not only apparent to the most superficial observation of man, but many of them remain inexhaustible funds of successive discovery, perhaps as long as the continued existence of man upon earth. What an unknown world of mind, for example, is yet teeming in the womb of time, to be revealed in tracing the causes of the sympathy between the magnet and the pole—that unseen, immaterial spirit, which walks with us through the most entangled forests, over the most interminable wilderness, and across every region of the pathless deep, by day, by night, in the calm serene of a cloudless sky, and in the howling of the hurricane or the typhoon? Who can witness the movements of that tremulous needle, poised upon its centre, still tending to the polar star, but obedient to his distant hand, armed with a metallic guide, round every point of the compass, at the fiat of his will, without feeling a thrill of amazement approaching to superstition? The discovery of the attractive power of the magnet was made before the invention of the alphabet, or the age of hieroglyphics. No record of the event is found upon the annals of human history. But seven hundred years have scarcely passed away since its polarity was first known to the civilized European man. It was by observation of the periodical revolution of the earth in her orbit round the sun, compared with her daily revolution round her axis, that was disclosed the fact that her annual period was composed of three hundred and sixty-five of her daily revolutions; or, in other words, that the year was composed of three hundred and sixty-five days. But the shepherds of Egypt, watching their flocks by night, could not but observe the movements of the dog-star, next to the sun the most brilliant of the luminaries of heaven. They worshipped that star as a god; and, losing sight of him for about forty days every year, during his conjunction with the sun, they watched with intense anxiety for his reäppearance in the sky, and with that day commenced their year. By this practice it failed not soon to be found that, although the reäppearance of the star for three successive years was at the end of three hundred and sixty-five days, it would, on the fourth year, be delayed one day longer; and, after repeated observation of this phenomenon, they added six hours to the computed duration of the year, and established the canicular period of four years, consisting of one thousand four hundred and sixty-one days. It was not until the days of Julius Cæsar that this computation of time was adopted in the Roman calendar; and fifteen centuries from that time had elapsed before the yearly celebration of the Christian paschal festivals, founded upon the Passover of the Levitical law, revealed the fact that the annual revolution of the earth in her orbit round the sun is not precisely of three hundred and sixty-five days and one quarter, but of between eleven and twelve minutes less; and thus the duration of the year was ascertained, as a measure of time, to an accuracy of three or four seconds, more or less—a mistake which would scarcely amount to one day in twenty thousand years.

100

"It is, then, to the successive discoveries of persevering astronomical observation, through a period of fifty centuries, that we are indebted for a fixed and permanent standard for the measurement of time. And by the same science has man acquired, so far as he possesses it, a standard for the measurement of space. A standard for the measurement of the dimensions and distances of the fixed stars from ourselves is yet to be found; and, if ever found, will be through the means of astronomical observation.

"The influence of all these discoveries upon the condition of man is no doubt infinitely diversified in relative importance; but all, even the minutest, contribute to the increase and diffusion of knowledge. There is no richer field of science opened to the exploration of man in search of knowledge than astronomical observation; nor is there, in the opinion of this committee, any duty more impressively incumbent upon all human governments than that of furnishing means, and facilities, and rewards, to those who devote the labors of their lives to the indefatigable industry, the unceasing vigilance, and the bright intelligence, indispensable to success in these pursuits."

These remarks are succeeded by others on the Royal Observatory of Greenwich, on the connection of astronomy with the art of navigation, on the increase of observatories in the British Islands, in France, and in Russia; and, after repeating the objections to applying the fund of Mr. Smithson to a school devoted to any particular branch of science, or for general education, Mr. Adams, in behalf of the committee, submitted a bill for the consideration of the house, embracing the principles maintained in his report.

On May 8th, 1840, a bill to insure a more faithful execution of the laws relating to the collection of duties on imports being under consideration of the house, Mr. Adams, after commenting on the nature and injurious consequences of the fraud which it was the object of the bill to prevent, said that this practice was "a sort of national thing," to such an extent were the citizens of Great Britain accustomed to come over to this country to cheat us out of our revenue, and to defraud our manufacturing interest, and added:

"I have said that there is something national in this matter, and I will now proceed to state what, in my judgment, lies at the bottom of this proceeding. It is a maxim of British commercial law that it is lawful for the citizens of one nation to defraud the revenues of other nations. The author of the maxim was a man famous throughout the civilized world,— a man of transcendent talents, who fixed, more, perhaps, than any other man of the same century, his impress on the age in which he lived, and upon the laws of England,—I mean Lord Mansfield. In some respects it has been greatly to the advantage of those laws, but in others as much to their disadvantage and discredit, of which the maxim of which I now speak is a signal instance. He was the first British judge who established the principle that it is a lawful thing for Englishmen to cheat the revenue laws of other nations, especially those of Spain and Portugal.

"This principle was first settled in an act of Parliament, the object of which was to suppress what are denominated wager policies of insurance—a species of instrument well known to lawyers as gambling policies, being entered into when the party insuring has no interest in the property insured. It had been a question whether such policies were lawful by the common law. The practice had greatly increased, insomuch that wager policies had become a common thing. It was with a view to suppress these that the statute of the nineteenth of George the Second, chapter thirty-seventh, was passed. The object of that statute was good; it was remedial in its character; it went to suppress a public evil; but, while it prohibited wager policies in all other cases, it contained *an express exception in favor of those made on vessels trading to Spain and Portugal.*"

After commenting on this act of the British Parliament, he quotes the words of Blackstone, who, after stating the nature of these smuggling policies, and dwelling upon their immorality and pernicious tendency, refers to the law above mentioned, which enacts "that they shall be totally null and void, except as to policies on privateers in the Spanish and Portuguese trade, *for reasons sufficiently obvious.*" (2 Blackstone, ch. XXX., p. 4, § 1.) On this statement of Blackstone Mr. Adams remarks:

"It is an old maxim of the schools that frauds are always concealed under generalities. What were these *obvious reasons?* Why were they concealed? It is known to the committee that, in the celebrated controversy of the man in the mask,—I mean Junius with

101

Blackstone,—he said, that for the defence of law, of justice, and of truth, let any man consult the work of that great judge, his Commentaries upon the laws of England; but, if a man wanted to cheat his neighbor out of his estate, he should consult the doctor himself. I go a little further than Junius, although I do it with great reluctance, for I hold the book to be one of the best books in the world. I say that the observation of Junius applies to the book as much as to the judge, when, from reasons like those with which scoundrels cover their consciences, that book evades telling why the exception was made in regard to Spain and Portugal, and what those reasons were which the judge declares to be '*sufficiently obvious.*'

"This exception of the British law was *infectious*; it spread into France, whose government adopted the same provision by way of *reprisal.*"

Mr. Adams then read from Emerigon, the principal authority of French lawyers on insurance, who denies the principles of the English statute; and M. Pothier, not a mere lawyer, but a philosopher and moralist, who protests against this doctrine, and appeals to the eternal laws of morality. He then cites the second volume *Term Reports*, p. 164, in which Judge Buller states, "I have heard Lord Mansfield say that the reason of that allowance was to favor the smuggling of bullion from those countries." On which Mr. Adams remarks:

"This is the sum of the whole matter. Judge Buller heard Lord Mansfield say that the object of the exception in regard to Spain and Portugal was to encourage—yes, to *encourage*—the smuggling trade. The object was that smugglers should not only escape the effect of their villany, but should be actually encouraged by government in its perpetration.

"I think I have now established the position which I assumed, that the lawfulness of violating the revenue laws of other nations is a principle of English law,—a principle sanctioned by the Legislature and the judicial courts of Great Britain,—but one which the best elementary writers, proceeding on the great and eternal principles of morality, have condemned as a false principle; and I have thought it necessary to do this with a view to trace these frauds upon our revenue, committed by British subjects, to what I believe to be their original source in the false morality in the English Parliament and English judges. What is the natural effect of the promulgation of such principles by such authority? What can it be but to encourage frauds on the revenue of other nations? When a principle like this goes out, sanctioned with the legislative authority, it will have its effect on the nation.

"'*Quid leges sine moribus.*' The whole moral principle of a nation is contaminated by the legislative authorization and judicial sanction of a practice dishonest in itself, which necessarily includes not merely a permission, but a stimulant, to perjury. If an English merchant, subscribing to this principle, goes to establish himself in a foreign country, he goes as an enemy, warranted, by the sanction of his own courts and Parliament, to do anything that can defraud its revenue. Perhaps this may be one of the causes of the vulgar saying,—which all must have heard, but which, thank God, I still hope is not warranted by the practice of the native merchants of our country,—that custom-house oaths have no validity. There is a feeling, but too prevalent, which distinguishes between custom-house oaths and other oaths. It is obvious that smuggling can not be carried on to any extent without the commission of perjury. There must be false swearing; and it is that false swearing which the British laws have sanctioned. None of this bullion, of which Justice Buller speaks, could be smuggled out of Spain and Portugal without false oaths; and you will find, from the details of a case which I shall presently call to your attention, that false swearing is at the bottom of the frauds which this bill seeks to correct—frauds in consequence of which seven eighths of all the woollens imported into New York escaped the payment of the duty charged by law. These people do not hold themselves bound to respect our revenue laws, and thus proceed without scruples to the perpetration of perjury in order to carry on with success the evasion of them."

In the conclusion of his speech Mr. Adams paid the following tribute to the English nation, saying:

"That of the English nation he entertained sentiments of the most exalted admiration; that he was proud of being himself descended from that stock, although two hundred years had passed away, during which all his ancestors had been natives of this country. He claimed the great men of England of former ages as his countrymen, and could say with the poet Cowper, in hearty concurrence with the sentiment, that it is

'Praise enough
To fill the ambition of a common man,
That Chatham's language was his mother tongue,
And Wolfe's great name compatriot with his own.'

"He believed that no nation, of ancient or modern times, was more entitled to veneration for its exertion in the cause of human improvement than the British. He thought their code of laws admirable; but, in the discussion of the bill before the committee, he had been compelled, in the discharge of his duty, to expose one great erroneous principle of morals incorporated into their laws; a principle, the natural and necessary consequence of which had been the occasion of the bill now before the committee; a principle enacted by the British Parliament, and sanctioned by the decision of their highest judicial tribunals, with the express and avowed purpose of encouraging the subjects of Great Britain to the practice of defrauding, even by the commission of perjury, the revenues of a foreign country."

In July, 1840, a memorial was presented to Congress, from the American Philosophical Society of Philadelphia, asking the aid of government to carry on a series of magnetic and meteorological observations. This application was made in coöperation with the Royal Society of Great Britain, and at their solicitation, and had for its object an extended system of magnetic observations at fixed magnetic observatories in different quarters of the globe. Mr. Adams, having been appointed chairman of a committee on the memorial, made a report setting forth at large the motives for concurrence, and the importance of the object asked for. The following extracts illustrate his comprehensive views and appreciation of the subject:

"Among the most powerful, most wonderful, and most mysterious agents in the economy of the physical universe, is the magnet. Its attractive properties, its perpetual tendency to the poles of the earth and of the heavens, and its exclusive sympathies with one of the mineral productions of the earth, have been brought within the scope of human observation at different periods of the history of mankind, separated by the distance of many centuries from each other. The attractive power of the magnet was known in ages of antiquity so remote that it transcends even the remembrance of the name of its first discoverer, and the time of its accession to the mass of human knowledge. Its polarity, or, at least, the application of that property to the purposes of navigation beyond the sight of land, was unknown in Europe, and probably throughout the world, until the twelfth or thirteenth century of the Christian era; and its horizontal variation from the tendency directly to the pole was first perceived by Christopher Columbus, in that transcendent voyage of discovery which gave a new hemisphere to the industry and intelligence of civilized man;—an incident then so alarming to him and his company, that, but for the inflexible and persevering spirit of this intrepid and daring mariner, it would have sunk them into despair, and buried the New World for ages upon ages longer from the knowledge of the Old. Centuries have again passed away, disclosing gradually new properties of the magnet to the ardent and eager pursuit of human curiosity, still stimulated by constant observation of the phenomena connected with this metallic substance, dug from the bowels of the earth, yet seeming more and more to elude or defy all the ordinary laws of matter. Thus, in the process of observation to ascertain the horizontal variation of the needle from its polar direction, it was found that it differed in intensity in the different regions of the earth and the seas; that its variations were affected by different causes, some tending in the same direction, alternately east and west, through a succession of years, of ages, even of centuries, and others accomplishing their circle of existence from day to day, perhaps from hour to hour, or at stated hours of the day. It was found that there was a perpendicular as well as a horizontal deviation from the polar direction; and it became a matter of anxious inquiry to ascertain the intensity both of the dip and variation of the needle at every spot on the surface of the globe. It was inferred, from the different intensities of variation in different latitudes, that there were magnetic poles not coïncident with those of the earth; and the northern of these poles has been recently traced to its actual location by the British circumnavigators, Parry and Ross.

"The attractive power, the polarity, the deviations from the polar direction, horizontal and perpendicular, the varieties even of these deviations, and the detection of the northern magnetic pole, have still left materials for further observation, and suggested problems for solution to the perseverance and ingenuity of the human mind.

"In the spring of 1836 that illustrious philosopher and statesman, Baron Alexander Von Humboldt, addressed to the Duke of Sussex, then President of the Royal Society, a letter upon the means of perfecting the knowledge of terrestrial magnetism, by the establishment of magnetic stations and corresponding observations; and solicited the powerful concurrence of the Royal Society in favor of the labors then already undertaken by a learned association in Germany, and which, radiating at once from several great scientific central points in Europe, might lead progressively to the more precise knowledge of the laws of nature."

Mr. Adams then proceeds to state the subsequent proceedings of the Royal Society, and the measures the British government had taken to carry into effect the views of that society, earnestly recommending the compliance with the request of the American Philosophical Society, and adds:

"The committee would hail, with feelings of hope and encouragement, the virtual alliance of great and mighty nations for this union of efforts in the promotion of the cause of science. Long enough have the leagues and federations between the potentates of the earth been confined to alliances, offensive and defensive, to promote purposes of mutual hatred and hostility. It is refreshing to the friends of humanity to witness the rise and progress of a spirit of common and concerted inquiry into the secrets of material nature, the results of which not only go to accumulate the mass of human knowledge, but to harmonize in a community of enjoyments the varied tribes of man throughout the habitable globe. The invitation to participate in these labors, and to acquire the credit and reputation of having contributed to the beneficial results which may confidently be expected from them, is itself creditable to the character of our own country."

In conclusion, the committee recommend the adoption of a resolution, which they report, appropriating twenty thousand dollars for the establishment of five several stations for making observations on terrestrial magnetism and meteorology, conformably to the invitation of the Royal Society of Great Britain to the American Philosophical Society of Philadelphia.

In July, 1840, at the closing of the congressional session, Mr. Adams thus expressed his opinion of the state of public affairs: "The late session of Congress has been painful to me beyond all former experience, by the demonstration it has given of degenerating institutions. Parties are falling into profligate factions. I have seen this before; but the worst symptom now is the change in the manners of the people. The continuance of the present administration will, if accomplished, open wide all the floodgates of corruption. Will a change produce a reform? Pause and ponder! Slavery, the Indians, the public lands, the collection and disbursement of public moneys, the tariff, and foreign affairs—what is to become of them?"

In September, 1840, Mr. Adams remarked, on the electioneering addresses then made, preparatory to the next election of President: "This practice of itinerant speech-making has suddenly broken out in this country to a fearful extent. Electioneering for the Presidency has spread its contagion to the President himself, to his now only competitor, to his immediate predecessor, to the candidates Henry Clay and Daniel Webster, and to many distinguished members of both branches of Congress. The tendency of all this is to the corruption of popular elections both by violence and fraud."

Again, in October ensuing: "One of the peculiarities of the present time is that the principal leaders of the political parties are travelling about the country from state to state, and holding forth, like Methodist preachers, to assembled multitudes, under the broad canopy of heaven. Webster, Clay, W. C. Rives, Silas Wright, and James Buchanan, are among the first and foremost in this canvassing oratory; while Andrew Jackson, and Martin Van Buren, with his heads of departments, are harping on another string of the political accordion, by writing controversial electioneering letters. Besides the principal leaders of the parties, numerous subaltern officers of the administration are summoned to the same service, and, instead of attending to the duties of their offices, roam, recite, and madden, round the land."

In a speech made on the 28th of December, 1840, Mr. Adams severely denounced the policy pursued by the government in respect of the navy pension fund; stating that it amounted to one million two hundred thousand dollars; that, without any authority, it had been loaned to different states, and vested in their stocks, which, for the most part, were either depreciated in value, wholly lost, or unsalable. That fund, he maintained, was a sacred trust, and proceeded to state fully and at large the manner in which it had been violated without authority.

Mr. Adams then went on to state the proceedings of the Executive relative to the Smithsonian fund. He said that about the 1st of September, 1838, the sum of five hundred and nine thousand dollars had been deposited in the Mint of Philadelphia in gold,—in mint-drops;—a sacred trust, which the United States had accepted, on the pledge of their faith to keep it whole, entire, for the purpose for which it had been given by a foreigner. Within three days the five hundred thousand dollars were on their way to Arkansas to make a bank. The members of the Senate and of the House from Arkansas had a quick scent of these moneys coming into the Treasury; and care had been taken to insert into a bill for a very different object a provision authorizing the President and Secretary of the Treasury to loan to the states that sum of money when it should come into the Treasury. This was three months beforehand; and three days after the money was received the plan was carried into execution.

"Now, we had heard," said Mr. Adams, "of British gold carrying the elections, which had resulted, not in favor of the present incumbent of the presidential chair, but against him. There he could put his finger upon five hundred and nine thousand dollars of British gold, which contributed, so far as it could go, to the election of the present executive magistrate; and he thought he had shown the means by which it was done. Go to the State of Arkansas. The dollars are not there, but they *were* there, and they were sent there from the Mint of the United States. Here was policy—profound policy—economy—democracy; and all this accompanied with so great a horror at the idea of assuming state debts, that the hair of the gentlemen stood on end at the mere mention of the possibility of such a thing. Was not here a debt of the State of Arkansas of half a million of dollars? Had not the general government assumed that debt? Had they not employed trust-money? If Arkansas should declare herself insolvent to-morrow, Congress must pay that debt; they had assumed it."

About this time, Mr. Adams, in some of his writings, thus graphically illustrates the political influences which have mainly shaped the destinies of the United States: "A very curious philosophical history of parties might be made by giving a *catalogue raisonné* of the candidates for the Presidency voted for in the electoral colleges since the establishment of the constitution of the United States. It would contain a history of the influences of the presidential office. Would not the retrospect furnish practical principles concerning the operation of the constitution?—1st. That the direct and infallible path to the Presidency is military service, coupled with demagogue policy. 2d. That, in the absence of military service, demagogue policy is the first and most indispensable element of success, and the art of party drilling the second. 3d. That the drill consists in combining the Southern interest in domestic slavery with the Northern riotous democracy. 4th. That this policy and drill, first organized by Thomas Jefferson, accomplished his election, and established the Virginia dynasty of twenty-four years;—a perpetual practical contradiction of its own principles. 5th. That the same policy and drill, invigorated by success and fortified by experience, has now placed Martin Van Buren in the President's chair, and disclosed to the unprincipled ambition of the North the art of rising upon the principles of the South. And 6th. That it has exposed in broad day the overruling influence of the institution of domestic slavery upon the history and policy of the Union."

In the case of a contested election Mr. Adams remarked: "The conduct of a majority of the House has, from beginning to end, been governed by will, and not by judgment; and so I fear it will be always in every case of contested elections."

"The speech of Horace Everett, of Vermont," (made on the 8th June, 1836, on the Indian annuity bill,) said Mr. Adams, "gives a perfectly clear and distinct exposition of the origin and causes of the Florida war, and demonstrates, beyond all possibility of being gainsaid, that the wrong of the war is on our side. It depresses the spirits, and humiliates the soul, that this war is now running into its fifth year, has cost thirty millions of dollars, has successively baffled and disgraced all our chief military generals,—Gaines, Scott, Jesup, and Macomb,—and that our last resources now are bloodhounds and no quarter. Sixteen millions of Anglo-Saxons unable to subdue, in five years, by force and by fraud, by secret treachery and by open war, sixteen hundred savage warriors! There is a disregard of all appearance of right, in our transactions with the Indians, which I feel as a cruel disparagement of the honor of my country."

On the 1st of January, 1841, Mr. Adams, referring to the accounts he had received that the attendance at the Presidential levees was much smaller than usual, and that the visitors were chiefly from among the President's old adversaries, the Whigs, remarked:

"'*Donec eris felix multos numerabis amicos Tempora si fuerint nubila solus eris.*'

There is, perhaps, no occasion in human affairs," he added, "which more uniformly exemplifies this propensity of human nature than the exit of a President of the United States from office."

On the 4th of February, 1841, there arose, incidentally, in the House of Representatives, a debate upon the act to suppress duelling. Mr. Wise, of Virginia, had said, in the course of a former debate: "The anti-duelling law is producing its bitter fruits. It is making this house a bear-garden. We have an example in the present instance. Here, with permission of the chair and committee, and without a call to order from anybody, we see and hear one member (Mr. Johnson) say to another (Mr. Duncan) that he had been branded as a coward on this floor. The other says back that 'he is a liar!' And, sir, there the matter will stop. There will be no fight." Before proceeding to comment, Mr. Adams called for the reading of this statement, as reported in the *National Intelligencer*. On which Mr. Wise said publicly, in the house, "That is a correct report."[45]

After this acknowledgment, Mr. Adams proceeded to remark with severity on this statement and language, occasioning an excitement in the house, particularly among the duellists, which belongs to the history of the period. After stating that he understood that statement and language "as maintaining that duelling, between members of this house, for matters passing within this house, is a practice that ought not to be suppressed," he continued: "I maintain the contrary; and I maintain it for the independence of this house, for my own independence, for the independence of those with whom I act, for the independence of the members from the Northern section of this country, who not only abhor duelling in theory, but in practice; in consequence of which members from other sections are perpetually insulting them on this floor, under the impression that the insult will not be resented."

Here Mr. Campbell, of South Carolina, as the reporter states, called Mr. Adams to order. The chairman said something, of which not a word could be heard, the house being in such a state of tempestuous uproar. When the voice of Mr. Adams again caught the ear of the reporter, he was proceeding as follows:

"Would you smother discussion on the duelling law? There is not a point in the affairs of this nation more important than this very practice of duelling,—considered as a point of honor in one part of the Union, and a point of infamy in another,—with its consequences. I say there is no more important subject that can go forth, North and South, East and West; and I therefore take my issue upon it. I have come here determined to do so between the different portions of this house, in order to see whether this practice is to be continued; whether the members from that section of the Union whose principles are against duelling are to be insulted, upon every topic of discussion, because it is supposed that the insult will not be resented, and that 'there will be no fight.'"

Mr. Adams here called for the reading of "the act to suppress duelling;" which the clerk having read, he proceeded:

"I was going on to say that the reason why I had brought this subject into the discussion is because it is most intimately connected with all the transactions in this house and this nation; and because I think it time to settle this question between the duellists and non-duellists, whoever they may be. I say that, in consequence of my principles, and what I believe to be the principles of a very large portion of the people in that part of the country from which I came, I will not, as regards the approaching administration, put myself under

106

the lead of any man who considers the duelling law in this district as having borne any bitter fruits whatever. It may not, indeed, be sufficiently potent in its operation to prevent the thirst for blood which follows offensive words; but I believe it has prevented, and will prevent, any such occurrences as we have witnessed here. But, as it bears upon the affairs of the nation, I am not willing to sit any longer here, and see other members from my own section of the country, or those who may be my successors here, made subject to any such law as the law of the duellist. I am unwilling that they should not have full freedom of speech in this house on all occasions—as much so as the primest duellist in the land. I do not want to hear perpetual intimations, when a man from one part of the country means to insult another coming from other parts of the country, as, 'I am ready to answer here or elsewhere;' and 'The gentleman knows where I am to be found;' saying, as the gentleman from Maryland (Mr. W. C. Johnson) did just now, that he would call to account any person who dared make allusion to what had taken place between him and another member of this house. I do not intend to hear that any more, for myself or others, if I can help it. Therefore I move to bring the matter up for full discussion here, whether we are to be twitted and taunted with remarks that a man is ready to meet us here or elsewhere. It goes to the independence of this house; it goes to the independence of every individual member of this house; it goes to the right of speech and freedom of debate in this house; and I felt myself bound to bear my testimony in the most decided manner against the practice of duelling, or anything in the shape of even a virtual challenge taking place in this house, now and forever. If the committee think proper to put me down, after a debate of three weeks, involving almost every topic under the sun, and in which not one man has been called to order, I must submit. It shall go out to the country, and I am willing that the sober sentiment of the whole nation shall be my final judge on this subject."

Mr. Adams, after having recapitulated his course of proceedings on various topics, and explained his motives and their relations on former occasions, and his present general views on those subjects, closes his remarks on duelling by declaring that what he had said had been from motives of pure public spirit, with no disposition to offend any gentleman, and least of all the gentleman from Virginia (Mr. Wise); but that he had felt it his duty to say what he had said, because he believed that the application of the principle of duelling, as regards different portions of this house, is such that it must be discarded; that duelling must be considered as a crime, and that it must not be countenanced by professions of any necessity for its existence.

In January and March, 1841, Mr. Adams delivered his celebrated argument before the Supreme Court of the United States, in the case of the United States, appellants, against Cinque and others, appellees. This was afterwards published at length. In it he publicly arraigned before that court and the civilized world the conduct of the then existing administration, for having, in all their proceedings relating to these unfortunate Africans, exhibited sympathy for one of the parties, and antipathy for the other; sympathy for the white, antipathy to the black; sympathy for the slaveholders, in place of protection for the unfortunate and oppressed. It is impossible by any abstract or outline to do justice to the laborious ability with which this argument is sustained. The just severity with which he scrutinizes the proceedings of the Executive and the demands of the Spanish Minister, the completeness with which he vindicates for these Africans their right to freedom,—the extensive research into the law of nations, and the broad principles of eternal justice, on which he supports their claim to be liberated, were probably not excelled by any public effort at that period, whether of the bar or the senate. He concluded with the following touching reminiscences of distinguished members of the bench and the bar, with whom in former times he had been associated:

"May it please your honors: On the 7th of February, 1804, now more than thirty-seven years past, my name was entered, and yet stands recorded, on both the rolls, as one of the attorneys and counsellors of this court. Five years later, in February and March, 1809, I appeared for the last time before this court, in defence of the cause of justice and of important rights, in which many of my fellow-citizens had property to a large amount at stake. Very shortly afterwards I was called to the discharge of other duties, first in distant lands, and in later years within our own country, but in different departments of her government. Little did I imagine that I should ever again be required to claim the right of appearing in the capacity of an officer of this court; yet such has been the dictate of my destiny, and I appear again to plead the cause of justice, and now of liberty and life, in behalf of many of my fellow-men, before that same court which, in a former age, I had addressed in support of rights of property. I stand again, I trust for the last time, before the same court. '*Hic cæstus, artemque repono.*' I stand before the same court, but not before the same judges, nor aided by the same associates, nor resisted by the same opponents. As I cast my eyes along those seats of honor and of public trust now occupied by you, they seek in vain for one of those honored and honorable persons whose indulgence listened then to my voice. Marshall, Cushing, Chase, Washington, Johnson, Livingston, Todd,—where are they? Where is that eloquent statesman and learned lawyer who was my associate counsel in the management of that cause, Robert Goodloe Harper? Where is that brilliant luminary, so long the pride of Maryland and of the American bar, then my opposing counsel, Luther Martin? Where is the excellent clerk of that day, whose name has been inscribed on the shores of Africa as a monument of his abhorrence of the African slave-trade, Elias B. Caldwell? Where is the marshal—where are the criers of the court? Alas! where is one of the very judges of the court, arbiter of life and death, before whom I commenced this anxious argument, even now prematurely closed? Where are they all? Gone—gone—all gone! Gone from the services which in their day and generation they faithfully tendered to their country. From the excellent characters which they sustained in life, so far as I have had the means of knowing, I humbly hope, and fondly trust, they have gone to receive the rewards of blessedness on high.

"In taking, then, my final leave of this bar, and of this honorable court, I can only ejaculate a fervent petition to Heaven that every member of it may go to his final account with as little of earthly frailty to answer for as those illustrious dead; and that every one, after the close of a long and virtuous career in this world, may be received at the portals of the next with the approving sentence, 'Well done, good and faithful servant; enter thou into the joy of thy Lord.'"

CHAPTER XII.

WILLIAM HENRY HARRISON PRESIDENT OF THE UNITED STATES.— HIS DEATH.— VICE-PRESIDENT JOHN TYLER SUCCEEDS.—REMARKS OF MR. ADAMS ON THE OCCASION.—HIS SPEECH ON THE CASE OF ALEXANDER M'LEOD.—HIS VIEWS CONCERNING COMMONPLACE BOOKS.—HIS LECTURE ON CHINA AND CHINESE COMMERCE.—REMARKS ON THE STATE OF THE COUNTRY, AND HIS DUTY IN RELATION TO IT.—HIS PRESENTATION OF A PETITION FOR THE DISSOLUTION OF THE UNION, AND THE VOTE TO CENSURE HIM FOR DOING IT.—HIS THIRD REPORT ON MR. SMITHSON'S BEQUEST.—HIS SPEECH ON THE MISSION TO MEXICO.

On the 4th of March, 1841, William Henry Harrison, of Ohio, was inaugurated President of the United States, and John Tyler, of Virginia, Vice-President; each of whom had two hundred and thirty-four out of two hundred and ninety-four votes,—the whole number,—and Martin Van Buren, the only other candidate for the Presidency, had sixty. Mr. Adams remarked that this inauguration was celebrated with demonstrations of popular feeling unexampled since that of Washington, in 1789, and at the same time with so much order and tranquillity that not the slightest symptom of conflicting passions occurred to disturb the enjoyments of the day. Many thousands of people from the adjoining, and considerable numbers from distant states, were assembled to witness the ceremony.

On the 4th of April, 1841,—precisely one calendar month after his inauguration,— President Harrison died. On this occasion Mr. Adams thus expressed himself:

"The first impression of this event here, where it occurred, is of the frailty of all human enjoyments, and the awful vicissitudes woven into the lot of mortal man. He had reached, but one short month since, the pinnacle of honor and power in his own country. He lies a lifeless corpse in the palace provided by his country for his abode. He was amiable and benevolent. Sympathy for his suffering and his fate is the prevailing sentiment of his fellow-citizens. The bereavement and distress of his family are felt intensely, albeit they are strangers here, and known scarcely to any one.

"The influence of this event upon the condition and history of the country can scarcely be foreseen. It makes the Vice-President of the United States, John Tyler, of Virginia, acting President of the Union for four years, less one month.

"Tyler is a political sectarian, of the slave-driving, Virginian, Jeffersonian school; principled against all improvement; with all the interests and passions and vices of slavery rooted in his moral and political constitution; with talents not above mediocrity, and a spirit incapable of expansion to the dimensions of the station on which he has been cast by the hand of Providence, unseen, through the apparent agency of chance. To that benign and healing hand of Providence I trust, in humble hope of the good which it always brings forth out of evil. In upwards of half a century this is the first instance of a Vice-President being called to act as President of the United States, and brings to the test that provision of the constitution which places in the executive chair a man never thought of for it by anybody.

"Tyler deems himself qualified to perform the duties and exercise the powers and office of President, on the death of President Harrison, without any other oath than that which he has taken as Vice-President; yet, as doubts might arise, and for greater caution, he will take and subscribe the oath as President. May the blessing of Heaven upon this nation attend and follow this providential revolution in its government! For the present it is not joyous, but grievous.

"The moral condition of this country is degenerating, and especially through the effect of that part of its constitution which is organized by the process of unceasing elections. The spirit of the age and country is to accumulate power in the hands of the multitude: to shorten terms of service in high public places; to multiply elections, and diminish executive power; to weaken all agencies protective of property, or repressive of crime; to abolish capital punishments and imprisonment for debt. Slavery, intemperance, land-jobbing, bankruptcy, and sundry controversies with Great Britain, constitute the materials for the history of John Tyler's administration. But the improvement of the condition of man will form no part of his policy, and the improvement of his country will be an object of his most inveterate and inflexible opposition."

In September, 1841, one Alexander McLeod was imprisoned at Lockport, in the State of New York, under an indictment for murder. The following circumstances were the occasion of these proceedings. A steamer, called the Caroline, owned and fitted out at Buffalo, had been engaged in aiding certain insurgents against the Canadian government with military apparatus and provisions; and an expedition, sent by the British authorities, had cut the Caroline out of the port of Buffalo, set her on fire, and sent her floating over the Niagara Falls. In the fight which occurred one of the men on board the Caroline was killed.

The excitement was general and excessive throughout the State of New York. McLeod was the leader in this expedition, and having, after the lapse of some time, visited that state, he was arrested, imprisoned, indicted, and the popular voice was clamorous that he should be *hanged*. Notwithstanding the British government had declared that he had acted under their authority as a military man, simply obeying the order of his superiors, a like state of feeling and purpose had extended to Congress, and a resolution had been introduced requesting the President to inform the House "whether any officer of the army, or the Attorney-General, had been directed to visit the State of New York for any purpose connected with the imprisonment or trial of Alexander McLeod; or whether, by any executive measures, the British government had been given to understand that McLeod would be released."

Fearing that the result of these proceedings might lead to a great and most formidable issue of peace and war between the United States and Great Britain, Mr. Adams took this occasion to express his views on the subject.

"The first question which occurs to me is," he said, "what is the object of this resolution, and for what purpose has the house been agitated with it from the commencement of the session to this day? The gentleman who offered it has disclaimed all party purposes; he breathes in a lofty atmosphere, elevated high above that of party. But what sort of comprehension had both the friends and the opponents of the resolution put upon it? No party complexion! O, no! No; it was patriotism—pure patriotism—patriotism pure and undefiled! Well; I am disposed to give gentlemen on all sides of the house credit for whatever patriotism they profess; but sure it is that patriotism is a coat of many colors, and suited to very different complexions; and, if it had not been for that unqualified profession of patriotism and no party, which had rung through this house, from every gentleman who had supported this resolution, I should have felt bound to believe it the rankest party measure that ever was introduced into this house.

"What is the object of this resolution? It is to make an issue with Great Britain—an issue of right or wrong—upon the affair of burning the Caroline. No, sir; never shall my voice be for going to war upon that issue. I will not go to war upon an issue upon which, when we go to a third power to arbitrate upon it, they will say we are wrong. The issue will be decided against us. We shall be told it is not the thing for us to quarrel about.

"I have not the time, were I possessed of the information, to give a history of the affair of the Caroline; and it is known as much to every member of the house as it is to me. We have heard a great deal of talk about territorial rights, and independence, and of state rights. But, in a question of that kind, other nations do not look much to your state rights nor to your independence questions. They will not talk of your independence; but they will say who is right, and who is wrong. Who struck the first blow? I take it, will be the main question with them. I take it that in the late affair the Caroline was in hostile array against the British government, and that the parties concerned in it were employed in acts of war against it; and I do not subscribe to the very learned opinion of the Chief Justice of the State of New York (not, I hear, the Chief Justice, but a Judge of the Supreme Court of that state), that there was no act of war committed. Nor do I subscribe to it that every nation goes to war only on issuing a declaration or proclamation of war. This is not the fact. Nations often wage war for years without issuing any declaration of war. The question is here not upon a declaration of war, but acts of war. And I say that, in the judgment of all impartial men of other nations, *we* shall be held as a nation responsible; that the Caroline there was in a state of war against Great Britain; for purposes of war, and the worst kind of war,—to sustain an insurrection—I will not say rebellion, because rebellion is a crime, and because I heard them talked of as 'patriots.' Yes; and I have heard, in the course of the discussion here, these patriots represented as carrying on a righteous cause, and that we ought to have assisted them; that we ought to have given them that assistance that a nation fighting for its liberty is entitled to from the generosity of other nations. Well, admit that merely for a moment. If we were bound to do it, we were bound to do it avowedly and above-board. But we disclaimed all intention of taking any part in it; and yet there was very little disguise about this expedition, and that this vessel was there for the purposes of hostility against the Canadian government. I say, therefore, that we struck the first blow; and if, instead of pressing this matter to a war, we were to refer it to a third power, even if it should be to a European republic,—if any such thing is remaining,—and should say there had been an invasion of our territory, they would ask us a question something like that which was put to a character in a play of Molière: *Que diable allait il faire dans cette galère?*—What the devil had we to do in that galley?

"Now, I think the arbitrator would say, "What the devil had you to do with that steamboat?" He would say that we struck the first blow. Now, admit that,—and none of your state rights men can deny it,—admit that, and all the rest follows of course. They will say it was wrong—abstractly, if you please. Talking of abstractions, it was wrong for an expedition to come over and burn the steamboat, and send her over the falls. But what was your steamboat about? What had she been doing? What was she to do the next morning? And what ought you to do? You have reparation to make for all the men, and for all the arms and implements of war, which we were transporting, and going to transport, to the other side, to foment and instigate rebellion in Canada. That is what the third party would say to us. And it would come, in the end, after all the blood and treasure had been wasted by a war between the two countries, to this, that we must shake hands and drink champagne together, after having made a mutual apology for mutual transgression. That is the way things are settled between individuals,—'If you said so, why, I said so,'—and thus the dispute is amicably settled. So we should have to do with this national matter; for there is not any great difference in the essentials of quarrelling and making up between nations and individuals."

Mr. Adams then proceeded to another point of view in which he objected to this resolution. He said:

"A prodigious affair has been made of this matter, as if the government of the United States had outraged the State of New York, because the great empire State of New York had undertaken to say that she would *hang* McLeod, whatever Great Britain or the general government might do. Yes; whatever they might do, the great empire State of New York would *hang* McLeod! That was the language.

"What, sir, I ask, is the object of this resolution? To inquire of the President of the United States whether any officer of the army, or the Attorney-General of the United States, since the 4th of March last, has visited the State of New York for any purpose connected with the trial of Alexander McLeod. What then? Has not the President a right to send the Attorney-General to New York on that or any other subject? Where is the constitutional provision prohibiting him from sending the Attorney-General to New York on that or any other of the subjects which are before the judicial courts of that state? Yes, the Attorney-General has been sent there, and we have his instructions. And I have heard here, on the part of some of my forty friends from New York, a great deal about the conscious dignity and honor of this *Empire State* of New York. I am not very fond of that term 'empire state,' in the language of this Union; and I say that if there is an 'empire state' in the Union, it is Delaware. To be magniloquent, and talk about the empire state, may well become the forty gentlemen who represent the state on this floor, having reference to their own numbers, and the numbers of their constituents, or to the extent, fertility, and beauty, of her soil; yet this is a distinction not recognized in the constitution of the United States. They are all, as members of this Union, equal, and the State of Delaware has as good a right to be called the 'empire state' as New York. Now, if my forty friends from New York choose to call it the 'empire state,' I will not quarrel with them. It is only as to consequences that I enter my caveat against the too frequent use of those terms on this floor; for there is meaning in those words, 'empire state,' when used among co-estates, more than meets the ear.

"Suppose that it was in Delaware that such an event had occurred; do you suppose my friend here (Mr. Rodney) from Delaware would have offered such a resolution as this? And, by the terms of the resolution, I should presume my friends from New York think there is a little more dignity and power in forty representatives than only one."

In September, 1841, a plan for a newly-invented Commonplace Book, as an improvement upon Locke's, was brought to Mr. Adams for his recommendatory notice; which he declined, from a general rule he had adopted on the subject, but said he thought it might be very useful, if a practical system of such a manual could be simplified to the intellect and industry of common minds, which he doubted. "I had occupied and amused a long life," said he, "in the search of such a compendious wisdom-box, but without being able to find or make it. I had made myself more than one of Locke's Commonplace Books, but never used any one of them. I had learnt and practised Byrom's Shorthand Writing, but no one could read it but myself. I had kept accounts by double entry,—day-book, journal, and ledger, with cash-book, bank-book, house-book, and letter-book. I had made extracts, copies, translations, and quotations, more perhaps than other man living, without ever being able to pack up my knowledge or my labors in any methodical order; and now doubt whether I might not have employed my time more profitably in some one great, well-compacted, comprehensive pursuit, adapting every hour of labor to the attainment of some great end."

In December, 1841, Mr. Adams delivered before the Massachusetts Historical Society a lecture on the war then existing between Great Britain and China. The principles stated and maintained in that lecture were so much in advance of the opinions entertained at the time, that it is believed to have been published in but a single newspaper in this country or in Europe, and never in a pamphlet form, except by the proprietors of the *Chinese Repository*, published in Macao, China, in May, 1842. Though his views were ridiculed or repudiated by many when delivered, they are at this day acknowledged; and are made some of the chief grounds of the justification of that invasion of the Chinese empire now apparently in successful progress. The subject is of preëminent importance, and is canvassed with that laborious research and independence eminently characteristic of the author.

In this lecture, after controverting the doctrine of an eminent French writer, who contended that there was no such thing as international law, and that the word law is not applicable to the obligations incumbent upon nations, on the ground that law is a rule of conduct prescribed by a superior; and that nations, being independent, acknowledge no superior, and have no common sovereign from whom they can receive law,—Mr. Adams proceeds to maintain that "by the law of nations is to be understood, not one code of laws, binding alike on all the nations of the earth, but a system of rules varying according to the character and condition of the parties concerned." There is a law of nations, among Christian communities, which is the law recognized by the constitution of the United States as obligatory upon them in their intercourse with European states and colonies. But we have a different law of nations regulating our intercourse with the Indian tribes on this continent; another, between us and the woolly-headed natives of Africa; another, with the Barbary powers; another, with the flowery land, or Celestial empire. This last is the nation with which Great Britain is now at war. Then, reasoning on the rights of property, established by labor, by occupancy, and by compact, he maintains that the right of exchange, barter,—in other words, of commerce,—necessarily follows; that a state of nature among men is a state of peace; the pursuit of happiness man's natural right; that it is the duty of men to contribute as much as is in their power to one another's happiness, and that there is no other way by which they can so well contribute to the comfort and well-being of one another as by commerce, or the mutual exchange of equivalents. These views and principles he thus illustrates:

"The duty of commercial intercourse between nations is laid down in terms sufficiently positive by Vattel, but he afterwards qualifies it by a restriction, which, unless itself restricted, annuls it altogether. He says that, although the general duty of commercial intercourse is incumbent upon nations, yet every nation may exclude any particular branch or article of trade which it may deem injurious to its own interest. This cannot be denied. But, then, a nation may multiply these particular exclusions, until they become general, and equivalent to a total interdict of commerce; and this, time out of mind, has been the inflexible policy of the Chinese empire. So says Vattel, without affixing any note of censure upon it. Yet it is manifestly incompatible with the position which he had previously laid down, that commercial intercourse between nations is a moral obligation incumbent upon them all.

"The empire of China is said to extend over three hundred millions of human beings. It is said to cover a space of seven millions of square miles—about four times larger than the surface of these United States. The people are not Christians, nor can a Christian nation appeal to the principles of a common faith to settle the question of right and wrong between them. The moral obligation of commercial intercourse between nations is founded entirely and exclusively upon the Christian precept to love your neighbor as yourself. With this principle, you cannot refuse commercial intercourse with your neighbor, because, commerce consisting of a voluntary exchange of property mutually beneficial to both parties, excites in both the selfish and the social propensities, and enables each of the parties to promote the happiness of his neighbors by the same act whereby he provides for his own. But, China not being a Christian nation, its inhabitants do not consider themselves bound by the Christian precept to love their neighbors as themselves. The right of commercial intercourse with them reverts not to the execrable principle of Hobbes, that the state of nature is a state of war, where every one has a right to buy, but no one is obliged to sell. Commerce becomes altogether a matter of convention. The right of each party is only to propose; that of the other is to accept or refuse, and to his result he may be guided exclusively by the consideration of his own interest, without regard to the interests, the wishes, or other wants, of his neighbor.

"This is a churlish and unsocial system; and I take occasion here to say that whoever examines the Christian system of morals with a philosophical spirit, setting aside all the external and historical evidences of its truth, will find all its precepts tending to exalt the nature of the animal man; all its purpose to be peace on earth and good will towards men. Ask the atheist, the deist, the Chinese, and they will tell you that the foundation of their system of morals is selfish enjoyment. Ask the philosophers of the Grecian schools,—

112

Epicurus, Socrates, Zeno, Plato, Lucretius, Cicero, Seneca,—and you will find them discoursing upon the Supreme Good. They will tell you it is pleasure, ease, temperance, prudence, fortitude, justice: not one of them will whisper the name of love, unless in its gross and physical sense, as an instrument of pleasure; not one of them will tell you that the source of all moral relation between you and the rest of mankind is to love your neighbor as yourself—to do unto him as you would that he should do unto you.

"The Chinese recognize no such law. Their internal government is a hereditary patriarchical despotism, and their own exclusive interest is the measure of all their relations with the rest of mankind. Their own government is founded upon the principle that as a nation they are superior to the rest of mankind. They believe themselves and their country especially privileged over all others; that their dominion is the celestial empire, and their territory the flowery land.

"The fundamental principle of the Chinese empire is anti-commercial. It is founded entirely upon the second and third of Vattel's general principles, to the total exclusion of the first. It admits no obligation to hold commercial intercourse with others. It utterly denies the equality of other nations with itself, and even their independence. It holds itself to be the centre of the terraqueous globe,—equal to the heavenly host,—and all other nations with whom it has any relations, political or commercial, as outside tributary barbarians, reverently submissive to the will of its despotic chief. It is upon this principle, openly avowed and inflexibly maintained, that the principal maritime nations of Europe for several centuries, and the United States of America from the time of their acknowledged independence, have been content to hold commercial intercourse with the empire of China.

"It is time that this enormous outrage upon the rights of human nature, and upon the first principle of the rights of nations, should cease. These principles of the Chinese empire, too long connived at and truckled to by the mightiest Christian nations of the civilized world, have at length been brought into conflict with the principles and the power of the British empire; and I cannot forbear to express the hope that Britain, after taking the lead in the abolition of the African slave-trade and of slavery, and of the still more degrading tribute to the Barbary African Mahometans, will extend her liberating arm to the furthest bound of Asia, and at the close of the present contest insist upon concluding the peace upon terms of perfect equality with the Chinese empire, and that the future commerce shall be carried on upon terms of equality and reciprocity between the two communities parties to the trade, for the benefit of both; each retaining the right of prohibition and of regulation, to interdict any article or branch of trade injurious to itself, as for example the article of opium, and to secure itself against the practices of fraudulent traders and smugglers. This is the truth, and I apprehend the only question at issue between the governments and nations of Great Britain and China. It is a general, but I believe altogether a mistaken opinion, that the quarrel is merely for certain chests of opium, imported by British merchants into China, and seized by the Chinese government for having been imported contrary to law. This is a mere incident to the dispute, but no more the cause of war than the throwing overboard of the tea in Boston harbor was the cause of the North American Revolution.

"The cause of the war is the pretension on the part of the Chinese that in all their intercourse with other nations, political or commercial, their superiority must be implicitly acknowledged, and manifested in humiliating forms. It is not creditable to the great, powerful, and enlightened nations of Europe, that for several centuries they have, for the sake of a profitable trade, submitted to these insolent and insulting pretensions, equally contrary to the first principles of the law of nature and of revealed religion—the natural equality of mankind—

"'*Auri sacra fames, quid non mortalia pectora cogis?*'

"This submission to insult is the more extraordinary for being practised by Christian nations, which, in their intercourse with one another, push the principle of equality and reciprocity to the minutest punctilios of form."

This lecture concludes with a sketch of the treatment of Lord Macartney by the Chinese emperor, in 1792, when sent to that court as ambassador from Great Britain, illustrating and supporting its general argument. The remarks of Mr. Adams upon the distinction with a very small difference between "the bended knee" and "entire prostration," as a token of homage,—admitted as to the first, denied as to the last, by the British ambassador,—are characteristic.

"The narrative of Sir George Staunton distinctly and positively affirms that Lord Macartney was admitted to the presence of the Emperor Kienlung, and presented to him his credentials, without performing the prostration of the Kotow—the Chinese act of homage from the vassal to the sovereign lord. Ceremonies between superiors and inferiors are the personification of principles. Nearly twenty-five years after the repulse of Lord Macartney, in 1816, another splendid embassy was despatched by the British government, in the person of Lord Amherst, who was much more rudely dismissed, without even being admitted to the presence of the emperor, or passing a single hour at Pekin. A Dutch embassy instituted shortly after the failure of that of Lord Macartney, fared no better, although the ambassador submitted with a good grace to the prostration of the Kotow. A philosophical republican may smile at the distinction by which a British nobleman saw no objection to delivering his credentials on the bended knee, but could not bring his stomach to the attitude of entire prostration. In the discussion which arose between Lord Amherst and the celestials on this question, the Chinese, to a man, insisted inflexibly that Lord Macartney had performed the Kotow; and Kiaking, the successor of Kienlung, who had been present at the reception of Lord Macartney, personally pledged himself that he had seen his lordship in that attitude. Against the testimony to the fact of the imperial witness in person, it may well be conjectured how impossible it was for the British noble to maintain his position, which was, after all, of small moment. The bended knee, no less than the full prostration to the ground, is a symbol of homage from an inferior to a superior, and if not equally humiliating to the performer, it is only because he has been made familiar by practice with one, and not with the other. In Europe, the bended knee is exclusively appropriated to the relations of sovereign and subject; and no representative of any sovereign in Christendom ever bends his knee in presenting his credentials to another. But the personal prostration of the ambassador before the emperor was, in the Chinese principle of exaction, symbolical not only of the acknowledgment of subjection, but of the fundamental law of the empire prohibiting all official intercourse upon a footing of equality between the government of China and the government of any other nation. All are included under the general denomination of outside barbarians: and the commercial intercourse with the maritime or navigating nations is maintained through the exclusive monopoly of the Hong merchants."

At the opening of the session of Congress, on the 3d of December, 1841, Mr. Adams thus wrote concerning his own course and the country's prospects:

"Between the obligation to discharge my duty to the country and the obvious impossibility of accomplishing anything for the improvement of its condition by legislation, my deliberate judgment warns me to a systematic adherence to inaction upon all the controverted topics which cannot fail to be brought into debate. Upon the rule-question (that is, refusing to receive or refer petitions on the subject of slavery) I cannot be silent, but shall be left alone, as heretofore. I await the opening of the session with great anxiety; more from an apprehension of my own imprudence than from a belief that the fortunes of the country will be much affected, for good or evil, by anything that will be done. There is neither spotless integrity nor consummate ability at the helm of the ship, and she will be more than ever the sport of winds and waves, drifting between breakers and quicksands. May the wise and good Disposer send her home in safety!"

On the 24th of January, 1842, Mr. Adams presented the petition of forty-five citizens of Haverhill, Massachusetts, praying that Congress would immediately take measures peaceably to dissolve the Union of these States. 1st. Because no Union can be agreeable which does not present prospects of reciprocal benefits. 2d. Because a vast proportion of the resources of one section of the Union is annually drained to sustain the views and course of another section, without any adequate return. 3d. Because, judging from the history of past nations, that Union, if persisted in, in the present course of things, will certainly overwhelm the whole nation in utter destruction. Mr. Adams moved that the petition be referred to a select committee, with instructions to report an answer showing the reasons why the prayer of it ought not to be granted.

The excitement the presentation of this petition produced was immediate and intense. Mr. Hopkins, of Virginia, moved to burn it in presence of the house. Mr. Wise, of the same state, asked the speaker if it was in order to move to censure any member for presenting such a petition. Mr. Gilmer, also of Virginia, moved a resolution, that Mr. Adams, for presenting such a petition, had justly incurred the censure of the house. Mr. Adams said that he hoped the resolution would be received and discussed. A desultory debate ensued, and was continued until the house adjourned. A caucus was immediately held by the opponents of Mr. Adams among the representatives from the South and West, to take measures to effect his expulsion. It was feared that the two thirds vote requisite to expel a member could not be obtained. Three resolutions were therefore prepared, the adoption of which it was deemed would in popular effect be equivalent to an expulsion. Thomas F. Marshall, of Kentucky, consented to present them the next day. The consideration of these resolutions, which continued until the 5th of February, produced a series of as violent and personal debates as perhaps the halls of Congress ever witnessed. They were in these words:

"WHEREAS, The federal constitution is a permanent form of government, and of perpetual obligation, until altered or modified in the mode pointed out in that instrument; and the members of this House, deriving their political character and powers from the same, are sworn to support it; and the dissolution of the Union necessarily implies the destruction of that instrument, the overthrow of the American republic, and the extinction of our national existence: a proposition, therefore, to the representatives of the people, to dissolve the organic laws framed by their constituents, and to support which they are commanded by those constituents to be sworn before they can enter into the execution of the political powers created by it and intrusted to them, is a high breach of privilege, a contempt offered to this House, a direct proposition to the legislature and each member of it to commit perjury, and involving necessarily in its execution and its consequences the destruction of our country, and the crime of high treason.

"*Resolved, therefore,* That the Honorable John Quincy Adams, member from Massachusetts, in presenting for the consideration of the House of Representatives of the United States a petition praying for the dissolution of the Union, has offered the deepest indignity to the House of which he is a member, an insult to the people of the United States, of which that House is the legislative organ; and will, if this outrage be permitted to pass unrebuked and unpunished, have disgraced his country, through their representatives, in the eyes of the whole world.

"*Resolved, further,* That the aforesaid John Quincy Adams, for this insult, the first of the kind ever offered to the government, and for the wound which he has permitted to be aimed, through his instrumentality, at the constitution and existence of his country, the peace, the security, and liberty of the people of these States, might well be held to merit expulsion from the national councils; and the House deem it an act of grace and mercy when they only inflict upon him their severest censure for conduct so utterly unworthy of his past relations to the state, and his present position. This they hereby do, for the maintenance of their own purity and dignity. For the rest, they turn him over to his own conscience, and the indignation of all true American citizens."

The scene which occurred, on their presentation, is thus graphically described in the newspapers of the day:

"On the 25th of January, the whole body of Southerners came into the House, apparently resolved to crush Mr. Adams and his cause forever. They gathered in groups, conversed in deep whispers, and the whole aspect of their conduct at twelve o'clock indicated a conspiracy portending a revolution. Thomas F. Marshall, of Kentucky, rose, and, having asked and received of Mr. Gilmer leave to offer a substitute for his resolution of censure which was pending at the adjournment, presented the three prepared resolutions. He assumed a manner and tone as if he felt the historical importance of his position; spoke with great coolness and solemnity,—a style wholly unusual with him; assumed a solemn, magisterial air, and judicial elevation, as if he thought, in the insolence of his conceit, that he was about to pour down the thunder of condemnation on the venerable object of his attack, as a judge pronouncing sentence on a convicted culprit, in the sight of approving men and angels. Warming somewhat with the silent, imposing attention of the vast audience before

115

whom he spoke, he expanded into an inflated exhibition of his own past relations to the object of his attack, and thus represented himself eminently qualified to act the part he had assumed of prosecutor, judge, and executioner. When he finished, the speaker announced to Mr. Adams that his position entitled him to the floor, bringing up to the imagination a parallel scene: 'Then Agrippa said unto Paul, Thou art permitted to speak for thyself.'

"Up rose, then, that bald, gray old man, his hands trembling with constitutional infirmity and age, upon whose consecrated head the vials of tyrannic wrath had been outpoured. Among the crowd of slaveholders who filled the galleries he could seek no friends, and but a few among those immediately around him. Unexcited, he raised his voice, high-keyed, as was usual with him, but clear, untremulous, and firm. In a moment his infirmities disappeared, although his shaking hand could not but be noticed: trembling not with fear, but with age. At first there was nothing of indignation in his tone, manner, or words. Surprise and cold contempt were all. But anon a flash of withering scorn struck the unhappy Marshall. A single breath blew all his mock-judicial array into air and smoke. In a tone of insulted majesty and reinvigorated spirit, Mr. Adams then said, in reply to the audacious, atrocious charge of 'high treason:' 'I call for the reading of the first paragraph of the Declaration of Independence. Read it! read it! and see what that says of the right of a people to reform, to change, and to dissolve their government.'

"The look, the tone, the gesture, of the insulted patriot, at that instant were most imposing. The voice was that of sovereign command. The burthen of seventy-five winters rolled off, and he rose above the puny things around him, who thought themselves his equals, from being his associates.

"When the passage of the Declaration was read that solemnly proclaims the right of reform, revolution, and resistance to oppression, the old man thundered out, 'Read that again!' and he looked proudly round on the listening audience, as he heard his triumphant vindication sounded forth in the glorious sentences of the revolutionary Magna Charta.

"The sympathetic revulsion of feeling was intense, though voiceless. Every drop of free, honest blood in that vast assemblage bounded with high impulse, every fibre thrilled with excitement.

"A strong exhibition of the facts in the case, mostly in cold, calm, logical, measured sentences, concluded the high appeal of Mr. Adams, from the slaveholders of the present generation to the Father of that system of revolutionary liberty with which he is the coëval and the noblest champion. And then he sat down vindicated, victorious."

Apart from the excited interest of friends, the malign aspersions of political enemies, and his own indignant response to the hollow tirade of his assailants, his defence, reduced to its elements, was simply this: that the petition was sent to him for presentation; that it was a subject for which the signers of it had a constitutional right to petition, and that in presenting it he had proposed that the committee should be instructed to report reasons why it ought not to be granted. He said that he should not enter further into his self-defence at that time, but should wait to see the action of the house upon those resolutions. But whenever the proper time for his defence should come, he pledged himself to show that "a portion of the country from which the assailants came was endeavoring to destroy the right of habeas corpus, and of trial by jury, and all the rights in which the liberties of the country consist;"—"that there was in that portion of country a systematic attempt even to carry it to the dissolution of the Union, with a continual system and purpose to destroy all the principles of civil liberty among the free states, and by power to force the detested principles of slavery on the free States of this Union;" a pledge which in the course of his subsequent argument he fully redeemed.

The last of January, Mr. Adams thus expressed himself concerning these proceedings: "My occupations during the month have been confined entirely to the business of the house, and for the last ten days to the defence of myself against an extensive combination and conspiracy, in and out of Congress, to crush the liberties of the free people of this Union, by disgracing me with the brand of censure, and displacing me from the chair of the Committee on Foreign Affairs, for my perseverance in presenting abolition petitions. I am in the midst of that fiery ordeal, and day and night absorbed in the struggle against this attempt at my ruin. God send me a good deliverance!"

Intemperate debates, with violence undiminished, succeeded, in which all the topics of party censure, from the adoption of the constitution, were collected and heaped upon Mr. Adams by Marshall, Wise, Gilmer, and others.

On the 3d of February Mr. Adams took the floor, and spoke for two hours in his own defence, with an eloquence and effect to which no description can do justice. He touched the low underplot of the Committee on Foreign Affairs with pointed severity and bitter truth, and then gave amusing particulars of missives he had received from the South threatening him with assassination. Among other kindly hints sent through the post-office was a colored lithograph portrait of himself, with the picturesque annotation of a rifle-ball on the forehead, and a promise that such a remedy "would stop his music." He alluded to these communications with perfect good nature, some of them being identical with words used towards him by Mr. Gilmer. A further account of them will be given from the correspondent of the newspapers of the day.[46]

"Among the many strange impressions of these singular scenes, nothing is more striking than the total, disgraceful ignorance which prevails as to who John Quincy Adams *is*. That he has been President of the United States, and had previously borne high offices, seems occasionally to be vaguely remembered by a few of the most intelligent of his persecutors. But of the part which he has borne for half a century in the history of America and of the world they know no more than they do of the Vedas and Puránas.

"The thread of this great discourse was his present and past relations to Virginia and Virginians. After gratefully acknowledging his infinite obligations to the great Virginians of the first age of the federal republic, he modestly and unpretendingly recounted the unsought exalted honors heaped upon him by Washington, Madison, and Monroe, and detailed with touching simplicity and force some of his leading actions in the discharge of those weighty trusts. As he went back through the historic vista of patriotic achievements, he seemed to renew his youth like the eagles, and rose into a still loftier and bolder strain than in the withering retort with which he struck down Wise and Marshall. In passing over the preliminaries of his discourse, he chanced to fix his eye on the latter, who was moving down one of the side aisles. Instantly, at the suggestion of the moment, he burst forth into a beautiful appeal to the hallowed memory of the venerated and immaculate Virginian who once bore the name of Marshall through a long career of judicial honor and usefulness. The general interest in this appeal to the past was impressive. The members of the house drew together around him; even his persecutors paid an involuntary tribute to 'the old man eloquent.'

"Lord Morpeth was an attentive spectator and auditor of these scenes of turbulence; and it was interesting to see a British statesman looking up to learn from such a source the unwritten history of his own country, as well as of Europe. For such it was, when Mr. Adams gave the history of the movements at the court of the Emperor Alexander, and his connection with them, which resulted in the Russo-British alliance and in the overthrow of Napoleon. The early-chosen favorite of Washington, the trusted counsellor of Jefferson, the much-honored agent of Madison, the guide and chief support of Monroe, the restorer of the purity of the Washingtonian epoch to the Presidential chair, and for the last ten years the bold champion of universal liberty, stood there baited by absurd charges of perjury and treason, by insignificant beings of yesterday.

"The monument of a past age, a beacon to the present, a landmark to the future, he towered above the little things around him. The beautiful poetic appeal to Virginia, with which he concluded, caused a thrill of delighted admiration in the whole assembly. The emphasis, the pathetic intonation, touched every heart. The triumph of Mr. Adams was complete."

On the eleventh day of this debate, Mr. Adams, in opening his defence, said that he had been charged by his assailant with consuming an unreasonable portion of the time of the house with his own affairs; but he thought that six days could not be deemed an extravagant requirement for the defence of a man situated as he was, when a great portion of that period had been consumed by his assailants, their associates, and others. He did not desire to be responsible for any unnecessary consumption of the hours of debate. He wished, indeed, to state the whole affair; and, to accomplish this, he should require a great deal more time. He

117

had laid out a great platform for his defence, if he was forced to continue it; but he was willing to forego it all, provided it could be done without sacrificing his rights, the rights of his constituents, and those of the petitioners. He then stated that if any gentleman would make a motion to lay the whole subject on the table, he would forbear to proceed any further with his defence. This motion was immediately made by Mr. Botts, of Virginia, and the house decided in its favor, by a vote of *one hundred and six* to *ninety-three*. The petition from Haverhill was then taken up and refused to be received; one hundred and sixty-six in the affirmative to forty in the negative.

On the 12th of April, 1842, Mr. Adams, as chairman of the committee on the Smithsonian fund, made a report in the form of a bill, the object of which was to settle three fundamental principles for the administration and management of the fund in all after time. The bill provided, First, that the principal fund should be preserved and maintained unimpaired, with an income secured upon it at the rate of six per cent. a year, from which all appropriations for the purposes of the founder should be made. Second, that the portions of the income already accrued and invested in state stocks should be constituted funds, from the annual income of which an astronomical observer, with suitable assistants, should be supported. Third, that in the future management of this fund no part of it should be applied to any institution of education, or religious establishment.

To the persevering spirit with which Mr. Adams on every occasion urged upon Congress and the people of the United States the observance of those fundamental principles which he had first asserted and which he afterwards uninterruptedly maintained, notwithstanding a local and interested opposition to them, may be justly attributed the preservation of that fund, and its subsequent application to the objects of the founder's bequest, although in his prevailing desire that an astronomical observatory should be one of them, he did not succeed. Connected with this report, all the previous proceedings in relation to it were again published, for the information of Congress and the public.

On the 14th of the same month, a bill making appropriations for the civil and diplomatic expenses of government being under consideration, Mr. Linn, of New York, moved to strike out so much of it as related to a minister to Mexico, expressing his belief that the object of this mission was to bring about the annexation of Texas. A debate ensued, which was desultory and declamatory on the part of those advocating the appropriation. Mr. Wise, of Virginia, said that the tyrant of Mexico was now at war with Texas; that he threatened to invade her territory, and never stop until he had driven slavery beyond the Sabine; and that the gentlemen opposed to the mission would let him loose his servile horde, and yet send no minister to remonstrate or to threaten. Our citizens had claims on that government to the amount of twelve or thirteen millions. Ten or a dozen of our citizens—of our own native citizens—were in degrading bondage in the mines of Mexico, or sweeping its streets; and yet a minister to Mexico was opposed because the President and a party in this country wished to annex Texas to the Union. It was not only the duty of this government to demand the liquidation of our claims and the liberation of our citizens, but to go further, and demand the non-invasion of Texas. We should at once say to Mexico, "If you strike Texas, you strike us." And if England, standing by, should dare to intermeddle and ask, "Do you take part with Texas?" his prompt answer would be, "Yes, and against you."

Mr. Ingersoll, of Pennsylvania, followed on the same side, maintaining that Texas ought to be annexed to the Union, even at the risk of a war with Great Britain. He said that he was a man of peace, and was not insensible to the evils of war, but he contended that they were greatly exaggerated. He wished the British minister to understand that war would not do us so much harm as it would his own country. In the first place, if we chose to apply the principles of war, it paid all the state debts at once,—two hundred millions of dollars. At all events, it suspended the interest during the war. We had a sufficient population, the capacity of drilling that population, and all the materials for war. There were two vessels now within the sound of his voice to which there was nothing in a British or French navy to be compared. Our lakes were covered with transporting steamboats, which could easily be made effective for harbor defence. We lived in a republican country, in an armed nation; and he would rather take this nation as it was than the most completely armed nation in the world. Having proceeded at great length in this strain, stating various particulars, some of

118

which may be gathered from Mr. Adams' reply, he concluded by challenging opposition to the opinion that there was no right of search in time of war, and that such a claim was a monstrosity. The greatest question in the world, which now agitated nearly all Christendom, was this mixed question of the slave-trade and the right of visit and search. To statements and arguments of this force and nature Mr. Adams made a scrutinizing and unanswerable reply, of which the following extract will sufficiently exhibit the power and quality.

"The gentleman from Pennsylvania began by saying that he was for peace—for universal peace. Then followed a most learned dissertation to prove that it was an entire mistake to suppose that we are not now prepared for war; and to demonstrate that a nation which goes into a war unprepared will infallibly conquer; that it must be so; that every unarmed and unprepared nation always had conquered its armed opposers. No; we are not unprepared for war,—not at all,—because we have in sight of the windows of this capitol two armed steamers; one of them, as I am informed, nearly disabled, so that she will need, in a great measure, to be rebuilt, leaving for our use, in case of immediate hostilities, one entire steamer, and with that we are to burn London; and though the gentleman readily admitted that it was possible, nay, very probable, that New York would be burnt too, yet, as London was four or five times as large, we should have a great balance of burning on our side. Yes; we were to conquer Great Britain and burn London, and we were told that it would be a very cheap price for all this to have the city of New York burnt in turn, or burnt first. And this was an argument *for peace*!

"What else did the gentlemen say? What else did he not say? He made a great argument and a valorous display of zeal in relation to the right of search. O, that—that was a point never to be conceded—no, never. He maintained that there is no such thing as a right of search—no such right in time of war, none in time of peace. Well, I do agree with the gentleman partially on that one point, so far as to believe that there is no need of our coming to an issue with Great Britain there, and we have not as yet. After reading, as I have done, and carefully examining the papers put forth on both sides, I asked myself, What is the question between us? And I have heard men of the first intelligence say that they found themselves in the very same situation. The gentleman has made a total misrepresentation of the demand of Great Britain in the matter. She has never claimed the right to search American vessels—no such thing. On the contrary, she has explicitly disclaimed any such pretension, and that to the whole extent we can possibly demand. What is it we do demand? Not that Great Britain should disclaim the right to search American vessels, but we deny her the right to board pirates who hoist the American flag. Yes; and to search British vessels, too, that have been declared to be pirates by the laws of nations, pirates by the laws of Great Britain, pirates by the laws of the United States. That is the demand of our late minister to London, whose letters are so much admired by the gentleman from Pennsylvania. Now, it happens that behind all this exceeding great zeal against the right of search is a question which the gentleman took care not to bring into view, and that is the support and perpetuation of the African slave-trade. That is the real question between the ministers of America and Great Britain: whether slave-traders, pirates, by merely hoisting the American flag, shall be saved from capture.

"I say there is no such thing as an exemption from the right of search by the laws of nations, and I challenge and defy the gentleman to produce the proof. The right of search in time of war we have never pretended to deny. Nay, we ourselves exercised that right during the last war. And the Supreme Court of the United States, in their decisions of prize cases brought before them, sustained us in doing so, and said it was lawful according to the laws of nations. And, indeed, we should have had a very poor chance in a war with Great Britain, without it.

"But what is the right of search in time of peace? And how has Congress felt, and how has the American government acted, on this point? I have some knowledge on this subject. In the year 1817, when I was about to return from England to the United States, Mr. Wilberforce, then a member of the British Parliament, very celebrated for his long and persevering exertions to suppress the African slave-trade, wrote me a note requesting an interview. I acceded promptly to his request; and in conversation he stated to me that the British government had found that without a mutual right of search between this country and that, upon the coast of Africa, it would be impossible to carry through the system she had formed in connection with the United States for the suppression of that infamous traffic. I had then just signed with my own hand a treaty declaring 'the traffic in slaves (not the African slave-trade, but THE TRAFFIC IN SLAVES) unjust and inhuman,' and in which both nations engaged to do all in their power to suppress it. Mr. Wilberforce inquired of me whether I thought that a proposal for a mutual, restricted, qualified right of search would be acceptable to the American government. I had at that time a feeling to the full as strong against the right of search, as it had then been exercised by British cruisers, as ever the gentleman from Pennsylvania (Mr. Ingersoll) had, in all his life. I had been myself somewhat involved in the question as a public man. It constituted one of the grounds of my unfortunate difference from those with whom I had long been politically associated; and it was for the exertions I had made against the admission of that right that I forfeited my place in the other end of the capitol, and, which was infinitely more painful to me, for this I had differed with men long dear to me, and to whom I had also been dear, insomuch that for a time it interrupted all friendly relations between us.

"The first thing I said, in reply to Mr. Wilberforce, was: 'No; you may as well save yourselves the trouble of making any proposals on that subject; my countrymen, I am very sure, will never assent to any such arrangement.' He then entered into an argument, the full force of which I felt, when I said to him, 'You may, if you think proper, make the proposal; but I think some other mode of getting over the difficulty must be resorted to; for the prejudices of my country are so immovably strong on that point, that I do not believe they will ever assent.'

"I returned home, and, under the administration of Mr. Monroe, I filled the office of Secretary of State; and in that capacity I was the medium through which the proposal of the British government was afterwards made to the United States to arrange a special right of search for the suppression of the slave-trade. This proposition I resisted and opposed in the cabinet with all my power. And I will say that, although I was not myself a slaveholder, I had to resist all the slaveholding members of the cabinet, and the President also. Mr. Monroe himself was always strongly inclined in favor of the proposition, and I maintained the opposite ground against him and the whole body of his official advisers as long as I could.

"At that time there was in Congress, and especially in the House, a spirit of concession, which I could not resist. From the year 1818 to the year 1823, not a session passed without some movement on this point, and some proposition made to request the President to negotiate for the mutual concession of this right of search. I resisted it to the utmost; and so earnest did the matter become, that, on one occasion, at an evening party in the President's house, in a conversation between myself and a distinguished gentleman of Virginia,—a principal leader of this movement, now living, but not now a member of this house,—words became so warm that what I said was afterwards alluded to by another gentleman of Virginia, in an address to his constituents, against my election as President of the United States. It was made an objection against me that I was an enemy to the suppression of the slave-trade. That address and my reply to it are in existence, and the latter in the hands of a gentleman of Virginia now in this house, and who can correct me if I do not state the matter correctly. The address was written, and would have been published, with an allusion to what I had said in the conversation (which the writer heard, although it was not addressed to him), but the gentleman with whom I was conversing went to him, and told him that if he did refer in print to that private conversation, he would never speak to him; and so it was suppressed. I state these facts, sir, that I may set myself right on this question of the right of search.

"At that time a gentleman, who was the leader of one of the parties in this house, had endeavored from year to year to prevail with the house to require of the President a concession of the right asked. I name him to honor him; for he was one of the most talented, laborious, eloquent, and useful men upon this floor. I allude to Charles Fenton Mercer, of Virginia. Session after session, he brought forward his resolution; and he continued to press it, until, finally, in 1823, he brought the house by yeas and nays to vote their assent to it; and, strange to say, there were but nine votes against it. The same thing took place in the other house. The joint resolution went to the President, and he accordingly

120

entered into the negotiation. It was utterly against my judgment and wishes; but I was obliged to submit, and I prepared the requisite despatches to Mr. Rush, then our minister at the court of London. When he made his proposal to Mr. Canning, Mr. Canning's reply was, 'Draw up your convention, and I will sign it.' Mr. Rush did so, and Mr. Canning, without the slightest alteration whatever,—without varying the dot of an *i*, or the crossing of a *t*,—did affix to it his signature; thus assenting to our own terms in our own language.

"The convention came back here for ratification; but, in the mean time, another spirit came over the feelings of this house, as well as of the Senate. A party had been formed against the administration of Mr. Monroe; the course of the administration was no longer favored, and the house came out in opposition to a convention drawn in conformity to its own previous views.

"But now, as I do not wish to intrude on the attention of this committee a single moment longer than is necessary, I will pass over the rest of what I might say on this subject, and recur, in a few observations, to the other war-trumpet which we have heard within the last two days.

"They unite in one purpose, though they seem to be pursuing it by different means. The gentleman from Virginia (Mr. Wise), confining his observations to our relations with Mexico, also urges us to war with the same professions of a disposition for peace as were so often repeated by the gentleman from Pennsylvania in regard to Great Britain. He does not immediately connect the questions of war with Mexico and war with Great Britain, but apparently knows and feels that they are in substance and in fact but one and the same question; and that, so surely as we rush into a war with Mexico, we shall shortly find ourselves in a war with England. The gentleman appeared entirely conscious of that; and I hope that no member of this committee will come to the conclusion that it is possible for us to have a war with Mexico without at the same time going to war with Great Britain. On that subject I will venture to say that the minister from England has no instructions. That is not one of the five points on which the gentleman from Pennsylvania tells us our controversy with England rests, and the surrendering of which is to open to that minister so easy a road to an earldom. The war with Mexico is to be produced by different means, and for different purposes. I think the gentleman from Virginia, in his speech, rested the question of the war with Mexico upon three grounds: 1st, That our citizens had claims against the Mexican government to the amount of ten or twelve millions; 2d, That some ten or twelve of our citizens had been treated with great severity, and suffered disgrace and abuse from the Mexican government, having been made slaves, and compelled to work at cleansing the streets; that these citizens were detained in servitude, while one British subject had been promptly released on the first demand of the British minister there; and, 3d, That a war with Mexico would accomplish the annexation of Texas to the Union. The gentleman was in favor of war, not merely for the abstract purpose of annexing Texas to the Union, but he was for war by peremptorily prohibiting Santa Anna from invading Texas.

"I will take up these reasons in order. And, first, as to going to war for the obtaining of these ten or twelve millions of dollars, being the claims of our own citizens on Mexico. This seems a very extraordinary reason, when, according to the doctrine of the gentleman from Pennsylvania, a state of war at once extinguishes all national debts. If we go to war with Mexico, her debts to our citizens will be expunged at once, if the doctrine of the gentleman from Pennsylvania be true. He did, to be sure, qualify the position by saying that war would at least suspend the payment of interest. If so, then it would equally suspend interest in the case of Mexico. The arguments of the two war gentlemen happen to cross each other, though they are directed to the same end. One of them will have us go to war with Mexico to recover twelve millions of dollars; the other would have us go to war with England to wipe out a debt of two hundred millions. I will not compare the arguments of the two gentlemen together; but I will say, in regard to the doctrine of the gentleman from Pennsylvania, that it has quite too much of repudiation in it for my creed. I do not think that a war with England would extinguish these two hundred millions, but that, on the contrary, Great Britain would be likely to say to us, 'We will go to war to recover the money you owe us.' That is one of the questions which we must settle if we go to war, but which we might otherwise, at least for a time, stave off. But, if we go to war, what must be the effect of the peace that follows? We must pay our two hundred millions, with the interest. As to our debt from Mexico, I believe the way to recover it is not to go to war for it; for war, besides failing to recover the money, will occasion us the loss of ten times the amount in other ways.

"As to war producing a suspension of interest on a national debt, let the gentleman look back a little to the wars of France. In 1793 France was at war with almost all the countries of Europe, and she immediately confiscated all her debts to them. But what happened thirty years after, when the reäction came? The allies took Paris, and, in the settlement which then took place, they compelled France to pay all her debts, with full interest on the whole period during which payment had been suspended. That was the consequence to France of going to war to extinguish debts. And, if we go to war with Great Britain to-morrow, she will make us, as one of the conditions of peace, pay our whole debt of two hundred millions, with interest. And what shall we gain? Spend millions upon millions every year, as long as the war continues; and, unless it is greatly successful, have to pay our debt at last, principal and interest. This would depend on the chances of war, or the issues of battle. And, as our contests would be chiefly on the ocean, we must first obtain a superiority on the seas before we can put her down and vanquish her; and this to save ourselves from the payment of two hundred millions justly due from our citizens to hers!

"There is a second reason given by the gentleman from Virginia in favor of war. He reminds us, with great warmth, that there are some ten or twelve citizens of the United States now prisoners in the city of Mexico, and dragging chains about the streets of that city; that a British subject taken with them has been liberated, while they are kept in bondage. Now, if I am correctly informed, one American citizen, a son of General Coombs, has been liberated on the application of the minister of the United States, who was as fairly a subject of imprisonment as the British subject of whom the gentleman speaks. I certainly have no objections to our minister's making such representations as he can in favor of the release of citizens of the United States, although taken in actual war against Mexico, in association with Texian forces; but I am not prepared to go to war to obtain their liberation. I must first be permitted to ask how it is that these men happen to be in the streets of Mexico. Is it not because they formed part of an expedition got up in Texas against the Mexican city of Santa Fé? Were they not taken *flagrante bello*, actually engaged in a war they had nothing to do with, to which the United States were no party? In all this great pity and sympathy for American citizens made to travel hundreds of miles barefoot and in chains, the question 'How came they there?' seems never to be asked. And yet, so far as the interposition of this nation for their recovery is concerned, that is the very first question to be asked.

"I come now to the third ground for war urged by the gentleman from Virginia, and I hope I do not misrepresent him when I say that I understood him to affirm that if he had the power he would prohibit the invasion of Texas by Mexico; and if Mexico would not submit to such a requirement, and should persist in her invasion, he would go to war. The gentleman stated, as a ground for war, that Santa Anna had avowed his determination to 'drive slavery beyond the Sabine.' That was what the gentleman from Virginia most apprehended—that slavery would be abolished in Texas; that we should have neighbors at our doors not contaminated by that accursed plague-spot. He would have war with Mexico sooner than slavery should be driven back to the United States, whence it came. If that is to be the avowed opinion of this committee, in God's name let my constituents know it! The sooner it is proclaimed on the house-tops, the better—the house is to go to war with Mexico for the purpose of annexing Texas to this Union!"

CHAPTER XIII.

REPORT ON PRESIDENT TYLER'S APPROVAL, WITH OBJECTIONS, OF THE BILL FOR THE APPORTIONMENT OF REPRESENTATIVES.—REPORT ON HIS VETO OF THE BILL TO PROVIDE A REVENUE FROM IMPORTS.— LECTURE ON THE SOCIAL COMPACT, AND THE THEORIES OF FILMER, HOBBES, SYDNEY, AND LOCKE.—ADDRESS TO HIS CONSTITUENTS ON THE POLICY OF PRESIDENT TYLER'S ADMINISTRATION.—ADDRESS TO THE NORFOLK COUNTY TEMPERANCE SOCIETY.—DISCOURSE ON THE NEW ENGLAND CONFEDERACY OF 1643.—LETTER TO THE CITIZENS OF

On the 23d of June, 1842, President Tyler announced to the House of Representatives that he had signed and approved an act for the apportionment of representatives among the several states, and had deposited the same in the office of the Secretary of State, accompanied with his reasons for giving to it his sanction; by which it appeared that, after having officially "approved" that act, he had declared, in effect, that *he did not approve of it*, having doubts concerning both its constitutionality and expediency, and that he had signed it only in deference to the opinions of both houses of Congress. Mr. Adams, from the committee to whom these proceedings of the President had been referred, in a report to the House severely scrutinizes the course of the President in this respect. He declares that the duty of the President, in exercising the authority given him by the constitution to sign and approve acts of Congress, is prescribed in terms equally concise and precise; and that it has given him no power to alter, amend, comment upon, or assign his reasons for the performance of his duty. These views he illustrates by a minute examination of the language of that instrument, and shows that what the President had done was a departure not only from the language but from the substance of the law prescribing to him his duties in that respect. Mr. Adams then, in behalf of the committee, after showing that the proceeding of the President in this instance is without precedent or example, and imminently dangerous in its tendencies, proceeds to remark:

"The entry upon the bill is, 'Approved: John Tyler;' and that entry makes it the law of the land; and then, by a private note deposited with the law in the Department of State, the same hand which, under the sacred obligation of an official oath, has written the word '*approved*,' and added the sign-manual of his name, feels it due to himself to declare that the bill is not approved, and that he doubts both its constitutionality and its policy, and that he signs it only in deference to the declared *will* of both houses of Congress; not from assent to their reasons, but in submission to their *will*.

"And he feels it due to himself to say this,—first, that his motives for signing it may be rightly understood; secondly, that his opinions may not be liable to be misunderstood; or, thirdly, quoted hereafter erroneously as a precedent. The motives of a President of the United States for signing an act of Congress can be no other than because he approves it; and because, in that event, the constitution enjoins it upon him to sign it as a duty, which he has sworn to perform, and with which he cannot dispense.

"But no; in the present case the President feels it due to himself to say that his motives for signing the bill were not because he approved it, or because it was made by the constitution his duty to sign it, but to prove his submission to the will of Congress. He feels it due also to himself to guard against the liability of his opinions to misconstruction, or to be quoted hereafter erroneously as a precedent. His signature to the bill, preceded by the word '*approved*,' taken in connection with the duties prescribed to the President of the United States by the constitution, certainly was liable to the construction that his opinions were favorable to the bill. They were, indeed, liable to no other construction respectful to him, or trustful to his honor and sincerity; nor can there be a doubt that they would have been quoted hereafter as a precedent. No man living could have imagined that the word '*approved*' could be construed to mean either doubt or obsequious submission to the will of others; and it is with extreme regret that the committee see, in the President's exposition of his reasons for signing an act of Congress, the open avowal that, in his vocabulary, used in the performance of one of the most solemn and sacred of his duties, the word '*approved*' means not approval, but doubt; not the expression of his own opinions, but mere obsequiousness to the will of Congress."

The report proceeds to deny that the example of the advice given by the first Secretary of State to the first President of the United States, which the President adduces in his support, and the following that advice by that President, gave any "sanction to such recorded duplicity." It asserts that such an example is of dangerous tendency—an encroachment by the Executive on legislative functions; that the reasons given by President Tyler are a running commentary against the law, against its execution according to the intention of the legislature, and forestalling the appropriate action of the judicial tribunals in

123

expounding it. These and consentaneous views the report largely illustrates, and concludes with a resolution declaring the proceedings of the President in this case to have been unwarranted by the constitution and laws of the United States, injurious to the public interest, and of evil example in future; solemnly protesting against its ever being repeated, or adduced as a precedent hereafter.

On the 9th of August, 1842, President Tyler returned to the House of Representatives the bill to provide a revenue from imports, and changing the existing laws imposing duties on them, accompanied with his objections to it. The house referred the subject to a select committee, of which Mr. Adams was chairman. On the 16th of August he reported that the message was the last of a series of executive measures, the result of which had been to defeat and nullify the whole action of the legislative authority of the Union upon the most important interests of the nation;—that, at the accession of the late President Harrison, the revenue and the credit of the country were so completely disordered, that a suffering people had commanded a change in the administration; and the elections throughout the Union had placed in both houses of Congress majorities, the natural exponents of the principles which it was the will of the people should be substituted instead of those which had brought the country to a condition of such wretchedness and shame;— that there was a perfect harmony between the chosen President of the people and this majority; but that, by an inscrutable decree of Providence, the chief of the people's choice, in harmony with whose principles the majorities of both houses had been constituted, was laid low in death. A successor to the office had assumed the title, with totally different principles, who, though professing to harmonize with the principles of his immediate predecessor, and with the majorities in both houses of Congress, soon disclosed his diametrical opposition to them.

The report then proceeds to show the several developments of this new and most unfortunate condition of the general government, effected by "a system of continual and unrelenting exercise of executive legislation,"—by the alternate gross abuse of constitutional power, and bold assumption of powers never vested in him by any law,—resulting in four several vetoes, which, in the course of fifteen months, had suspended the legislation of the Union. It then states and comments upon the reasons assigned by the President for returning this bill to the House of Representatives, with his objections to it, as specified in the veto message referred to this committee; and, after a rigid analysis and course of argument, pronounces them "feeble, inconsistent, and unsatisfactory;" after which the report proceeds:

"They perceive that the whole legislative power of the Union has been, for the last fifteen months, with regard to the action of Congress upon measures of vital importance, in a state of suspended animation, strangled by the *five* times repeated stricture of the executive cord. They observe that, under these unexampled obstructions to the exercise of their high and legitimate duties, they have hitherto preserved the most respectful forbearance towards the Executive Chief; that while he has time after time annulled, by the mere act of his will, their commission from the people to enact laws for the common welfare, they have forborne even the expression of their resentment for these multiplied insults and injuries. They believed they had a high destiny to fulfil, by administering to the people, in the form of law, remedies for the sufferings which they had too long endured. The will of one man has frustrated all their labors, and prostrated all their powers. The majority of the committee believe that the case has occurred, in the annals of our Union, contemplated by the founders of the constitution, by the grant to the House of Representatives of the power to impeach the President of the United States; but they are aware that the resort to that expedient might, in the present condition of public affairs, prove abortive. They see the irreconcilable difference of opinion and of action between the legislative and executive departments of the government is but sympathetic with the same discordant views and feelings among the people. To them alone the final issue of the struggle must be left. In sorrow and mortification, under the failure of all their labors to redeem the honor and prosperity of their country, it is a cheering consolation to them that the termination of their own official existence is at hand; that they are even now about to return to receive the sentence of their constituents upon themselves; that the legislative power of the Union, crippled and disabled as it may now be, is about to pass, renovated and revivified by the will of the people, into other hands, upon whom will devolve the task of providing that remedy for the public distempers which their own honest and agonizing energies have in vain endeavored to supply.

"The power of the present Congress to enact laws essential to the welfare of the people has been struck with apoplexy by the executive hand. Submission to his will is the only condition upon which he will permit them to act. For the enactment of a measure, earnestly recommended by himself, he forbids their action, unless coupled with a condition declared by himself to be on a subject so totally different that he will not suffer them to be coupled in the same law. With that condition Congress cannot comply. In this state of things he has assumed, as the committee fully believe, the exercise of the whole legislative power to himself, and is levying millions of money upon the people, without any authority of law. But the final decision of this question depends neither upon legislative nor executive, but upon judicial authority; nor can the final decision of the Supreme Court upon it be pronounced before the close of the present Congress. In the mean time, the abusive exercise of the constitutional power of the President to arrest the action of Congress upon measures vital to the welfare of the people has wrought conviction upon the minds of a majority of the committee that the veto power itself must be restrained and modified by an amendment of the constitution itself; a resolution for which they accordingly herewith respectfully report."

The report was signed by ten members of the committee, including the chairman. The resolution with which it closed provided for submitting to the States a proposed modification of the constitution, by substituting the words "majority of the whole number," instead of the words "two thirds," by which the power of the House of Representatives to pass a law, notwithstanding the veto of the President, is at present restricted.

The report was agreed to in the house by a majority of one hundred ayes to ninety nays, and the resolution itself passed by a majority of ninety-eight ayes to ninety nays; but the constitution, in such cases, requiring two thirds majority, it was of consequence rejected.

In November, 1842, Mr. Adams delivered a lecture before the Franklin Lyceum, at Providence, Rhode Island, on the Social Compact, in which he enters into "an examination of the principles of democracy, aristocracy, and universal suffrage, as exemplified in a historical review of the present constitution of the Commonwealth of Massachusetts, with some notice of the origin of human government, and remarks on the theories of divine right, as maintained by Hobbes and Sir Robert Filmer, on one side, and by Sydney, Locke, Montesquieu, and Rousseau, on the other."

He shows, from the history of Massachusetts, that the fundamental principle asserted in the fifth article of our declaration of rights, that all power resides originally in *the people*, is derived from the above-named writers, and explains how this power has been practically exercised by the people of that state. The assertion of Rousseau, that the social compact can be formed only by unanimous consent, because the rule itself that a majority of votes shall prevail can only be established by agreement, that is, by compact, Mr. Adams controverts, maintaining in opposition to it that the social compact constituting the body-politic is, and by the law of nature must be, a compact not merely of individuals, but of families. On this view of the subject he largely animadverts. The philosophical examination of the foundations of civil society, of human governments, and of the rights and duties of man, he views as among the consequences of the Protestant Reformation. The question raised by Martin Luther involved the whole theory of *the rights* of individual man, paramount to all human authority. The talisman of *human rights* dissolved the spell of political as well as of ecclesiastical power. The Calvinists of Geneva and the Puritans of England contested the right of kings to prescribe articles of faith to their people, and this question necessarily drew after it the general question of the origin of all human government. In search of its principle, Hobbes, a royalist, affirmed that the state of nature between man and man was a state of war, whence it followed that government originated in *conquest*. This theory is directly opposite to that of Jesus Christ. It cuts the gordian knot with the sword, extinguishes all the rights of man, and makes fear the corner-stone of government. It is the only theory upon which slavery can be justified, as conformable to the law of nature. This is Sir John Falstaff's law, when, speaking of Justice Shallow, he says, "If the young dace be a bait for the old pike,

I see no reason in *the law of nature* why I may not snap at *him*." Sir Robert Filmer, by a theory far more plausible, though not more sound, than that of Hobbes, derived the origin of human government from the Scriptures of the Old Testament, from the grant of the earth to Adam, and afterwards to Noah.

But the vital error of Filmer was in assuming that the natural authority of the father over the child was either permanent or unlimited; and still more that the authority of the husband over the wife was unlimited. Sir Robert Filmer did not perceive that by the laws of nature and of God every individual human being is born with rights which no other individual, or combination of individuals, can take away; that all exercise of human authority must be under the limitation of right and wrong; and that all despotic power over human beings is exercised in *defiance* of the laws of nature and of God—all, Sir John Falstaff's law of nature between the young dace and the old pike.

The history of Filmer's work was remarkable. It was composed and published in the heat of the struggle between King Charles the First and the Commons of England, which terminated in the overthrow of the monarchy, and in the death of King Charles upon the scaffold. It was the theory of government on which *the cause* of the house of Stuart was sustained. No man can be surprised that such a cause was swept away by a moral and political whirlwind; that it carried with it all the institutions of civil society, so that its march was a wild desolation. James, by relying on the principles of Filmer's theory, fell back into the arms of the Church of Rome, and vainly struggled to turn back the tide of religious reformation, and revive the divine right of kings, and passive obedience, and non-resistance. The republican spirit had slumbered on the white cliffs of Albion, and in his sleep, like the man-mountain in Lilliput, had been pinned down to the earth by the threads of a spider's web for cords. On the first reäppearance of Filmer's book, he awoke, and, like the strong man in Israel, at the cost of his own life, shook down the temple of Dagon, and buried himself and the Philistines again under its ruins.

The discourses of John Locke concerning government demolished while they immortalized the work of Filmer, whose name and book are now remembered only to be detested. But the first principles of morals and politics, which have long been settled, acquire the authority of self-evident truths, which, when first discussed, may have been vehemently and portentously contested. John Locke, a kindred soul to Algernon Sydney, seven years after his death published an elaborate system of government, in which he declares the "false principles and foundation of Sir Robert Filmer and his followers are detected and overthrown." Subsequently, he published an essay concerning the true original extent and end of civil government. "The principles," says Mr. Adams, "of Sydney and Locke constitute the foundation of the North American Declaration of Independence; and, together with the subsequent writings of Montesquieu and Rousseau, that of the constitution of the Commonwealth of Massachusetts, and of the constitution of the United States." Neither of these constitutions separately, nor the two in combined harmony, can, without a gross and fraudulent perversion of language, be termed a *Democracy.* They are neither democracy, aristocracy, nor monarchy. They form together a mixed government, compounded not only of the three elements of democracy, aristocracy, and monarchy, but with a fourth added element, *Confederacy.* The constitution of the United States when adopted was so far from being considered as a democracy, that Patrick Henry charged it, in the Virginia Convention, with an awful squinting towards monarchy. The tenth number of the Federalist, written by James Madison, is an elaborate and unanswerable essay upon the vital and radical difference between a democracy and a republic. But it is impossible to disconnect the relation between names and things. When the anti-federal party dropped the name of Republicans to assume that of *Democrats,* their principles underwent a corresponding metamorphosis; and they are now the most devoted and most obsequious champions of executive power—the very life-guard of the commander of the armies and navies of this Union. The name of Democracy was assumed because it was discovered to be *very taking* among the multitude; yet, after all, it is but the investment of the *multitude* with absolute power. The constitutions of the United States and of the Commonwealth of Massachusetts are both the work of the people—one of the Union, the other of the State—not of the whole people by the phantom of universal suffrage, but of the whole people by that portion of them capable of contracting for the

126

whole. They are not democracy, nor aristocracy, nor monarchy, but a compound of them all, of which democracy is the oxygen, or vital air, too pure in itself for human respiration, but which in the union of other elements, equally destructive in themselves and less pure, forms that moral and political atmosphere in which we live, and move, and have our being.

The preceding abstract, given almost wholly in the language of Mr. Adams, shows the general drift of this characteristic essay.

On the 17th of September, 1842, a convention of delegates from the district he represented received Mr. Adams at Braintree, and expressed their thanks for his services on the floor of Congress, especially for his fidelity in their defence "against every attempt of Southern representatives and their Northern allies to sacrifice at the altar of slavery the freedom of speech and the press, the right of petition, the protection of free labor, and the immunities and privileges of Northern citizens." Mr. Adams, in reply, after expressing his sensibility at their unabated confidence in the integrity of his intentions, and in his capacity to serve them, declared that it had been his endeavor to discharge all the duties of his station "faithfully and gratefully to them; faithfully to our native and beloved Commonwealth; faithfully to our whole common country, the North American Union; faithfully to the world of mankind, in every quarter of the globe, and under every variety of condition or complexion; faithfully to that creator, God, who rules the world in justice and mercy, and to whom our final account must be made up by the standard of those attributes." He then proceeded to state, that on receiving their invitation to attend that meeting, it had been his intention to avail himself of the opportunity to unfold to them the professions, principles, and practices, of the federal administration of these United States, under the successive Presidents invested with executive power, from the day when he took his seat as their representative in Congress to the then present hour.

"I trusted it would be in my power to present to your contemplation, not only the outward and ostensible indications of federal policy, proclaimed and trumpeted abroad as the maxims of the Jackson, Van Buren, and Tyler administrations, but to lay bare their secret purposes, and never yet divulged designs for the future government or dissolution of this Union.

"Further reflection convinced me that this exposition would require more time than you could possibly devote to one meeting to hear me. My friend and colleague, Mr. Appleton, has, in an answer to an invitation of his constituents to a public dinner, lifted a corner of the veil, and opened a glance at the monstrous and horrible object beneath it; but South Carolina nullification itself, with its appendages of separation, secession, and the forty-bale theory, was but the struggles of Quixotism dreaming itself Genius, to erect on the basis of state sovereignty a system for seating South Carolina slavery on the throne of this Union in the event of success; or of severing the present Union, and instituting, with a tier of embryo Southern States to be wrested from the dismemberment of Mexico, a Southern slaveholding confederation to balance the free Republic of the North.

"'The passage,' says Mr. Appleton, 'of the revenue bill imposing discriminating duties with a view to the protection and encouragement of American industry, is, under the circumstances, an event of the very highest importance. Notwithstanding the system had been formerly established in 1816, and fortified by succeeding legislation; notwithstanding its success in the development of our resources and the establishment of manufactures and arts, surpassing the expectation of the most sanguine; notwithstanding the immense investments of capital made on the faith of the national legislation inviting such application, the attempt was seriously entertained of breaking down this whole system, with a reckless disregard of consequences, either in the wanton destruction of capital, or, what is far more important, in the general paralysis of the industry of the country. *The origin of this attempt may be traced to the mad ambition of certain politicians of South Carolina, who, in 1832, formed the project of a Southern Confederacy, severed from the rest of the Union, with that state for its centre, as affording more security to the slave states for their peculiar institutions than exist under the general government.*

"'This project led to the invention of a theory of political economy, which was maintained with an ingenuity and perseverance worthy of a better cause, founded on the assumption that all imports are, in effect, direct taxes upon exports. So indefatigable were the promulgators of this theory, that the whole South was made to believe that a protective

127

tariff was a system of plunder levied upon their productions of cotton, rice, and tobacco, which constituted the bulk of our exports to foreign markets.'"

Mr. Adams then proceeds to state that the principles of nullification were never more inflexibly maintained, never more inexorably pursued, than they had been by all that portion of the South which had given them countenance, from the day of the death of William Henry Harrison to the present, and that nullification is the creed of the executive mansion at Washington, the acting President's *conscience*, and the woof of all his vetoes.

"Nullification," he adds, "portentous and fatal as it is to the prospects and welfare of this Union, is not the only instrument of Southern domination wielded by the executive arm at Washington. The dismemberment of our neighboring republic of Mexico, and the acquisition of an immense portion of her territories, was a gigantic and darling project of Andrew Jackson, and is another instrument wielded for the same purpose.

"Within five weeks after the proclamation of the constitution of the Republic of Texas followed the battle of San Jacinto; and from that day the struggles of the Southern politicians, who ruled the councils of this nation, were for upwards of two years unremitting, and unrestrained by any principles of honor, honesty, and truth: openly avowed, and audaciously proclaimed, whenever they dared; clandestinely pursued, under delusive masks and false colors, whenever the occasion required.

"No sooner was the event of the battle of San Jacinto known than memorials and resolutions, from various parts of the Union, were poured in upon Congress, calling upon that body for the immediate recognition of the independence of the Republic of Texas. Many of these memorials and resolutions came from the free states, and one of them from the Legislature of Connecticut, then blindly devoted to the rank Southern, sectional policy of the Jackson administration, by that infatuation of Northern sympathy with Southern interests, which Mr. Appleton points out to our notice, and the true purposes of which had already been sufficiently divulged in an address of Mr. Clement C. Clay to the Legislature of Alabama. But there was another more hidden impulse to this extreme solicitude for the recognition of the independence of Texas working in the free states, quite as ready to assume the mask and cap of liberty as the slave-dealing champions of the rights of man. The Texan land and liberty jobbers had spread the contagion of their land-jobbing traffic all over the free states throughout the Union. Land-jobbing, stock-jobbing, slave-jobbing, rights-of-man-jobbing, were all, hand in hand, sweeping over the land like a hurricane. The banks were plunging into desperate debts, preparing for a universal suspension of specie payment, under the shelter of legislative protection to flood the country with irredeemable paper. Gambling speculation was the madness of the day; and, in the wide-spread ruin which we are now witnessing as the last stage of this moral pestilence, Texan bonds and Texan lands form no small portion of the fragments from the wreck of money corporations contributing their assets of two or three cents to the dollar. All these interests furnished vociferous declaimers for the recognition of Texan independence."

Mr. Adams next states the proceedings of Congress on this subject during the whole of the residue of the Jackson administration, terminating with the recognition by Congress of the independence of Texas. At this period Mr. Van Buren—a Northern man with Southern principles—assumed the functions of President of the United States. But the recognition of the independence of Texas availed nothing without her annexation to the United States. In October, 1837, a formal proposition from the Republic of Texas for such annexation was communicated to Congress, with the statement that it had been declined by Mr. Van Buren. But the passion for the annexation of Texas was not to be so disconcerted. Memorials for and against its annexation poured into Congress, and were referred to the Committee on Foreign Affairs. "In the debate which arose from their report," says Mr. Adams, "I exposed the whole system of duplicity and perfidy towards Mexico, which had marked the Jackson administration from its commencement to its close. It silenced the clamors for the annexation of Texas to this Union for three years, till the catastrophe of the Van Buren administration. The people of the free states were lulled into the belief that the whole project was abandoned, and that they should hear no more of the slave-trade cravings for the annexation of Texas. Had Harrison lived, they would have heard no more of it to this day. But no sooner was John Tyler installed into the President's house than nullification, and

Texas, and war with Mexico, rose again upon the surface, with eye steadily fixed upon the polar star of Southern slave-dealing supremacy in the government of the Union."

Mr. Adams then comments upon the history of the Santa Fé expedition, which was fitted out in the summer of 1841, shortly after the accession of Mr. Tyler, by the then President of Texas, having been originated and concerted within these states, and carried on chiefly by citizens of the United States. That it was known, countenanced, and encouraged, at the presidential house, was, said Mr. Adams, more than questioned; for, while it was on foot, and before it was known, frequent hints were given in public journals, moved by Executive impulse, that at the coming session the annexation of Texas was to be introduced by a citizen of the highest distinction. "But the Texan expedition was ill-starred. Instead of taking and rioting upon the beauty and booty of Santa Fé, they were all captured themselves, without even the glory of putting a price on their lives. They surrendered without firing a gun." The failure of this expedition discomfited the war faction in Congress, and injured for a moment, and only for a moment, the project to which Southern nullification clung with the grasp of death.

Mr. Adams next proceeds to exhibit the evidence to show "the participation of the administration at Washington with this incursion of banditti from Texas against Santa Fé," and to explain "the legislative exploit" by which the treasury of the United States was made to contribute to "the dismemberment of Mexico, and the annexation of an immense portion of its territory to the slave representation of the Union." The internal evidence he regarded as irresistible that "the expedition against Santa Fé was planned within your boundaries, and committed to the execution of your citizens, under the shelter of Mexican banners and commissions."

In the subsequent portion of this address Mr. Adams, regarding the principles of nullification as being at the basis of Mr. Tyler's whole policy, enters at large into its nature, and thus speaks of its origin and association with democracy:

"Let me advert again to the important disclosure in the letter of Mr. Appleton to his constituents, from which I have taken the liberty of reading to you an extract. Nullification was generated in the hot-bed of slavery. It drew its first breath in the land where the meaning of the word democracy is that a majority of the people are the goods and chattels of the minority; that more than one half of the people are not men, women, and children, but things, to be treated by their owners, not exactly like dogs and horses, but like tables, chairs, and joint-stools; that they are not even fixtures to the soil, as in countries where servitude is divested of its most hideous features,—not even beings in the mitigated degradation from humanity of beasts, or birds, or creeping things,—but destitute not only of the sensibilities of our own race of men, but of the sensations of all animated nature. That is the native land of nullification, and it is a theory of constitutional law worthy of its origin. *Democracy*, pure democracy, has at least its foundation in a generous theory of human rights. It is founded on the natural equality of mankind. It is the corner-stone of the Christian religion. It is the first *element* of *all* lawful government upon earth. Democracy is self-government of the community by the conjoint will of the majority of numbers. What communion, what affinity, can there be between that principle and nullification, which is the despotism of a corporation—unlimited, unrestrained, *sovereign* power? Never, never was amalgamation so preposterous and absurd as that of nullification and democracy."

Of the hostility of nullification to the prosperity of the free states he thus speaks:

"The root of the doctrine of nullification is that if the internal improvement of the country should be left to the legislative management of the national government, and the proceeds of the sales of the public lands should be applied as a perpetual and self-accumulating fund for that purpose, the blessings unceasingly showered upon the people by this process would so grapple the affections of the people to the national authority, that it would, in process of time, overshadow that of the state governments, and settle the preponderancy of power in the free states; and then the undying worm of conscience twinges with terror for the fate of *the peculiar institution*. Slavery stands aghast at the prospective promotion of the general welfare, and flies to nullification for defence against the energies of freedom, and the inalienable rights of man."

After stating and commenting upon the policy of General Jackson, as having for its object the "dismembering of Mexico, and restoring slavery to Texas, and of surrounding the South with a girdle of slave states, to eternize the blessings of the peculiar institution, and spread them like a garment of praise over the whole North American Union," he explained the effect of party divisions always operating in the United States, and the character of the several proportions of their power. Their results, in tending to revive and strengthen slavery and the slave-trade, which Mr. Adams then foretold, excited melancholy anticipations in the mind of every reflecting freeman. What was then prophecy is now history.

"There are two different party divisions always operating in the House of Representatives of the United States,—one sectional, North and South, or, in other words, slave and free; the other political—both sides of which have been known at different times by different names, but are now usually denominated Whigs and Democrats. The Southern or slave party, outnumbered by the free, are cemented together by a common, intense interest of property to the amount of twelve hundred millions of dollars in human beings, the very existence of which is neither allowed nor tolerated in the North. It is the opinion of many theoretical reasoners on the subject of government that, whatever may be its form, the ruling power of every nation is its property. Mr. Van Buren, in one of his messages to Congress, gravely pointed out to them the anti-republican tendencies of associated wealth. Reflect now upon the tendencies of twelve hundred millions of dollars of associated wealth, directly represented in your national legislature by one hundred members, together with one hundred and forty members representing persons only—freemen, not chattels. Reflect, also, that this twelve hundred millions of dollars of property is peculiar in its character, and comes under a classification once denominated by a Governor of Virginia *property acquired by crime*; that it sits uneasy upon the conscience of its owner; that, in the purification of human virtue, and the progress of the Christian religion, it has become, and is daily becoming, more and more odious; that Washington and Jefferson, themselves slaveholders, living and dying, bore testimony against it; that it was the dying REMORSE of John Randolph; that it is renounced and abjured by the supreme pontiff of the Roman Church, abolished with execration by the Mahometan despot of Tunis, shaken to its foundations by the imperial autocrat of all the Russias and the absolute monarch of Austria;—all, all bearing reluctant and extorted testimony to the self-evident truth that, by the laws of nature and nature's God, man cannot be the property of man. Recollect that the first cry of human feeling against this unhallowed outrage upon human rights came from ourselves—from the Quakers of Pennsylvania; that it passed from us to England, from England to France, and spread over the civilized world; that, after struggling for nearly a century against the most sordid interests and most furious passions of man, it made its way at length into the Parliament, and ascended the throne, of the British Isles. The slave-trade was made piracy first by the Congress of the United States, and then by the Parliament of Great Britain.

"But the curse fastened by the progress of Christian charity and of human rights upon the African slave-trade could not rest there. If the African slave-trade was piracy, the coasting American slave-trade could not be innocent, nor could its aggravated turpitude be denied. In the sight of the same God who abhors the iniquity of the African slave-trade, neither the American slave-trade nor slavery itself can be held guiltless. From the suppression of the African slave-trade, therefore, the British Parliament, impelled by the irresistible influence of the British people, proceeded to point the battery of its power against slavery itself. At the expense of one hundred millions of dollars, it abolished slavery, and emancipated all the slaves in the British transatlantic colonies; and the government entered upon a system of negotiation with all the powers of the world for the ultimate extinction of slavery throughout the globe.

"The utter and unqualified inconsistency of slavery, in any of its forms, with the principles of the North American Revolution, and the Declaration of our Independence, had so forcibly struck the Southern champions of our rights, that the abolition of slavery and the emancipation of slaves was a darling project of Thomas Jefferson from his first entrance into public life to the last years of his existence. But the associated wealth of the slaveholders outweighed the principles of the Revolution, and by the constitution of the United States a compromise was established between slavery and freedom. The extent of the sacrifice of principle made by the North in this compromise can be estimated only by its practical effects. The principle is that the House of Representatives of the United States is a representation only of the persons and freedom of the North, and of the persons, property, and slavery, of the South. Its practical operation has been to give the balance of power in the house, and in every department of the government, into the hands of the minority of numbers. For practical results look to the present composition of your government in all its departments. The President of the United States, the President of the Senate, the Speaker of the House, are all slaveholders. The Chief Justice and four out of the nine Judges of the Supreme Court of the United States are slaveholders. The commander-in-chief of your army and the general next in command are slaveholders. A vast majority of all the officers of your navy, from the highest to the lowest, are slaveholders. Of six heads of the executive departments, three are slaveholders; securing thus, with the President, a majority in all cabinet consultations and executive councils. From the commencement of this century, upwards of forty years, the office of Chief Justice has always been held by slaveholders; and when, upon the death of Judge Marshall, the two senior justices upon the bench were citizens of the free states, and unsurpassed in eminence of reputation both for learning in the law and for spotless integrity, they were both overlooked and overslaughed by a slaveholder, far inferior to either of them in reputation as a lawyer, and chiefly eminent for his obsequious servility to the usurpations of Andrew Jackson, for which this unjust elevation to the Supreme Judicial bench was the reward.

"As to the house itself, if an article of the constitution had prescribed, or a standing rule of the house had required, that no other than a slaveholder should ever be its Speaker, the regulation could not be more rigorously observed than it is by the compact movements of the slave representation in the house. Of the last six speakers of the house, including the present, every one has been a slaveholder. It is so much a matter of course to see such a person in the chair, that, if a Northern man but thinks of aspiring to the chair, he is only made a laughing-stock for the house.

"With such consequences staring us in the face, what are we to think when we are told that the government of the United States is a democracy of numbers—a government by a majority of the people? Do you not see that the one hundred representatives of persons, property, and slavery, marching in solid phalanx upon every question of interest to their constituents, will always outnumber the one hundred and forty representatives only of persons and freedom, scattered as their votes will always be by conflicting interests, prejudices, and passions?

"But this is not all. The second party division in the house to which I have alluded is political, and known at present by the names of Whigs and Democrats, or Locofocos. The latter are remarkable for an exquisite tenderness of affection for *the people*, and especially for the poor, provided their skins are white, and against the rich. But it is no less remarkable that the princely slaveholders of the South are among the most thoroughgoing of the Democrats; and their alliance with the Northern Democracy is one of the cardinal points of their policy."

The residue of this address is devoted to a searching and severe examination of the whole course of President Tyler's administration, showing that "the sectional division of parties—in other words, the conflict between freedom and slavery—is the axle round which the administration of the national government revolves." "The political divisions with him, and with all Southern statesmen of his stamp, are mere instruments of power to purchase auxiliary support to the cause of slavery even from the freemen of the North."

In closing this most illustrative address, he apologizes to his constituents for any language he may have used in debate which might be deemed harsh or acrimonious, and asks them to consider the adversaries with whom he had to contend; the virulence and rancor, unparalleled in the history of the country, with which he had been pursued; and to remember that, "for the single offence of persisting to assert the right of the people to petition, and the freedom of speech and of the press, he had been twice dragged before the house to be censured and expelled." One of his assailants, Thomas F. Marshall, had declared, in an address to his constituents, his motives for the past, and his purposes for the future, in the following words:

"Though petitions to dissolve the Union be poured in by thousands, I shall not again interfere on the floor of Congress, since the house have virtually declared that there is nothing contemptuous or improper in offering them, and are willing again to afford Mr. Adams an opportunity of sweeping all the strings of discord that exist in our country. I acted as I thought for the best, being sincerely desirous to check that man, who, if he could be removed from the councils of the nation, or *silenced* on the exasperating subject to which he seems to have devoted himself, *none other, I believe, could be found hardy enough, or bad enough, to fill his place.*"

"Besides this special and avowed malevolence against me," Mr. Adams remarks,— "this admitted purpose to expel or silence me, for the sake of brow-beating all other members of the free representation, by establishing over them the reign of terror,—a peculiar system of tactics in the house has been observed towards me, by *silencers* of the slave representation and their allies of the Northern Democracy."

The system of tactics to which he alludes was, first, to turn him out of the office of chairman of the Committee on Foreign Affairs, and, this failing, to induce a majority of the servile portion of that committee to refuse any longer to serve with him; their purpose being exactly that of Mr. Marshall, to remove him from the councils of the nation, or to silence him, for the sake of *intimidating* all others by "an ostentatious display of a common determination not to serve with any man who would not submit to the gag-rule, and would persist in presenting abolition petitions." Mr. Adams then illustrates the powerful effect of such movements to overawe members from the free states.

"Another practice," he observed, "of this communion of Southern, sectional, and Locofoco antipathy against me, is that I never can take part in any debate upon an important subject, be it only upon a mere abstraction, but a pack opens upon me of personal invective in return. Language has no word of reproach or railing that is not hurled at me; and the rules of the house allow me no opportunity to reply till every other member of the house has had his turn to speak, if he pleases. By another rule every debate is closed by a majority whenever they get weary of it. The previous question, or a motion to lay the subject on the table, is interposed, and I am not allowed to reply to the grossest falsehoods and most invidious misrepresentations."

This course of party tactics Mr. Adams exhibits by a particular narrative of the misrepresentation to which he had been subjected, closing his statement with the following acknowledgment: "I must do many of the members of the House of Representatives from the South the justice to say that their treatment of me is dictated far more by the passions and prejudices of their constituents than by their own. Were it not for this curse of slavery, there are some of them with whom I should be on terms of the most intimate and confidential friendship. There are many for whom I entertain high esteem, respect, and affectionate attachment. There are among them those who have stood by me in my trials, and scorned to join in the league to sacrifice me as a terror to others."

In September, 1842, at the invitation of the Norfolk County Temperance Society, Mr. Adams delivered at Quincy an address,—not perhaps in coïncidence with the prevailing expectations of that society, but in perfect unison with his own characteristic spirit of independence. He instituted an inquiry into the effect of the *principles* of total abstinence from the use of spirituous liquors, the administration of pledges, or, in other words, the contracting of engagements by vows; and examined the whole subject with reference to the essential connection which exists between temperance and religion. In the course of his argument he maintains that the moral principles inculcated by the whole tenor of the Old Testament, with regard to temperance, are,—1. That the *temperate* use of wine is innocent, and without sin. 2. That excess in it is a heinous sin. 3. That the voluntary assumption of a vow or pledge of total abstinence is an effort of exalted virtue, and highly acceptable in the sight of God. 4. That the habit of excess in the use of wine is an object of unqualified abhorrence and disgust. He concluded with a warning to his fellow-citizens to "stand fast in the liberty wherewith Christ has made you free, and be not entangled again with the yoke of bondage;" and, after applauding the members of the Norfolk County Temperance Society for their attempts to suppress intemperance, declaring it a holy work, and invoking the blessing of Heaven on their endeavors, he bids them "go forth as missionaries of Christianity among their own kindred. Go, with the commendation of the Saviour to his apostles when he first sent them forth to redeem the world: 'Be ye therefore wise as serpents, and harmless as doves.' In the ardor of your zeal for moral reform forget not the rights of personal freedom. All *excess* is of the nature of intemperance. Self-government is the foundation of all our political and social institutions; and it is by self-government alone that the laws of temperance can be enforced.... Above all, let no tincture of party politics be mingled with the pure stream from the fountain of temperance."

The spirit of this address, and the intimate knowledge of the Scriptures Mr. Adams possessed, will be illustrated by the following extract:

"Throughout the whole of the Old Testament the vine is represented as one of the most precious blessings bestowed by the Creator upon man. In the incomparable fable of Jotham, when he lifted up his voice on the summit of Mount Gerizim, and cried to the men of Shechem, 'Hearken unto me, ye men of Shechem, that God may hearken unto you,' he told them that when the trees of the forest went forth to anoint them a king to reign over them, they offered the crown successively to the olive-tree, the fig-tree, and the *vine*. They all declined to accept the royal dignity; and when it came to the turn of the vine to assign the reasons for his refusal, he said, 'Should I leave my *wine*, which cheereth God and man, and go to be promoted over the trees?' In the one hundred and fourth Psalm,—that most magnificent of all descriptions of the glory, the omnipotence, and the goodness of the Creator, God,—wine is enumerated among the richest of his blessings bestowed upon man. 'He causeth the grass to grow,' says the Psalmist, 'for the cattle, and herb for the service of man, that he may bring forth food out of the earth, and wine that maketh glad the heart of man, and oil to make his face to shine, and bread that strengtheneth man's heart.'

"But, while wine was thus classed among the choicest comforts and necessaries of life, the cautions and injunctions against the inordinate use of it are repeated and multiplied in every variety of form. 'Wine is a mocker,' says Solomon (Prov. 20:1); 'strong drink is raging; and whosoever is deceived thereby is not wise.' 'He that loveth pleasure shall be a poor man; he that loveth wine and oil shall not be rich.' (21:17.) 'Who hath woe? who hath sorrow? who hath contentions? who hath babbling? who hath wounds without cause? who hath redness of eyes? They that tarry *long* at the wine; they that go *to seek* mixed wine. Look not thou upon the wine when it is red, when it giveth its color in the cup, when it moveth itself aright,'—say, like sparkling Champagne.—'At the *last* it biteth like a serpent, and stingeth like an adder. Thine eyes shall behold strange wonders, and thine heart shall utter perverse things; yea, thou shalt be as he that lieth down in the midst of the sea, or as he that lieth on the top of a mast. They have stricken me, shalt thou say, and I was not sick; they have beaten me, and I felt it not: when shall I awake? I will seek it yet again.' Never was so exquisite a picture of drunkenness and the drunkard painted by the hand of man.

"Yet in all this there is no interdict upon the *use* of wine. The caution and the precept are against excess."

On the 29th of May, 1843, Mr. Adams delivered before the Massachusetts Historical Society a discourse in celebration of the Second Centennial Anniversary of the New England Confederacy of 1643. This work is characterized by that breadth and depth of research for which he was distinguished and eminently qualified. It includes traces of the early settlements of Virginia, New England, Pennsylvania, and New York; of the causes of each, and the spirit in which they were made and conducted, and of the principles which they applied in their intercourse with the aboriginals of the forest. He then proceeds to give an account of the confederation of the four New England colonies, Plymouth, Massachusetts, Connecticut, and New Haven, in 1643, with appropriate statements of the principles and conduct of the founders of each settlement, and of the character and motives of the leaders of each of them.

The origin, motives, and objects of that confederation, he explains; analyzing the distribution of power between the commissioners of the whole confederacy and among the separate governments of the colonies, and showing that it combined the same identical principles with those which gathered and united the thirteen English colonies as the prelude to the Revolution which severed them forever from their national connection with Great

Britain; and that the New England Confederacy of 1643 was the model and prototype of the North American Confederacy of 1774.

His sketch of the founder of the Colony of Rhode Island will give a general idea of the spirit and bearing of this discourse:

"Roger Williams was a man who maybe considered the very impersonation of a combined conscientious and contentious spirit. Born in the land of Sir Hugh Evans and Captain Fluellen, educated at the University of Oxford, at the very period when the monarchical Episcopal Church of England was purging herself, as by fire, from the corruptions of the despotic and soul-degrading Church of Rome, he arrived at Boston in February, 1630, about half a year after the landing of the Massachusetts Colony of Governor Winthrop. He was an eloquent preacher, stiff and self-confident in his opinions; ingenious, powerful, and commanding, in impressing them upon others; inflexible in his adherence to them; and, by an inconsistency peculiar to religious enthusiasts, combining the most amiable and affectionate sympathies of the heart with the most repulsive and inexorable exclusions of conciliation, compliance, or intercourse, with his adversaries in opinion.

"On his first arrival he went to Salem, and there soon made himself so acceptable by his preaching, that the people of Mr. Skelton's church invited him to settle with them as his colleague. But he had broached, and made no hesitation in maintaining, two opinions imminently dangerous to the very existence of the Massachusetts Colony, and certainly not remarkable for that spirit of charity or toleration upon which he afterwards founded his own government, and which now, in after ages, constitutes his brightest title to renown. The first of these opinions was that the royal charter to the Colony of Massachusetts was a nullity, because the King of England had no right to grant lands in foreign countries, which belonged of right to their native inhabitants. This opinion struck directly at all right of property held under the authority of the royal charter, and, followed to its logical conclusions, would have proved the utter impotence of the royal charter to confer power of government, any more than it could convey property in the soil.

"The other opinion was that the Church of Boston was criminal for having omitted to make a public declaration of repentance for having held communion with the Church of England before their emigration; and upon that ground he had refused to join in communion with the Church of Boston.

"By the subtlety and vehemence of his persuasive powers he had prevailed upon Endicott to look upon the cross of St. George in the banners of England as a badge of idolatry, and to cause it actually to be cut out of the flag floating at the fort in Salem. The red cross of St. George in the national banner of England was a grievous and odious eye-sore to multitudes, probably to a great majority, of the Massachusetts colonists; but, in the eyes of the government of the colony, it was the sacred badge of allegiance to the monarchy at home, already deeply jealous of the purposes and designs of the Puritan colony."

On the 4th of July, 1843, Mr. Adams, in a letter addressed to the citizens of Bangor, in Maine, declining their invitation to deliver an address on the 1st of August, the anniversary of British emancipation of slavery in the West Indies, thus expressed his views on that subject:

"The extinction of SLAVERY from the face of the earth is a problem, moral, political, religious, which at this moment rocks the foundations of human society throughout the regions of civilized man. It is indeed nothing more nor less than the consummation of the Christian religion. It is only as *immortal* beings that all mankind can in any sense be said to be born equal; and when the Declaration of Independence affirms as a self-evident truth that all men are born equal, it is precisely the same as if the affirmation had been that all men are born with immortal souls; for, take away from man his soul, the immortal spirit that is within him, and he would be a mere tamable beast of the field, and, like others of his kind, would become the property of his tamer. Hence it is, too, that, by the law of nature and of God, man can never be made the property of man. And herein consists the fallacy with which the holders of slaves often delude themselves, by assuming that the test of property is human law. The soul of one man cannot by human law be made the property of another. The owner of a slave is the owner of a living corpse; but he is not the owner of a man."

134

In illustration of this principle he observes that "the natural equality of mankind, affirmed by the signers of the Declaration of Independence to be *held up* by them as self-evident truth, was not so held by their enemies. Great Britain held that sovereign power was unlimitable, and the natural equality of mankind was a fable. France and Spain had no sympathies for the rights of human nature. Vergennes plotted with Gustavus of Sweden the revolution in Sweden from liberty to despotism. Turgot, shortly after our Declaration of Independence, advised Louis Sixteenth that it was for *the interest* of France and Spain that the insurrection of the Anglo-American colonies *should be suppressed.* But none of them foresaw or imagined what would be the consequence of the triumphant establishment in the continent of North America of an Anglo-Saxon American nation on the foundation of the natural equality of mankind, and the inalienable rights of man."

Mr. Adams then states and reasons upon these consequences in Europe and the United States: the abolition of slavery by the judicial decision of the Supreme Court of Massachusetts, three years after the Declaration of Independence. Since that day there has not been a slave within that state. The same principle is corroborated by the fact that the Declaration of Independence imputes slavery in Virginia to George the Third, as one of the crimes which proved him to be a tyrant, unfit to rule a free people; and that at least twenty slaveholders, if not thirty, among whom were George Washington and Thomas Jefferson, avowed abolitionists, were signers of that Declaration.

He next states that "the result of the North American revolutionary war had prepared the minds of the people of the British nation to contemplate with calm composure the new principle engrafted upon the association of the civilized race of man, the self-evident truth, the natural equality of mankind and the rights of man." He then introduces Anthony Benezet, a member of the society of Friends, and Granville Sharp, an English philanthropist, "blowing the single horn of human liberty and the natural equality of mankind against the institution of slavery, practised from time immemorial by all nations, ancient and modern; supported by the denunciation of the traffic in slaves by the popular writers both in France and England,—by Locke, Addison, and Sterne, as well as by Raynal, Rousseau, Montesquieu, and Voltaire; succeeded by the association of Thomas Clarkson and two or three Englishmen together, for the purpose of arraying the power of the British empire for the total abolition of slavery throughout the earth." The success of that association he next illustrates,—until this "emanation of the Christian faith is now, under the cross of St. George, overflowing from the white cliffs of Albion, and sweeping the slave-trade and slavery from the face of the terraqueous globe." He proceeds:

"People of that renowned island!—children of the land of our forefathers!—proceed, proceed in this glorious career, till the whole earth shall be redeemed from the greatest curse that ever has afflicted the human race. Proceed until millions upon millions of your brethren of the human race, restored to the rights with which they were endowed by your and their Creator, but of which they have been robbed by ruffians of their own race, shall send their choral shouts of redemption to the skies in blessings upon your names. O, with what pungent mortification and shame must I confess that in the transcendent glories of that day our names will not be associated with yours! May Heaven in mercy grant that we may be spared the deeper damnation of seeing our names recorded, not among the liberators, but with the oppressors of mankind!"

After inquiring what we have done in the United States to support "the principle proclaimed to the world as that which was to be the vital spark of our existence as a community among the nations of the earth," and declaring that we have done nothing, he thus enumerates the proceedings which disqualify us from presuming to share in the festivities and unite in the songs of triumph of the 1st of August, and shows how little we have concurred with Great Britain in her attempts to break the chain of slavery. He inquires into what we are doing:

"Are we not suffering our own hands to be manacled, and our own feet to be fettered, with the chains of slavery? Is it not enough to be told that, by a fraudulent perversion of language in the constitution of the United States, we have falsified the constitution itself, by admitting into both the legislative and executive departments of the government an overwhelming representation of one species of *property*, to the exclusion of all others, and that the odious property in slaves?

"Is it not enough that, by this exclusive privilege of property representation, confined to one section of the country, an irresistible ascendency in the action of the general government has been secured, not indeed to that section, but to an oligarchy of slaveholders in that section—to the cruel oppression of the poor in that same section itself? Is it not enough that, by the operation of this radical iniquity in the organization of the government, an immense disproportion of all offices, from the highest to the lowest, civil, military, naval, executive, and judicial, are held by slaveholders? Have we not seen the sacred right of petition totally suppressed for the people of the free states during a succession of years, and is it not yet inexorably suppressed? Have we not seen, for the last twenty years, the constitution and solemn treaties with foreign nations trampled on by cruel oppression and lawless imprisonment of colored mariners in the Southern States, in cold-blooded defiance of a solemn adjudication by a Southern judge in the Circuit Court of the Union? And is not this enough? Have not the people of the free states been required to renounce for their citizens the right of habeas corpus and trial by jury; and, to coërce that base surrender of the only practical security to all personal rights, have not the slave-breeders, by state legislation, subjected to fine and imprisonment the colored citizens of the free states, for merely coming within their jurisdiction? Have we not tamely submitted for years to the daily violation of the freedom of the post-office and of the press by a committee of seal-breakers? And have we not seen a sworn Postmaster-general formally avow that, though he could not license this cut-purse protection of the peculiar institution, the perpetrators of this highway robbery must justify themselves by the plea of necessity? And has the pillory or the penitentiary been the reward of that Postmaster-general? Have we not seen printing-presses destroyed; halls erected for the promotion of human freedom levelled with the dust, and consumed by fire; and wanton, unprovoked murder perpetrated with impunity, by slave-mongers? Have we not seen human beings, made in the likeness of God, and endowed with immortal souls, burnt at the stake, not for their offences, but for their color? Are not the journals of our Senate disgraced by resolutions calling for *war*, to indemnify the slave-pirates of the Enterprise and the Creole for the self-emancipation of their slaves; and to inflict vengeance, by a death of torture, upon the heroic self-deliverance of Madison Washington? Have we not been fifteen years plotting rebellion against our neighbor republic of Mexico, for abolishing slavery throughout all her provinces? Have we not aided and abetted one of her provinces in insurrection against her for that cause? And have we not invaded openly, and sword in hand, another of her provinces, and all to effect her dismemberment, and to add ten more slave states to our confederacy? Has not the cry of war for the conquest of Mexico, for the expansion of reïnstituted slavery, for the robbery of priests, and the plunder of religious establishments, yet subsided? Have the pettifogging, hair-splitting, nonsensical, and yet inflammatory bickerings about the right of search, pandering to the thirst for revenge in France, panting for war to prostrate the disputed title of her king—has the sound of this war-trumpet yet faded away upon our ears? Has the supreme and unparalleled absurdity of stipulating by treaty to keep a squadron of eighty guns for five years without intermission upon the coast of Africa, to suppress the African slave-trade, and at the same time denying, at the point of the bayonet, the right of that squadron to board or examine any slaver all but sinking under a cargo of victims, if she but hoist a foreign flag—has this diplomatic bone been yet picked clean? Or is our *indirect* participation in the African slave-trade to be protected, at whatever expense of blood and treasure? Is the supreme Executive Chief of this commonwealth yet to speak not for himself, but for her whole people, and pledge *them* to shoulder their muskets, and to endorse their knapsacks, against the fanatical, non-resistant abolitionists, whenever the overseers may please to raise the bloody flag with the swindling watch-word of 'Union'? O, my friends, I have not the heart to join in the festivity on the First of August—the British anniversary of disenthralled humanity—while all this, and infinitely more that I could tell, but that I would spare the blushes of my country, weigh down my spirits with the uncertainty, sinking into my grave as I am, whether she is doomed to be numbered among the first liberators or the last oppressors of the race of immortal man!

"Let the long-trodden-down African, restored by the cheering voice and Christian hand of Britain to his primitive right and condition of manhood, clap his hands and shout for joy on the anniversary of the First of August. Let the lordly Briton strip off much of his pride on other days of the year, and reserve it all for the pride of conscious beneficence on this day. What lover of classical learning can read the account in Livy, or in Plutarch, of the restoration to freedom of the Grecian cities by the Roman consul Flaminius, without feeling his bosom heave, and his blood flow cheerily in his veins? The heart leaps with sympathy when we read that, on the first proclamation by the herald, the immense assembled multitude, in the tumult of astonishment and joy, could scarcely believe their own ears, and made him repeat the proclamation, and then '*Tum ab certo jam gaudio, tantus cum clamore, plausus est ortus, totiesque repetitus, ut facile appararet nihil omnium bonorum multitudini gratius quam libertatem esse.*—Then rang the welkin with long and redoubled shouts of exultation, clearly proving that, of all the enjoyments accessible to the hearts of men, nothing is so delightful to them as liberty.' Upwards of two thousand years have revolved since that day, and the First of August is to the Briton of this age what the day of the proclamation of Flaminius was to the ancient Roman. Yes! let them celebrate the First of August as the day to them of deliverance and glory; and leave to us the pleasant employment of commenting upon their motives, of devising means to shelter the African slaver from their search, and of squandering millions to support, on a pestilential coast, a squadron of the stripes and stars, with instructions sooner to scuttle their ships than to molest the pirate slaver who shall make his flagstaff the herald of a lie!"

In July, 1843, the Cincinnati Astronomical Society earnestly solicited Mr. Adams to lay the corner-stone of their Observatory. No invitation could have been more coïncident with the prevailing interest of his heart, and he immediately accepted it, notwithstanding his advanced age, and the great distance which the performance of the duty required him to travel. Some of his constituents having questioned the propriety of this acceptance, and expressed doubts whether the duties it imposed were compatible with his other public obligations, Mr. Adams, in an address to them, at Dedham, on the 4th of July, took occasion to state that the encouragement of the arts and sciences, and of all good literature, is expressly enjoined by the constitution of Massachusetts. The patronage and encouragement of them is therefore one of the most sacred duties of the people of that state, and enjoined upon them and their children as a part of their duty to God. "The voices of your forefathers, founders of your social compact, calling from their graves, command you to this duty; and I deem it, as your representative, a tacit and standing instruction from you to perform, as far as may be my ability, that part of your constitutional duty for you. It is in this sense that, in accepting the earnest invitation from a respectable and learned society, in a far distant state and city of the Union, to unite with them in the act of erecting an edifice for the observation of the heavens, and thereby encouraging the science of astronomy, I am fulfilling an obligation of duty to you, and in your service." The nature of this duty he thus illustrates:

"From the Ptolemies of Egypt and Alexander of Macedon, from Julius Cæsar to the Arabian Caliphs Haroun al Raschid, Almamon, and Almansor, from Alphonso of Castile to Nicholas, the present Emperor of all the Russias,—who, at the expense of one million of rubles, has erected at Pulkova the most perfect and best-appointed observatory in the world,—royal and imperial power has never been exercised with more glory, never more remembered with the applause and gratitude of mankind, than when extending the hand of patronage and encouragement to the science of astronomy. You have neither Cæsar nor Czar, Caliph, Emperor, nor King, to monopolize this glory by largesses extracted from the fruits of your industry. The founders of your constitution have left it as their dying commandment to you, to achieve, as the lawful sovereigns of the land, this resplendent glory to yourselves—to patronize and encourage the arts and sciences, and all good literature."

Mr. Adams left Quincy for Cincinnati on the 25th of October, and returned to Washington on the 24th of November. At Saratoga, Rochester, Buffalo, he was received with marked attention; and in every place where he rested assemblages of the inhabitants took occasion to evidence their respect and interest in his character by congratulatory addresses, and welcomed his presence by every token of civility and regard. At Columbus he was met by a deputation from Cincinnati, and, in approaching that city, he was escorted into it by a procession and cavalcade. No demonstration of honor and gratitude for the exertion he had made, and the fatigues he had undergone, for their gratification, was omitted. His whole progress was an ovation.

In the presence of a large concourse of the citizens of Cincinnati, Mr. Adams was introduced to the Astronomical Society by its president, Judge Burnet, who gave, in an appropriate address, a rapid sketch of the history of his life and his public services, touching with delicacy and judgment on the trials to which his political course had been subjected. The following tributes, from their truth, justice, and appropriateness, are entitled to distinct remembrance:

"Being a son of one of the framers and defenders of the Declaration of Independence, his political principles were formed in the school of the sages of the Revolution, from whom he imbibed the spirit of liberty while he was yet a boy.

"Having been brought up among the immediate descendants of the Puritan fathers, whose landing in Massachusetts in the winter of 1620 gave immortality to the rock of Plymouth, his moral and religious impressions were derived from a source of the most rigid purity; and his manners and habits were formed in a community where ostentation and extravagance had no place. In this fact we see why it is that he has always been distinguished for his purity of motive, simplicity of manners, and republican plainness in his style of living and in his intercourse with society. To the same causes may be ascribed his firmness, his directness of purpose, and his unyielding adherence to personal as well as political liberty. You have recently seen him stand as unmoved as the rock of Gibraltar, defending the right of petition, and the constitutional privileges of the representatives of the people, assembled in Congress, though fiercely assailed by friends and by foes.

"It is a remarkable fact that during the whole of his public life, which has already continued more than half a century, he never connected himself with a political party, or held himself bound to support or oppose any measure for the purpose of advancing or retarding the views of a party; but he has held himself free at all times to pursue the course which duty pointed out, however he may have been considered by some as adhering to a party. This fact discloses the reason why he has been applauded at times, and at other times censured, by every party which has existed under the government. The truth is that, while the American people have been divided into two great political sections, each contending for its own aggrandizement, Mr. Adams has stood between them, uninfluenced by either, contending for the aggrandizement of the nation. His life has been in some respects *sui generis*; and I venture the opinion that, generally, when his course has differed most from the politicians opposed to him, it has tended most to the advancement of the public good.

"As a proof of the desire Mr. Adams has always cherished for the advancement of science, I might refer to his annual message to Congress in December, 1825, in which he recommended the establishment of a National University, and an Astronomical Observatory, and referred to the hundred and thirty of those 'light-houses of the skies' existing in Europe, as casting a reproach on our country for its unpardonable negligence on that important subject. The manner in which that recommendation was received and treated can never be forgotten. It must at this day be a source of great comfort to that devoted friend of science that those who yet survive of the highly-excited party which attempted to cast on him reproach and ridicule for that proposition, and especially for assimilating those establishments to light-houses of the skies, have recently admitted the wisdom of his advice by making ample appropriations to accomplish the very object he then proposed."

The oration Mr. Adams delivered on that occasion is, perhaps, the most extraordinary of his literary efforts, evidencing his comprehensive grasp of the subject, and the intensity of his interest in it. It embraces an outline of the history of astronomy, illustrated by an elevated and excited spirit of philosophy. Those who cultivated, those who patronized, and those who advanced it, are celebrated, and the events of their lives and the nature of their services are briefly related. The operations of the mind which are essential to its progress are touched upon. The intense labor and peculiar intellectual qualifications incident to and required for its successful pursuit are intimated. Nor are the inventors of those optical instruments, who had contributed to the advancement of this science beyond all previous anticipation, omitted in this extensive survey of its nature, progress, and history.

After celebrating "the gigantic energies and more than heroic labors of Copernicus, Tycho Brahe, Kepler, and Galileo," he pronounced Newton "the consummation of them all."

"It was his good fortune," observed Mr. Adams, "to be born and to live in a country where there was no college of cardinals to cast him into prison, and doom him to spend his days in repeating the seven penitential psalms, for shedding light upon the world, and publishing mathematical truths. Newton was not persecuted by the dull and ignorant instruments of political or ecclesiastical power. He lived in honor among his countrymen; was a member of one Parliament, received the dignity of knighthood, held for many years a lucrative office, and at his decease was interred in solemn state in Westminster Abbey, where a monument records his services to mankind, among the sepulchres of the British kings.

"From the days of Newton down to the present hour, the science of astronomy has been cultivated, with daily deepening interest, by all the civilized nations of Europe—by England, France, Prussia, Sweden, several of the German and Italian states, and, above all, by Russia, whose present sovereign has made the pursuit of knowledge a truly imperial virtue."

After speaking of the patronage extended to this science by the nations and sovereigns of Europe, he terminates his developments with this stirring appeal to his own countrymen:

"But what, in the mean time, have we been doing? While our fathers were colonists of England we had no distinctive political or literary character. The white cliffs of Albion covered the soil of our nativity, though another hemisphere first opened our eyes on the light of day, and oceans rolled between us and them. We were Britons born, and we claimed to be the countrymen of Chaucer and Shakspeare, Milton and Newton, Sidney and Locke, Arthur and Alfred, as well as of Edward the Black Prince, Harry of Monmouth, and Elizabeth. But when our fathers abjured the name of Britons, and 'assumed among the nations of the earth the separate and equal station to which the laws of nature and of nature's God entitled them,' they tacitly contracted the engagement for themselves, and above all for their posterity, to contribute, in their corporate and national capacity, their full share, ay, and more than their full share, of the virtues that elevate and of the graces that adorn the character of civilized man. They announced themselves as *reformers* of the institution of civil society. They spoke of the laws of nature, and in the name of nature's God; and by that sacred adjuration they pledged us, their children, to labor with united and concerted energy, from the cradle to the grave, to purge the earth of all slavery; to restore the race of man to the full enjoyment of those rights which the God of nature had bestowed upon him at his birth; to disenthrall his limbs from chains, to break the fetters from his feet and the manacles from his hands, and set him free for the use of all his physical powers for the improvement of his own condition. The God in whose name they spoke had taught them, in the revelation of the Gospel, that the only way in which man can discharge his duty to Him is by loving his neighbor as himself, and doing with him as he would be done by; respecting his rights while enjoying his own, and applying all his emancipated powers of body and of mind to self-improvement and the improvement of his race."

CHAPTER XIV.

REPORT ON THE RESOLVES OF THE LEGISLATURE OF MASSACHUSETTS PROPOSING AN AMENDMENT OF THE CONSTITUTION OF THE UNITED STATES IN EFFECT TO ABOLISH A REPRESENTATION FOR SLAVES.—FOURTH REPORT ON JAMES SMITHSON'S BEQUEST. —INFLUENCE OF MR. ADAMS ON THE ESTABLISHMENT OF THE NATIONAL OBSERVATORY AND THE SMITHSONIAN INSTITUTION.—GENERAL JACKSON'S CHARGE THAT THE RIO GRANDE MIGHT HAVE BEEN OBTAINED, UNDER THE SPANISH TREATY, AS A BOUNDARY FOR THE UNITED STATES, REFUTED.—ADDRESS TO HIS CONSTITUENTS AT WEYMOUTH. —REMARKS ON THE RETROCESSION OF ALEXANDRIA TO VIRGINIA.—HIS PARALYSIS. —RECEPTION BY THE HOUSE OF REPRESENTATIVES.—HIS DEATH.—FUNERAL HONORS. —TRIBUTE TO HIS MEMORY.

139

In April, 1844, certain resolves of the Legislature of Massachusetts, proposing to Congress to recommend, according to the provisions of the fifth article of the constitution of the United States, an amendment to the said constitution, in effect abolishing the representation for slaves, being under consideration, and a report adverse to such amendment having been made by a majority of the committee, Mr. Adams, and Mr. Giddings, of Ohio, being a minority, united in a report, in which, concurring in the opinion of the majority so far as to believe that it was not, at that time, expedient to recommend the amendment proposed by the Legislature of Massachusetts, they were compelled to dissent from the views and the reasons which had actuated them in coming to that conclusion.

"The subscribers are under a deep and solemn conviction that the provision in the constitution of the United States, as it has been and yet is construed, and which the resolves of the Legislature of Massachusetts propose to discard and erase therefrom, is repugnant to the first and vital principles of republican popular representation; to the self-evident truths proclaimed in the Declaration of Independence; to the letter and spirit of the constitution of the United States itself; to the letter and spirit of the constitutions of almost all the states in the Union; to the liberties of the whole people of all the free states, and of all that portion of the people of the states where domestic slavery is established, other than owners of the slaves themselves; that this is its essential and unextinguishable character in principle, and that its fruits, in its practical operation upon the government of the land, as felt with daily increasing aggravation by the people, correspond with that character. To place these truths in the clearest light of demonstration, and beyond the reach of contradiction, the subscribers proceed, in the order of these averments, to adduce the facts and the arguments by which they will be maintained."

The report then proceeds, in reply to the reasoning of the majority of the committee, to maintain that "the principle of republican popular representation is that the terms of representative and constituent are correlative;" that "democracy admits no representation of property;" that "the slave representation is repugnant to the self-evident truths proclaimed in the Declaration of Independence." The truths in that Declaration the report illustrates from history, from Scripture, and from the teachings of Jesus Christ; who was aware that wars, and their attendant, slavery, would continue among men, and that the destiny of his Gospel itself was often to be indebted for its progressive advancement to war.

"'I came not,' said he, 'to send peace upon earth, but a sword;' meaning, not that this was the object of his mission, but that, in the purposes of the Divine nature, war itself should be made instrumental to promote the final consummation of universal peace. Slavery has not ceased upon the earth; but the impression upon the human heart and mind that slavery is a wrong,—a crime against the laws of nature and of nature's God,—has been deepening and widening, till it may now be pronounced universal upon every soul in Christendom not warped by personal interest, or tainted with disbelief in Christianity. The owner of ten slaves believes that slavery is not an evil. The owner of a hundred believes it a blessing. The philosophical infidel has no faith in Hebrew prophecies, or in the Gospel of Jesus. He says in his heart, though he will not tell you to your face, that the proclamation of the natural equality of mankind, in the Declaration of Independence, is untrue; that the African race are physically, morally, and intellectually, *inferior* to the white European man; that they are not of one blood, nor descendants of the same stock; that the African is born to be a slave, and the white man to be his master. The worshipper of mammon and the philosophical atheist hold no communion with the signers of the declaration that all men are created equal, and endowed by their Creator with unalienable rights. But, with these exceptions, poll the whole mass of Christian men, of every name, sect, or denomination, throughout the globe, and you will not hear a solitary voice deny that slavery is a wrong, a crime, and a curse."

This report then proceeds to maintain that the representation of slaves as persons, conferred not upon themselves but their owners, is repugnant to the self-evident truth proclaimed in the Declaration of Independence, and equally repugnant both to the spirit and letter of the constitution of the United States, and to the constitution of almost every state of the Union; that it is deceptive, and inconsistent with the principle of popular representation;—all which is supported by reference to the writings of Thomas Jefferson, a

140

slaveholder, concerning the relations of master and slave. It is shown how, by the effect of that article in the constitution, all political power in the states is absorbed and engrossed by the owners of slaves, and the cunning by which this has been effected is explained. The report then enters into the history of slavery, declaring that "the resolves of the Legislature of Massachusetts speak the unanimous opinions and sentiments of the people—unanimous, with the exception of the sordid souls linked to the cause of slavery by the hopes and expectations of patronage."

In June, 1844, Mr. Adams, as chairman of a select committee on the Smithsonian fund, reported a bill, in which he referred to its actual state, and proposed measures tending to give immediate operation to that bequest. In support of its provisions, he stated that, on the first day of September, 1838, there had been deposited in the mint of the United States, in gold, half a million of dollars,—the full amount of the bequest of Mr. Smithson,—which, on the same day, under the authority of an act of Congress, and with the approbation of the President, had been vested by the Secretary of the Treasury in bonds of the States of Arkansas, Michigan, and Illinois; that the payment of the interest on these bonds had been almost entirely neglected; that the principal and arrears of interest then accumulating amounted to upwards of six hundred and ninety-nine thousand dollars; that the payment of these bonds was remote, and unavailable by Congress for application to the objects of this bequest.

In accepting this legacy, the faith of the United States had been pledged that all money received from it should be applied to the humane and generous purpose prescribed by the testator; and he contended that, for the redemption of this pledge, it was indispensably requisite that the funds thus locked up in the treasury, in bonds of these states, with the accruing and suspended interest thereon, should be made available for the disposal of Congress, to enable them to execute the sacred trust they had assumed.

The committee then reported a bill providing, in effect, for the assumption by Congress of the whole sum and interest, as a loan to the United States, invested in their stock, bearing an annual interest of six per cent., payable half-yearly, and redeemable at the pleasure of Congress by the substitution of other funds of equal value. In connection with this purpose they reported a bill making appropriations to enable Congress to proceed immediately to the execution of the trust committed to them by the testator, and for the fulfilment of which the faith of the nation had been pledged.

In specifying the objects to which it should be applied, that of the establishment of an Astronomical Observatory was not omitted. This recommendation decided the fate of the bill; for there was no purpose on which the predominating party were more fixed than to prevent the gratification of Mr. Adams in this well-known cherished wish of his heart.

In October, 1823, Mr. Adams, being then Secretary of State, had addressed a letter to a member of the corporation of Harvard University, urging the erection of an Astronomical Observatory in connection with that institution, and tendering a subscription, on his own account, of one thousand dollars, on condition a requisite sum should be raised, for that purpose, within two years. His proposal not meeting correspondent spirit among the friends of science at that time, in October, 1825, he renewed the offer, on the same condition and limitation. In both cases a concealment of his name was made imperative.[47]

The establishment of an Astronomical Observatory was recommended in his first message to Congress, as President of the United States; but the proposition fell on a political soil glowing with a red heat, enkindled by disappointed ambition. Opposition to the design became identified with party spirit, and to defeat it no language of contempt or of ridicule was omitted by the partisans of General Jackson. In every appropriation which it was apprehended might be converted to its accomplishment, the restriction "*and to no other*" was carefully inserted. In the second section of an act passed on the 10th of July, 1832, providing for the survey of the coasts of the United States, the following limitation was inserted: "*Provided that nothing in this act, or in the act hereby revived, shall be construed to authorize the construction or maintenance of a permanent Astronomical Observatory.*" Yet, at the time of passing this act, it was well understood that the appropriation it contained was to be applied to that object; and subsequently, in direct defiance of this prohibition, Congress permitted that and other appropriations to be applied to the erection of an Astronomical Observatory in the city of

Washington, to which annual appropriations were successively granted in the bill providing for the navy department; the authors of the proviso being aware of the uses to which the fund would be applied, but causing its insertion for the purpose of preventing its erection from being attributed to the influence of Mr. Adams. To such disreputable subterfuges party spirit can condescend, to gratify malignity, or to obscure merit from the knowledge of the world, to the power of which it is itself compelled to yield.

Nothing was effectually done, on the subject of the Smithsonian fund, until the 22d of April, 1846, when a bill to carry into effect that bequest was reported by Mr. Owen, of Indiana, and earnestly supported by him and others. In its important general features it coincided with the views of Mr. Adams, except only that it made no provision for an Astronomical Observatory. After various amendments, it received the sanction of both houses of Congress, Mr. Adams voting in its favor. On the 10th of August, 1846, it received the signature of the President of the United States.

During the debate upon this bill, its supporters acknowledged "that Mr. Adams had labored in this good cause with more zeal and perseverance than any other man."

In the course of the same debate it was said by one member that, "inasmuch as the views of Mr. Adams had been carried out in respect of an Astronomical Observatory, by the government, in the District of Columbia,"—and by another, that, "as building light-houses in the skies had grown into popular favor,"—it was hoped he would find no difficulty in giving his vote for the bill. On which Mr. Adams observed, that "he was very glad to hear that the 'building light-houses in the skies had grown into popular favor.' The appropriation for this Astronomical Observatory had been clandestinely smuggled into the law, under the head of a *dépôt* for charts, when, a short time before, a provision had been inserted in a bill passed that *no appropriation should be applied to an Astronomical Observatory.* He claimed no merit for the erection of an Astronomical Observatory, but, in the course of his whole life, no conferring of honor, of interest, or of office, had given him more delight than the belief that he had contributed, in some small degree, to produce these Astronomical Observatories both here and elsewhere.[48] He no longer wished any portion of the Smithsonian fund to be applied to an Astronomical Observatory."

Notwithstanding this disclaimer, the four reports of Mr. Adams, on the Smithsonian fund, in 1836, 1840, 1842, and 1844, which were neither coincident with the views nor within the comprehension of his opponents, will remain imperishable monuments of the extent and elevation of his mind on this subject. When the continued and strenuous exertions with which Mr. Adams opposed, at every step, the efforts to convert that fund to projects of personal interest or ambition are appreciated, it will be evident that the people of the United States owe to him whatever benefit may result from the munificence of James Smithson. History will be just to his memory, and will not fail to record his early interest and strenuous zeal for the advancement of astronomical science, and the influence his eloquence and untiring perseverance, in illustrating its importance with an unsurpassed array of appropriate learning, exerted on the public mind in the United States, not only in effecting the establishment of other Astronomical Observatories, but absolutely compelling party spirit, notwithstanding its open, bitter animosity, to lay the foundation of that Observatory which now bears the name of "National."

In February, 1843, Andrew Jackson addressed a letter to Aaron Vail Brown, a member of Congress, strongly recommending the annexation of Texas, and giving his reasons for that measure, which he commenced by stating the following facts:

"Soon after my election, in 1829, it was made known to me by Mr. Erwin, formerly our minister at the court of Madrid, that whilst at that court he had laid the foundation of a treaty with Spain for the cession of the Floridas, and the settlement of the boundary of Louisiana, fixing the western limit of the latter at the Rio Grande, agreeably to the understanding of France; that he had written home to our government for power to complete and sign this negotiation; but that, instead of receiving such authority, the negotiation was taken out of his hands, and transferred to Washington, and a new treaty was there concluded, by which the Sabine, and not the Rio Grande, was recognized and established as the boundary of Louisiana. Finding that these statements were true, and that our government did really give up that important territory, when it was at its option to retain it, I was filled with astonishment. The right to the territory was obtained from France, Spain stood ready to acknowledge it to the Rio Grande, and yet the authority asked by our minister to insert the true boundary was not only withheld, but, in lieu of it, a limit was adopted which stripped us of the whole vast country lying between the two rivers."

The letter containing this statement Aaron Vail Brown kept concealed from the public until March, 1844, when he gave it publicity to counteract a letter from Mr. Webster against the annexation of Texas to the United States. This statement of Andrew Jackson having thus been brought to the knowledge of Mr. Adams, he took occasion, on the 7th of October in that year, in an address to a political society of young men in Boston, to contradict and expose it in the following terms:

"I have read the whole of this letter to you, for I intend to prolong its existence for the benefit of posterity." [After reading the above extract from the letter of Andrew Jackson, Mr. Adams proceeds.] "He was filled with astonishment, fellow-citizens! I am repeating to you the words of a man who has been eight years President of the United States; words deliberately written, and published to the world more than a year after they were written; words importing a statement of his conduct in his office as chief magistrate of this Union; words impeaching of treason the government of his predecessor, James Monroe, and in an especial manner, though without daring to name him, the Secretary of State,—a government to which he (Andrew Jackson) was under deep obligations of gratitude.

"In what language of composure or of decency can I say to you that there is in this bitter and venomous charge not one single word of truth; that it is from beginning to end grossly, glaringly, wilfully false?—false even in the name of the man from whom he pretends to have derived his information. There never was a minister of the United States in Spain by the name of Erwin. The name of the man who went to him on this honorable errand, soon after his election in 1829, was George W. Erving, of whom and of whose revelations I shall also have something to say. I do not charge this distortion of the name as wilfully made; but it shows how carelessly and loosely all his relations and intercourse with him hung upon his memory, and how little he cared for the man.

"The blunder of the name, however, is in itself a matter of little moment. Mr. George W. Erving never did make to Mr. Jackson any such communication as he pretends to have found true, and to have filled him with astonishment. Mr. Erving never did pretend, nor will he dare to affirm, that he had laid the foundation of a treaty with Spain for the cession of the Floridas, and the settlement of the boundary of Louisiana, fixing the western limit at the Rio Grande. The charge, therefore, that our government did really give up that important territory, when it was at its option to retain it, is purely and unqualifiedly untrue; and I now charge that it was known by Mr. Brown to be so when he published General Jackson's letter; for, in the postscript to Jackson's letter, he says 'the papers furnished by Mr. Erwin, to which he had referred in it, could be placed in Mr. Brown's possession, if desired.'

"They were accordingly placed in Mr. Brown's possession, who, when he published Jackson's letter to the *Globe*, alluding to this passage asserting that Erving had laid the foundation of a treaty with Spain, fixing the western limit at the Rio Grande, otherwise called the Rio del Norte, subjoined the following note: 'That this boundary could have been obtained was doubtless the belief of our minister; *but the offer of the Spanish government was probably to the Colorado—certainly a line far west of the Sabine.*'

"This is the note of Aaron Vail Brown, and my fellow-citizens will please to observe,—

"First, That it blows to atoms the whole statement of Andrew Jackson that Erving had laid the foundation of a treaty by which our western bounds upon the Spanish possessions should be at the Rio Grande; and, of course, grinds to impalpable powder his charge that our government did give up that important territory when it was at its option to retain it.

"Secondly, That this note of Aaron Vail Brown, while it so effectually demolishes Jackson's fable of Erving's treaty with Spain for the boundary of the Rio del Norte, and his libellous charge against our government for surrendering the territory which they had the option to retain, is, with this exception, as wide and as wilful a departure from the truth as the calumny of Jackson itself, which it indirectly contradicts."

143

Mr. Adams then enters into a lucid and elaborate statement of Erving's connection with this negotiation with the Spanish government, with minute and important illustrations, highly interesting and conclusive; severely animadverting upon the conduct of General Jackson and Mr. Brown. He says:

"The object of the publication of that letter of Andrew Jackson was to trump up a shadow of argument for a pretended reännexation of Texas to the United States, by a fabulous pretension that it had been treacherously surrendered to Spain, in the Florida treaty of 1819, by our government,—meaning thereby the Secretary of State of that day, John Quincy Adams,—in return for greater obligations than any one public servant of this nation was ever indebted for to another. The argument for the annexation, or reännexation, of Texas is as gross an imposture as ever was palmed upon the credulity of an honest people."

In conclusion Mr. Adams addresses in a serious and exciting strain of eloquence the young men of Boston; and, after recapitulating part of an oration which he delivered on the 4th of July, 1793, before their fathers and forefathers, in that city, he closes thus:

"Young men of Boston, the generations of men to whom fifty-one years bygone I gave this solemn pledge have passed entirely away. They in whose name I gave it are, like him who addresses you, dropping into the grave. But they have redeemed their and my pledge. They were your fathers, and they have maintained the freedom transmitted to them by their sires of the war of independence. They have transmitted that freedom to you; and upon you now devolves the duty of transmitting it unimpaired to your posterity. Your trial is approaching. The spirit of freedom and the spirit of slavery are drawing together for the deadly conflict of arms. The annexation of Texas to this Union is the blast of a trumpet for a foreign, civil, servile, and Indian war, of which the government of your country, fallen into faithless hands, have already twice given the signal: first by a shameless treaty, rejected by a virtuous Senate; and again by the glove of defiance hurled by the apostle of nullification at the avowed policy of the British empire peacefully to promote the extinction of slavery throughout the world. Young men of Boston, burnish your armor—prepare for the conflict; and I say to you, in the language of Galgacus to the ancient Britons, 'Think of your forefathers! think of your posterity!'"[49]

On the 30th of the same month Mr. Adams delivered to his constituents at Weymouth an address equally elaborate, comprehensive, and historical, in a like fervid and characteristic spirit,[50] which thus concludes:

"Texas and slavery are interwoven in every banner floating on the Democratic breeze. 'Freedom or death' should be inscribed on ours. A war for slavery! Can you enlist under such a standard? May the Ruler of the universe preserve you from such degradation! 'Freedom! Peace! Union!' be this the watchword of your camp; and if Ate, hot from hell, will come and cry 'Havoc!' fight—fight and conquer, under the banner of universal freedom."

In February, 1845, our title to Oregon being the subject of debate in Congress, Mr. Adams joined in it, displaying his full knowledge of the subject, and declaring that it was time to give notice to Great Britain that the affair must be settled. He was desirous as any man to bring this subject to an issue, but he did not wish to enter upon the discussion of this matter before the world until we could show that we had the best of the argument. He wished to have the reasons given to the world for our taking possession of seven degrees of latitude, and perhaps more; and whenever we took it, too, he hoped we should have it defined geographically, defined politically, and, more than all the rest, defined *morally*; and then, if we came to question with Great Britain, we should say, "Come on, Macduff!" In answer to the inquiry who had been the means of giving this country a title to Oregon, Mr. Adams answered, it was a citizen of Massachusetts that discovered the Columbia River; and that he (Mr. Adams) had the credit of inserting the clause in the treaty on which our right was based. If it had not been for the attacks which had been made upon him, the fact would have gone with him to the grave.

In February, 1845, in a speech on the army bill, he treated ironically the spirit of conquest then manifesting itself towards Mexico, Oregon, and California. He said, at some future day we might hear the Speaker not only announce on this floor "the gentleman from the Rocky Mountains," or "the gentleman from the Pacific," or "the gentleman from Patagonia," but "the gentleman from the North Pole," and also "the gentleman from the

South Pole;" and the poor original thirteen states would dwindle into comparative insignificance as parts of this mighty republic.

In November, 1845, in answer to a letter soliciting his opinion on the constitutionality of the law of Congress retroceding Alexandria to Virginia, Mr. Adams replied: "I have no hesitation to say I hold that act unconstitutional and void. How the Supreme Court of the United States would consider it I cannot undertake to judge, nor how they would carry it into execution, should they determine the act unconstitutional. The constitution of the United States '*Stat magna nominis umbra*.'"

In the great debate on the Oregon question, which commenced in January, 1846, the intellectual power of Mr. Adams, and the extent and accuracy of his acquaintance with the facts connected with that subject, were preëminently manifested. Though conscious, being then in his seventy-eighth year, that he stood on the threshold of human life, he sought no relaxation from duty, no exemption from its performance. To counteract the effect of a nervous tremor, to which he was constitutionally subject, he used for many years an instrument to steady his hand when writing, on the ivory label of which he inscribed the motto "'Toil and trust," indicative of the determined will, which had characterized his whole life, "to scorn delights and live laborious days." His step, however, now became more feeble, and his voice less audible, but his indomitable spirit never failed to uplift him in defence of liberty and the constitution of his country, when assailed.

In a debate on the Oregon question, in August, 1846, when Mr. Adams arose to speak, the hall was found too extensive for the state of his voice, and the members rushed to hear him, filling the area in front of the Speaker. That officer, in behalf of the few who remained in their seats, called the house to order, and Mr. Adams continued his remarks with his accustomed clearness and energy.

At the close of the session, in 1846, he returned to his seat in Quincy, with unimpaired intellectual powers, and with no perceptible symptom of immediately declining health, until the 19th of November, when, walking in the streets of Boston, an attack of paralysis deprived him of the power of speech, and affected his right side. In the course of three months, however, he was sufficiently recovered to resume his official duties at Washington.

On the 16th of February, 1847, as he entered the Hall of the House of Representatives for the first time since his illness, the house rose as one man, business was at once suspended, his usual seat surrendered to him by the gentleman to whom it had been assigned, and he was formally conducted to it by two members. After resuming it, Mr. Adams expressed his thanks to the member who had voluntarily relinquished his right in his favor, and said: "Had I a more powerful voice, I might respond to the congratulations of my friends, and the members of this house, for the honor which has been done me. But, enfeebled as I am by disease, I beg you will excuse me."

After this period, on one occasion alone he addressed the house. On the refusal of President Polk to give information, on their demand, as to the objects of the then existing war with Mexico, and the instructions given by the Executive relative to negotiations for peace, Mr. Adams rose, and maintained the constitutional power of the house to call for that information; denying that in this case the refusal was justified by that of President Washington on a similar demand; and declaring that the house ought to sustain, in the strongest manner, their right to call for information upon questions in which war and peace were concerned.

From this time, though daily in his seat in the House of Representatives, he took no part in debate. On the 21st of February, 1848, he answered to the call of his name in a voice clear and emphatic. Soon after, he rose, with a paper in his hand, and addressed the Speaker, when paralysis returned, and, uttering the words, "This is the last of earth; I am content," he fell into the arms of the occupant of an adjoining seat, who sprang to his aid. The house immediately adjourned. The members, greatly agitated, closed around him, until dispersed by their associates of the medical faculty, who conveyed him to a sofa in the rotundo, and from thence, at the request of the Speaker of the House of Representatives, Robert C. Winthrop, he was removed to the Speaker's apartment in the capitol. There Mrs. Adams and his family were summoned to his side, and he continued, sedulously watched and attended, in a state of almost entire insensibility, until the evening of the 23d of February, when his spirit peacefully departed.

The gate of fear and envy was now shut; that of honor and fame opened. Men of all parties united in just tributes to the memory of John Quincy Adams. The halls of Congress resounded with voices of apt eulogy. After a pathetic discourse by the Chaplain of the House of Representatives, the remains of the departed statesman were followed by his family and immediate friends, and by the senators and representatives of the State of Massachusetts, as chief mourners. The President of the United States, the heads of departments, both branches of the national legislature, the members of the executive, judicial, and diplomatic corps, the officers of the army and navy, the corporations of all the literary and public societies in the District of Columbia, also joined the procession, which proceeded with a military escort to the Congressional cemetery. From thence his remains were removed, attended by thirty members of the House of Representatives,—one from each state in the Union,—to Massachusetts.

Every token of honor and respect was manifested in the cities and villages through which they passed. In Boston they were received by a committee appointed by the Legislature of Massachusetts, and by the municipal government; and, passing through the principal streets, were deposited, under care of the mayor of the city, in Faneuil Hall, which was appropriately draped in mourning. Here they lay in state until the next day, when, attended by the representatives of the nation, the Executive and Legislature of Massachusetts, and the municipal authorities of Boston, they were removed to Quincy, the birthplace of Mr. Adams. There, in its Congregational church, after an eloquent address,[51] these national tributes to the departed patriot closed, beside the sepulchre of his parents, amidst the scenes most familiar and dear to his heart.

The life of a statesman second to none in diligent and effective preparation for public service, and faithful and fearless fulfilment of public duty, has now been sketched, chiefly from materials taken from his published works. The light of his own mind has been thrown on his labors, motives, principles, and spirit. In times better adapted to appreciate his worth, his merits and virtues will receive a more enduring memorial. The present is not a moment propitious to weigh them in a true balance. He knew how little a majority of the men of his own time were disposed or qualified to estimate his character with justice. To a future age he was accustomed to look with confidence. "*Alteri sæculo*" was the appeal made by him through his whole life, and is now engraven on his monument.

The basis of his moral character was the religious principle. His spirit of liberty was fostered and inspired by the writings of Milton, Sydney, and Locke, of which the American Declaration of Independence was an emanation, and the constitution of the United States, with the exception of the clauses conceded to slavery, an embodiment. He was the associate of statesmen and diplomatists at a crisis when war and desolation swept over Europe, when monarchs were perplexed with fear of change, and the welfare of the United States was involved in the common danger. After leading the councils which restored peace to conflicting nations, he returned to support the administration of a veteran statesman, and then wielded the chief powers of the republic with unsurpassed purity and steadiness of purpose, energy, and wisdom. Removed by faction from the helm of state, he re-entered the national councils, and, in his old age, stood panoplied in the principles of Washington and his associates, the ablest and most dreaded champion of freedom, until, from the station assigned him by his country, he departed, happy in a life devoted to duty, in a death crowned with every honor his country could bestow, and blessed with the hope which inspires those who defend the rights, and uphold, when menaced, momentous interests of mankind.

Footnotes

1

See "Letters of Mrs. Adams, with an Introductory Memoir," and "The Works of John Adams, Second President of the United States, with a Life of the Author," by their grandson, Charles Francis Adams.

2

John Quincy represented the town of Braintree in the colonial legislature forty years, and long held the office of speaker.

3

See *Niles' Weekly Register*, New Series, vol. xv., pp. 218, 219.

4

Sparks' Life and Writings of Washington, XI., p. 56, and p. 188.

5

The writer of this Memoir.

6

See pages 18 and 19.

7

The Report of Mr. Adams, when Secretary of State, on weights and measures, at the call of Congress, sufficiently evidences the ultimate usefulness of these researches.

8

A committee appointed by the House of Representatives, on McGregor's possession of Amelia Island, waited on Mr. Adams, and inquired concerning the proposed proceedings of the executive, and his powers in that respect. Mr. Adams took occasion to state and explain to them the effects of "the *secret laws*, as they were called, and which," he said, "were singular anomalies of our system, having grown out of that error in our constitution which confers upon the legislative assemblies the power of declaring war, which, in the theory of government, according to Montesquieu and Rousseau, is strictly an executive act. But, as we have made it legislative, whenever secrecy is necessary for an operation of the executive involving the question of peace and war, Congress must pass a *secret* law to give the President power. Now, secrecy is contrary to one of the first principles of legislation, but the absurdity flows from having given to Congress, instead of the executive, the power of declaring war. Of these secret laws there are four, and one resolution; and one of the laws, that of the 28th of June, 1812, is so secret, that to this day it cannot be found among the rolls of the department. Another consequence has followed from this clumsy political machinery. The injunction of secrecy was removed on the 6th of July, 1812, from the laws previously passed by a vote of the House of Representatives, and yet the laws have never been published."

9

This publication is contained in *Niles' Weekly Register*, vol. XXII., pp. 198, 209, 220, 296, 327, and continued in vol. XXIII., pp. 6 and 9.

10

Niles' Register, vol. XXVI., pp. 251-328.

11

Niles' Register, vol. XXVII., p. 387.

12

Ibid., vol. XXVII., p. 321.

13

Niles' Weekly Register, vol. XXVII., p. 386.

14

Niles' Weekly Register, vol. XXVIII., p. 71.

15

Ibid., p. 20.

16

In the year 1823 the State of South Carolina passed a law making it the duty of the sheriff of any district to apprehend any free negro or person of color, brought into that state by any vessel, and confine him in jail until such vessel depart, and then to liberate him only on condition of payment of the expenses of such detention. To this law William Johnson, a South Carolinian, and a judge of the Supreme Court of the United States, in a letter to Mr. Adams, then Secretary of State, called the attention of the President of the United States, as a violation of the constitution; and declared his belief "that it had been passed as much for the pleasure of bringing the functionaries of the United States into contempt, by exposing their impotence, as from any other cause whatsoever;" they being precluded from resorting

147

to the writ of habeas corpus and injunction because the cases assumed the form of state prosecutions. William Wirt, also, the Attorney-General of the United States, in a letter to Mr. Adams, then Secretary of State, pronounced that law "as being against the constitution, treaties, and laws, and incompatible with the rights of all nations in amity with the United States."

17
Niles' Weekly Register, vol. XXXII., p. 162.

18
Niles' Weekly Register, vol. XXXII., p. 316.

19
Ibid., p. 415.

20
Niles' Register, vol. XXXIII., p. 297.

21
Niles' Register, vol. XXXIII., p. 303.

22
Address of John Quincy Adams to his Constituents, at Braintree, September 17, 1842, p. 27.

23
See, for Crawford's letter and Calhoun's address, *Niles' Weekly Register*, vol. XL., p. 12.

24
Jackson's cabinet were, Martin Van Buren, Secretary of State; Samuel D. Ingham, Secretary of the Treasury; John H. Eaton, Secretary of War; John Branch, Secretary of the Navy; John M'P. Berrien, Attorney-General; William T. Barry, Postmaster-General.

25
For which see *Niles' Weekly Register*, vol. XL., pp. 12, 13.

26
See *Niles' Weekly Register*, vol. XL., pp. 129-145.

27
Ibid., pp. 152-3.

28
Niles' Register, vol. XL., p. 201.

29
Ibid., p. 220.

30
Ibid., p. 253.

31
Ibid., p. 304.

32
Niles' Weekly Register, vol. XL., p. 331.

33
Ibid., vol. XLI., pp. 5, 6.

34
The facts above stated are chiefly derived from a speech of Henry Clay, delivered at Lexington, Kentucky, on the 16th of May, 1829, in which all the topics here touched are forcibly and eloquently illustrated. It may be found at length in *Niles' Weekly Register*, vol. XXXVI., pp. 399 to 405.

35
Niles' Weekly Register, vol. XLII., pp. 86-88.

36
See this letter in *Niles' Weekly Register*, vol. XXXVII., pp. 91-93.

37
Niles' Weekly Register, vol. XLVII., p. 91.

38
Mr. Wirt was Attorney-General of the United States during the four last years of Mr. Monroe's and the whole of Mr. Adams' administration.

39

See *Congressional Debates*, vol. X., part 2d, p. 2758.

40

Niles' Weekly Register, N. S., vol. I., pp. 385—390, et seq.

41

Niles' Weekly Register, New Series, vol. III., pp. 167, 168.

42

Niles' Weekly Register, New Series, vol. III., p. 161.

43

Niles' Weekly Register, New Series, vol. V., p. 219.

44

For this letter see *Niles' Weekly Register*, New Series, vol. V., p. 55.

45

See, for all the proceedings on this subject, the *Congressional Globe*, vol. IX., pp. 320-322.

46

See the *Boston Courier* and *New York American* of the period.

47

Quincy's History of Harvard University, vol. II., p. 567.

48

Congressional Globe, vol. XV., p. 738.

49

Niles' National Register, Second Series, vol. XVII., pp. 105-111.

50

Niles' National Register, Second Series, vol. XVII., pp. 154-159.

51

By William P. Lunt, minister of the First Congregational Church in Quincy.